JOURNEY TO
NOBLE IDEALS

THE BROKEN JUG SERIES – 13

JOURNEY TO NOBLE IDEALS

Droplets of Wisdom from the Heart

M. Fethullah Gülen

TUGHRA
BOOKS
New Jersey

Copyright © 2014 by Tughra Books

Originally published in Turkish as *Mefkure Yolculuğu (Kırık Testi-13)*, Nil Yayınları, İstanbul, 2014

17 16 15 14   1 2 3 4

Translated by Korkut Altay

Published by Tughra Books
345 Clifton Ave., Clifton,
NJ, 07011, USA

www.tughrabooks.com

Library of Congress Cataloging-in-Publication Data Available

ISBN: 978-1-59784-348-5

Printed by
Imak Ofset, Istanbul - Turkey

Contents

Preface

"**My cause!**" cried out Bediüzzaman when he tripped over a rock and fell off the high bluff of the Van Castle where had gone on a meditative retreat. Miraculously, after a somewhat physically impossible death-defying tumble, Bediüzzaman (d. 1960), one of the most notable Islamic scholars of 20th century Turkey, landed at the mouth of another cave only three meters below. Still, it is remarkable that in a moment when death appeared so imminent, he remembered his "cause." What would make him do this? Would you be able to do the same? Do you have such a *cause* in your life? Do you have a *purpose* in your life? A purpose, not in the sense of achieving career goals, obtaining the power boat you have always wanted to own, or seeing your team break its losing streak to nab the championship title, but something deeper, something *higher*. What is that lifetime dream or the inner *call* hidden deep in your heart that would make you feel complete if it were to come true? If you do not have such a cause, or even if you have never thought about it, do not worry: you are among the overwhelming majority—or maybe you should worry, for it shows you live only for each day.

This book aims to raise awareness about that call. It is an awareness of an inner craving—whether we are aware of it or not—that is always right inside our chest. It is a permanent call, which we ignore more often than not, or work hard to suppress and turn away from. Whatever achievements we might attain in this life are unable to respond to it fully, for ephemeral things are unable to satisfy a permanent drive. Can you hear that call? Can you decipher its message?

It would seem that a lack of a well-established and worthwhile purpose lies at the very heart of many of the personal and social problems we face today. Graduating from college, deciding on a career, finding a job, traveling around the world... These are human conditions and short term goals, changing and evolving as we grow, and after each one is attained, we ask ourselves "Now what?" We are born into this world, grow from a child into a young man or woman, a college student, a professional, a father or a mother, an older person, and then we die... And then what? What is the meaning of this universe, and then what comes after it?

Pursuing a dream or an ideal is necessary for a meaningful life, but it begs the question about the nature of this ideal. Hitler had an ideal too, and he devoted his life to what he called "My Struggle" (Mein Kampf). Genghis Khan's great ambition was to conquer the world; he believed he'd been sent to be "God's punishment" over mankind for their sins.

On the other hand, you have the example of Prophet Muhammad, peace and blessings be upon him, who did not hesitate even for a blink of an eye when he rejected the best of all attractions this world can offer, such as titles and wealth, and said, "Even if they gave the sun to my right hand, and the moon to my left hand, I will not renounce my mission." When Dr. Martin Luther King cried out "I have a dream," he was not speaking of an illusion, nor was he giving the glad tidings of a false dawn, for his words resounded on the foundations of a lifetime's commitment, sweat, and candor.

So, what makes a goal an admirably virtuous one?

In this volume, Fethullah Gülen—a master in diverse fields of knowledge, an authority in religious thought, and a man who has devoted his entire life to a higher cause—offers us some useful devices to decipher that inner call, and to do it virtuously. To understand this calling, this is not the only book that you can hold in your hands, but a good number of Gülen's works are dedicated to discovering a higher purpose. His books are like signposts for seekers of a cause in this life, and each title is a milestone for a new phase. Gülen wishes people to become aware of their spiritual capacity and to explore the *Emerald Hills of the Heart*; he encourages them to work hard to unleash that capacity, so they can erect *The Statue of Our Souls*; he rejects being egotistical in order to pursue a selfless life *So That Others May*

Live; he envisions a future of peaceful coexistence and directs his readers *Toward a Global Civilization of Love and Tolerance*; and while doing all this, he vows to rely on the infinite powers of the Divine, which are like a flowing river, rather than on the illusionary powers of those other than him, which are nothing more than small jugs of water. This is why Gülen titles his sermons, "The Broken Jug."

Journey to Noble Ideals is yet another contribution by Gülen which provides guidelines to build our individual ladders to self-discovery. In Gülen's prescription, climbing this ladder requires "life-long contentedness," "a spirit of chivalry", "becoming soil to grow roses," "balance and moderation," "being self-critical," "not to be dizzy with worldly pleasures," and "sincerity of intention." Nourished from a millennium-old accumulation of knowledge and tradition, Gülen speaks of preserving one's "chastity of thoughts" but not lagging behind, and instead soaring across the "horizons of spiritual knowledge." For Gülen, a healthy society is built on a "happy marriage," observing the "rights of neighbors," "sound reason," "retreats to read," and "asking for forgiveness." Above all, his faith rests on a firm belief that "God is sufficient" for all.

The book is a compilation of sermons and lectures Gülen delivered in Turkish, which were then translated into English over the years. The primary audience of these sermons were Muslims; thus the content offers much in the way of reference and allusions to Islam and Islamic history, and, as such, some background knowledge would prove helpful for non-Muslim readers to fully grasp their message. However, we believe that this book can be instrumental for all English-speakers, for the underlying tone that shapes the content and the ultimate objective of enthusing a higher purpose to life are universally relevant and a source of inspiration for all.

God Is Sufficient for Us

Question: *All of the Prophets sought refuge in God's might and power in the face of misfortunes that befell them and pointed out that only God grants success. So, what is the role of reciting prayers of "hasbiya" (God's sufficiency) for devoted souls who face lots of difficulties and troubles?*

Answer: Human beings, who are essentially weak and needy, can overcome any kind of difficulty only by seeking refuge in God, Who is the All-Powerful and the All-Wealthy. It is essential for them to seek refuge in God against the troubles they face by saying, "*God is sufficient for us, how excellent a Guardian He is!*" (Al Imran 3:173). Above all, those who utter this phrase with sincerity have entrusted their affairs to Him and believe with conviction that only He is their Guardian and that He will never forsake them when they seek refuge in Him.

Confidence in God

When some people turned away from the Prophet and his way, God Almighty revealed the verse which means, "*Still, if they turn away from you (O Messenger), say: "God is sufficient for me; there is no deity but He. In Him have I put my trust, and He is the Lord of the Supreme Throne*" (at-Tawbah 9:129).

Bediüzzaman[1] wrote the following commentary on this verse: "If the people of misguidance turn away, diverge from your way, and do not heed the Qur'an, do not worry. Say, 'God Almighty is sufficient for me. In Him I put my trust. He will raise up others in your place who will follow me. His Throne of rule encompasses everything. Neither the rebellious can escape its bounds, nor are those who ask for help left unaided.'"[2]

There is a prayer of the Messenger of God that is to be recited in the morning and in the evening. It is as follows: "O the All-Living and Self-Subsistent One! It is Your Mercy that I hope for, so leave me not alone for the blinking of an eye and set right all my affairs! O Living, Self-Subsistent Lord!"[3]

Expounding on this, we can say: "O God, please, let not distractions corrupt my deeds while I strive on Your way. Do not leave me to my carnal self and the devil even for a moment; for if they take over, they might lead me straight to the pits of Hell. Since the carnal self can never be trusted, I will be a loser if it holds the reins. If You are my Guardian, however, then I can find guidance and walk on the true path. For neither the carnal self nor the devil can manipulate anything if there is strength and support from You."

God's Absolute Dominion

When their people turned away from them, Prophet Abraham and those who believed in his message relied on God as well. They said: "O

---

[1]   In the many dimensions of his lifetime of achievement, as well as in his personality and character, Bediüzzaman Said Nursi (1877–1960) was and, through his continuing influence, still is an important thinker and writer in the Muslim world. He represented in a most effective and profound way the intellectual, moral and spiritual strengths of Islam, evident in different degrees throughout its fourteen-century history. He lived for eighty-five years. He spent almost all of those years, overflowing with love and ardor for the cause of Islam, in a wise and measured activism based on sound reasoning and in the shade of the Qur'an and the Prophetic example. ("Bediüzzaman and the Risale-i Nur" in *Belief and Worship*, Said Nursi, translated from Turkish by Ali Ünal, New Jersey: The Light, 2006, p. ii). (All footnotes were added by the editor.)

[2]   Nursi, *The Gleams*, p. 66.

[3]   An-Nasa'i, *As-Sunanu'l-Kubra*, 6/147; Al-Bazzar, *Al-Musnad*, 13/49

Our Lord! It is in You that We have put our trust, and it is to You that we turn in utmost sincerity and devotion, and to You is the homecoming. O Our Lord! Do not make us a prey to those who disbelieve. And forgive us, our Lord. You are the All-Glorious with irresistible might, the All-Wise" (al-Mumtahanah 60:4–5).

Their words present an upright stance against the disbelievers and virtually challenged all their threats. At the same time, they proclaimed that anything worshipped other than God bears no true value and deserves no praise. Their words indicate their personal realization of the Divine Power's absolute dominion over all things, as well as the illumination of belief.

Here, I would like to draw attention to another point. When one reads about the behavior and words of our Prophet along with previous Prophets from a comparative perspective, it is apparent that the laudable virtues God granted him are repetitions of the prayers of the previous Prophets. For example, Moses prayed and asked God to grant him serenity in his heart saying, *"My Lord, expand my breast"* (Ta-Ha 20:25).

Indeed the Qur'an mentions this asking, *"Have not We expanded your breast?"* (al-Inshirah 94:1). This is one of the blessings granted to Prophet Muhammad, peace and blessings be upon him and all the Prophets. As we mentioned above, Prophet Abraham and his followers were in a position where they realized only God could change their situation. Similarly, another verse describes the situation of the Companions of the Prophet in the following way:

Those (believers) to whom some people said: "Look, those people have gathered against you, therefore be fearful of them." But it increased them only in faith, and they responded: *"God is sufficient for us; how excellent a Guardian He is"* (Al Imran 3:173).

As the above verse demonstrates, even in situations where people normally feel fear and distress over the unknown, the Companions of the Prophet had complete faith and trust in God. They faced the enemy unafraid because they were filled with spiritual alertness.

Complete Confidence in God

When Bediüzzaman was completely isolated during his exile, the world seemed exceedingly gloomy. It was during this gloomy period that he was inspired by the verse, *"God is sufficient for us; how excellent Guardian He is"* (Al Imran 3:173). Suddenly, a new understanding of this verse occurred to him. From that point on, he began reciting the verse five hundred times a day and, consequently, various mysteries revealed themselves in his soul. Indeed, the spiritual power he obtained through the lessons he garnered from this single verse gave him a powerful faith that sufficed him not only against his persecutors in the exiled land, but also against the entire world.[4] A person whose heart attains such a level of ease will neither be seized by worry and grief nor imprisoned or pressured to change his course.

Prisons become like a school of Joseph for Bediüzzaman, and he continued his mission there. When his release from prison was possible, he would opt to stay in prison for the sake of not leaving their fruitful services halfway and being beneficial to the inmates there. This is the meaning of ease, serenity, and inner peace in its truest sense. On the other hand, a person with a depressed heart and spirit experiences such stress, anxiety, and anguish that no possessions in the world can provide a cure for it. Those who are not awakened to the truth in their souls can never be saved from the spiritual darkness even if they manufacture thousands of yachts and luxurious cars every day. True serenity and happiness is in the God-granted peacefulness of the heart. Those who attain such a state can stand up against troubles of great magnitude, turn the fires into colored flames and sparks in their hearts, and let those around them enjoy the spectacular display of fireworks.

As a matter of fact, the moment when the impact of the troubles and sufferings we go through strikes the horizons of our imagination and batters the conception and reasoning processes in our mind, inspirations like those granted to Bediüzzaman may enter our heart as well. Particularly, those who eagerly seek perfect faith and sincer-

---

[4]   Nursi, *The Gleams*, p. 353; *The Rays*, p. 75

ity and strive to keep up a sound relationship with God Almighty may be honored with the experience of such manifestations. However, most of us overlook such manifestations since we do not listen to our inner voice or may perceive such inspirations as ordinary things that occur to everyone. Spiritual figures, however, view inspirations on a different wavelength of manifestations coming to them not as casual and ordinary, but rather as something with meaning and wisdom in them. Indeed, they take such occurrences as important signs and warnings. So Bediüzzaman appreciated the precious truth that occurred to his heart and concentrated on it; he recited this Qur'anic verse five hundred times every day in hopes of gaining wisdom and inspiration.

Given that he repeated the verse five hundred times, one can assume that there must be a mysterious wisdom in repetition in terms of feeling the truth of a matter profoundly. In that case, ordinary people should seek refuge in the Divine Power against the evil of their enemies, target high horizons and say five hundred or even perhaps a thousand times a day this supplication of the Prophet, *"God is sufficient for me; there is no deity but He. In Him have I put my trust, and He is the Lord of the Supreme Throne."*

As individuals, we can use the following method for realizing this lofty aim: When a group of people share a certain long prayer amongst themselves by reading smaller parts of it, they can complete it in an easier way, whereas each participant benefits from the total blessings that correspond to the collective deed. So this prayer can be recited in the same way. For example, if ten friends agree to recite it a hundred times per person, the collective deed—God willing—will gain each one of them the reward as if they recited it a thousand times individually.

Saying "God Is Sufficient for Us" in the Face of Achievements

A believer is supposed to seek refuge in God not only against trouble and misfortune, but also in times of success and achievement. In this respect, the profundity of the issue in question may differ from person to person, for some say *"God is sufficient for us; how excellent Guardian He is,"* against misfortunes only. By turning to God this way, they witness all their problems being solved with the help of Divine Providence. This is the refuge those in distress need. As for others, they make it their habitual prayer and seek refuge in God's Power with their supplications to Him day and night. Those whose spiritual faculties are open to the horizons of Divine mysteries sense the Power of God Almighty over everything, down to the most trivial matters of their personal lives. Even when performing simple tasks such as threading a needle or taking a morsel of food to one's mouth, these enlightened people seek refuge in the Divine Power. In fact, they hold the belief that God creates their actions when they choose to do anything, since they do not have any power to create their own actions save making a choice in favor of an thing or another; thus, they say, He is always "the One who creates" our acts. This belief reflects pure faith in the Oneness of God.

Indeed, when we follow the tradition of the Prophet and repeat the prayer "God is sufficient for me; there is no deity but He. In Him have I put my trust, and He is the Lord of the Supreme Throne" seven times in the morning, we proclaim our acknowledgement that He is the ultimate Guardian to eliminate the problems we face during the day. Then, when the evening comes, we entrust our night to the Lord of Infinite Mercy by repeating the same words. May God enable us to weave every moment of our lives with the radiant rays of the tradition of the Prophet!

The Most Eloquent Invitation
for Divine Providence

Question: *In The Gleams,[5] Bediüzzaman lists the basic principles to attain true sincerity (ikhlas) for the volunteers serving faith. He relates the fourth principle as such: "As if it were you who possess the merits and virtues of your brothers and sisters, take pride in them and be thankful to God for them." Taking into account the feeling of envy in human nature, what are your recommendations to ingrain this perspective in us?*

Answer: While the Qur'an emphasizes in different verses that worship must be carried out solely for the sake of God, the issue is mostly presented with reference to the notion of sincerity, as in: *"... so worship God, sincere in your faith in Him and practicing the Religion purely for His sake"* (az-Zumar 39:2). In the next page, the Qur'an draws attention to sincerity again: *"Say: "I am commanded to worship God, sincere in faith in Him and practicing the Religion purely for His sake"* (az-Zumar 39:11). A few verses later, the importance of sincerity is emphasized once more: *"Say: "I worship God, sincere in my faith in Him and practicing the Religion purely for His sake"* (az-Zumar 39:14).

---

[5]   *The Gleams* is one of the four main volumes of the collection of the *Risale-i Nur* (The Epistles of Light) by the leading Islamic scholar Bediüzzaman Said Nursi (1877–1960). The other three main volumes in this modern commentary of the Qur'an are *The Words*, *The Letters*, and *The Rays*.

The Most Important Means for Divine Support

Giving so much importance to the issue of sincerity, Bediüzzaman wrote two separate chapters in *The Gleams* on *Sincerity*, and summarized the essentials of this issue. The first principle to attain sincerity is, in the words of Bediüzzaman, "seeking good pleasure of God in one's actions."[6] That is, the volunteers not cherishing any worldly or otherworldly expectations while carrying out their duty and taking God's good pleasure as the essential purpose. If unintended fruits and rewards come along, they should be received with gratitude to God and by offering due praise to Him, within a consideration of acknowledging Divine blessings.

However, we should never forget that we are living in an age of arrogance, and we need to wonder whether the blessings showered upon us denote "*istidraj*"—everything going perfectly well before the wrath of God comes, as in the case of the Pharaoh. In order not to become a loser in a zone of winning, we must always say, "These are not the deserve of a humble slave like me; what could be the reason for bestowing all these blessings so benevolently?" We also need to be vigilant against the possibility of a "gradual advance toward perdition" (*istidraj*), as we have mentioned, like the calm before the storm. Obviously, we are being granted Divine favors far beyond our eligibility. It is seen that so many great figures of profound discernment could not achieve a service as carried out by today's volunteers, a great blessing God Almighty bestows by means of ordinary people. For this reason, we need to seek refuge in Him by opening our hands in prayer and saying, "O God, if these blessings we are granted are to pave the way for us toward growing insolent and arrogant, we seek refuge in You against it! Please do not let us go astray!"

Attaining sincerity, which is of central importance to one's spiritual life, is actually in direct proportion with the strength of a person's faith. For this reason, if believers gain insight into the creative commands (the laws of God's creation) and the commandments of the Religion and then seek the ways of progress from faith by imita-

---

[6] Nursi, *The Gleams*, p. 226

tion to faith based on verification, if they, at the same time, try to become constantly oriented toward God in words, actions, and state, as God Almighty has lit the torch of faith in their hearts, He can similarly light the torch of sincerity one day. Thus, you can be able, by God's grace and permission, to practice the values you believe with heartfelt sincerity.

Actually, suppressing the urges of placing emphasis on oneself, being able to see one's shortcomings, coming to one's senses after any assumptions of self-importance and seeking forgiveness from God immediately, and slamming a sledgehammer on the ego depends on two dynamics: becoming totally oriented to sincerity and attaining stronger certainty in faith. Someone who possesses these two qualities will be able to act in harmony with his or her fellow volunteers, because they know that it is not possible to realize anything of a grain's worth without the help of God. And the most important means of that person receiving Divine help is maintaining harmony and unity among the volunteers. It is for this reason that Bediüzzaman emphasized from different angles the importance of the collective spiritual person of the volunteers. He saw this collective person as a significant factor in terms of attaining sound faith and passing to the next world with faith.[7] In addition, he also stated that the good, righteous deeds of each person acting with such collective consciousness would be included in every member's record of good deeds.[8] Thus, the deeds of every single person will increase a thousand-fold through the secret of "shared blessings for good deeds realized collectively." For example, a man may have initiated a process in a certain place in the name of guiding others. If there are ten other fellow volunteers sharing the spirit of brotherhood and taking the same step, every one of them may gain blessings as if each took a thousand steps. Since such people gain so much blessings unawares, they are not in danger of feeling confident in their good deeds; they do not ruin the beautiful results realized through their hands by making a

---

[7]   Nursi, *Tarihçe-i Hayat*, (Kastamonu Hayatı), p. 309
[8]   Nursi, *The Gleams*, pp. 229–230

claim on them. The Almighty Creator who sees and knows all of these approves of their breaking into step in harmony. And He makes them succeed at their services for the good of humanity in both worlds, He includes the total blessings for their collective deeds, in each one's record of good deeds. Thus, even their seemingly little personal good deeds grow into a tremendous totality.

Surprise Rewards

Sometimes, God Almighty grants exceptionally abundant blessings for seemingly little deeds, in special conditions. For example, a soldier's keeping guard near the border for an hour may amount to a year's devotions. Similarly, martyrdom can raise him to the highest levels of human perfection. In the same way, one blessed Night of Qadr spent in devotions can bring a reward more than eighty years of worship. As it is seen in all of these examples, God Almighty may increase the worth of good, righteous deeds so greatly under certain conditions that they become fruitful like ripened ears yielding a thousand grains for a single grain sown. As in these examples, acting as a part of the collective person, which is a different dimension of sincerity, and even beyond that, taking thankful pride in the good, righteous deeds realized by their fellow volunteers, has an exceptionally high worth in the sight of God. One day, Bediüzzaman wished to test whether such brotherhood and sincerity existed among his disciples. He praised the calligraphic skills of a certain disciple in the presence of another. The one who heard this was sincerely pleased and proud of his brother's better skills. Bediüzzaman saw that it was genuine appreciation; he thanked God for granting his disciples such lofty feelings, which would be a means of great service by God's grace.[9] As a matter of fact, it does not really matter which person had the honor of writing a book, who printed the copies, and who distributed them... We can even say that it is safer to feel happy about somebody else's realizing the relevant achievement in terms of retaining one's modesty.

---

[9] Nursi, *Barla Lâhikası*, p. 119

Achievements bring along their risks, such as taking personal pride in them. Even though no pride is taken initially, others' appreciation and praises may lead one to ascribe the achievement to their own knowledge and abilities. Therefore, what befalls on a person in the name of being saved from such risks and not letting things go undone or unfulfilled is to feel happy about a fellow volunteer's realizing that task, taking thankful pride in the other's merits, and gaining due blessings for his or her sincere gratitude to God. One who behaves this way should know that the same reward for the good deeds realized by that fellow volunteer will be included in the record of his or her own deeds as well, as one of the virtues of acting collectively in the name of goodness. In addition, suppressing arrogant inclinations within one's self and applauding fellow volunteers instead will bring such a person a great reward of a very different kind. Furthermore, those who receive this kind of encouragement can develop their potentials and present better performance at more important actions and deeds, and those who give support will have their share again from consequent blessings.

Doors Opening to Perfect Sincerity through Discussion Groups

To reiterate, being sincere and true are in direct proportion with one's degree of faith. The sounder one's faith is, the more that person will succeed in acquiring sincerity. Believers should never stop striving to attain sounder faith; they should always ask for more, trying to gain insight into knowledge of the creative commands and the Religion, in an effort to make continuous progress at faith and knowing God. They should make a ceaseless effort in this regard, climbing degrees of certainty in faith, and ascending from one level to the next.

On the other hand, we need to support one another at making the principles of attaining purity of intention and sincerity prevalent in our lives. We need to discuss this issue when we get together. However, this does not mean making brusque remarks about one another. This evokes a memory from my school years: I used to have only one pair of trousers, and I put them under my mattress, so that they looked neat. Since I came from a poor family, you can take it as a weakness if you wish. One day, a good boy I knew came to me and, referring to my wearing ironed trousers, said, "Why don't you wear untidy clothes and become more pious?" May God bless him, he had no bad intentions, but I still cannot get the connection between wearing ironed trousers and being pious. Even if we are sincere in our remarks, it is not right to be as blunt as a kick in the shins. Moreover, considering oneself to be purely innocent and taking it to the degree of giving sanctimonious advice to others is obvious transgression. As for the commendable way to follow, it is talking matters over without offending anyone and discussing in the mildest and most befitting manner.

Considering the significance of the issue, Bediüzzaman recommended reading the treatise on *Sincerity* every fortnight.[10] I think some of the volunteers have already read it fifty to hundred times. If you only prompt the initial word of a paragraph, some people can recite the rest by heart. However, in order to attain sincerity as an ingrained character and establish it in one's heart and spirit, the issue needs to be considered with a profound and comprehensive approach, rather than doing a flat, shallow reading. People can, however, bring fresh profundity and liveliness to the subject by changing the format of their study. For example, the issue of sincerity can be studied with reference to the Qur'an and the Traditions of the Prophet. Also, this study can be realized in an interactive way with the contribution of people in the group. If that happens, you will most likely say, "Thank God, I have benefited from it. There was so much I did not know. It seems that Bediüzzaman drew attention to very profound and crucial issues at such an early period. Although I had read it so many times, I now understand the importance of the issue with its different aspects."

---

[10] Nursi, *The Gleams*, p. 225

It is so important to evaluate matters in discussions. There is an old saying about it: "Knowledge is a deep well, and discussion is its bucket." Therefore, [just like arriving at a source of water with a bucket to take some water,] obtaining the sweet water of faith down inside the well depends on discussion. The noble Messenger of God, millions of peace and blessings be upon him, referred to the issue with the word "*tadhakur*" (mutual discussion).[11] The inflection of the word denotes that the relevant act is done between two or more people. Accordingly, it is commendable to evaluate matters in circles. The late Muhammed Lütfi of Alvar was a great Sufi master and he voiced the significance of such circles as follows:

> *O seeker of Divine inspirations,*
> *Come and step into the circle.*
> *O lover of the Divine light,*
> *Come and step into the circle.*

As it is stated by the noble Prophet, angels honor such circles formed by seekers of knowledge and truth by visiting them and bearing witness for them before God Almighty.[12]

We should as well, in the name of attaining true faith and sincerity, act with a consciousness of brotherhood and practice the discipline of discussing matters in groups. As we do these in terms of fulfilling the requirements of causes, we should at the same time hold onto prayer and ask for Divine help. At such a difficult age where arrogance has become so widespread, may God Almighty grant all of us a spirit of true brotherhood and perfect sincerity!

---

[11] *Sahih Muslim*, Dhikr, 38; *Sunan at-Tirmidhi*, Qira'ah, 10; *Sunan Abu Dawud*, Witr, 14

[12] *Sahih al-Bukhari*, Da'awat, 66; *Sunan at-Tirmidhi*, Da'awat, 129; *Sahih Muslim*, Dhikr, 25; Ahmad ibn Hanbal, *Al-Musnad*, 2/251, 382

Spirit of Chivalry

Question: *We see that the religious notion of chivalry (futuwwa) is taken in an extensive frame with different definitions from past to present. Considering the conditions of our time, what is chivalry and what are its characteristics?*

Answer: The word *futuwwa*, or chivalry, is derived from the word *fata*, which means young man. It denotes to have sound faith, treat others kindly, devote oneself to living for others, undertake duties for serving humanity without any considerations of primacy, make sacrifices for the sake of sacred values, persevere in the face of crazing flow of time and show active patience, stand up to every kind of evil by taking conditions of the time into consideration and without being unreasonable or illogical, and not panic or shake when confronted with troubles and torments life brings.

One of the *hadiths* reads: "There is no chivalrous man like Ali, and no sword like Zulfiqar."[13] It draws attention to the fact that Ali ibn Abi Talib was a hero who represented chivalry in every way. Actually, Ali ibn Abi Talib was not the first who deserved to be called

---

[13] Ibn Asakir, *Tarikh Dimashq*, 39/201, 42/71; Adh-Dhahabi, *Mizanu'l-I'tidal*, 5/390; Al-Ajluni, *Kashfu'l-Khafa*, 2/488. *Zulfiqar* is the name of a famous sword that Ali ibn Abi Talib used.

chivalrous since *futuwwa* dates back to far earlier periods. Every one of the Prophets can be seen as a significant representative of chivalry on a very lofty level, since they did not live for themselves but for the cause they were devoted to. Some Prophets only had a few followers. And some had no followers at all.[14] However, they continued their mission unwaveringly without complaint.

Seeing Success as God's Grace

The Prophets' carrying out their mission in the best possible way, complying with the requirement of causes and keeping up acting sensibly, taking perfectly strategic action in every condition, and seeing consequent success as God's grace in spite of everything constitute an important profundity of their chivalry. Being fervently dutiful at the beginning and enjoying the gratification of having completed one's duty in the end is a significant indication of the spirit of chivalry. In other words, it is a very important principle of conveying the divine teaching to continue without giving in to disappointment and hopelessness, and to hold the consideration of being thankful to God for He enabled them to carry out their duty, even without people sometimes accepting the message. Furthermore, He did not take away this honor by discharging them from their duty. The true representatives of the spirit of chivalry kept on fulfilling their mission, even if they risked crucifixion. They disregarded the pressures and intimidations of those in power, did not worry about their lives, and always kept walking on the righteous path. In spite of severe oppression by the Romans, Jesus the Messiah did not hesitate risking his life, turned people's attention to the next world, and then ascended to heaven. In this respect, it can be said that the spirit of chivalry Jesus represented served like a launcher for his ascension to heaven.

The story of Moses and his young companion meeting Khadr, as narrated in the Qur'anic chapter of Kahf, points out another dimen-

---

[14] *Sahih al-Bukhari*, Tibb, 17, 41; Riqaq, 50; *Sahih Muslim*, Iman, 374

sion of chivalry. Accordingly, an important profundity of true chivalry is transcending the narrow forms of physicality and journeying into the immensities of metaphysics; it is an ascension from animal life to the realm of the heart and spirit, subsequently continuing that journey. Even though the physical dimension does not cease to exist on that level of life and continues within vital necessities, wishes and desires of the animal side are given secondary importance. For this reason, another important lesson we learn from the parables about the subject is that believers should not suffice by knowing sciences of the physical world; they should also try to gain insight into spiritual secrets by activating their heart and spirit in the true sense.

Devotion and Chivalry

One of the most important aspects of chivalry is keeping up a spirit of devotion. Namely, being devoted to one's sublime cause and pushing aside all other considerations. Truly devoted souls must think that their essential duty is to glorify the Name of God on this earth. Actually, as it was mentioned in other talks, the Name of God is already glorified in its essence;[15] however, efforts must be made for conveying the truth to everyone. People devoted to their cause are supposed to pursue this ideal in all of their feelings, thoughts, initiatives, and actions; they must entreat God Almighty so that He makes them steadfast on this path. Devoted souls must be full of the zeal to offer others true life so as to virtually forget the way to their home and the faces of their children. Let it not be misunderstood, however, that fulfilling one's responsibilities as much as possible—unwillingly or not—toward family members is essential to this path.

Chivalry and Being Upright

In addition to devotion, another very important aspect of chivalry is keeping up an unwavering course. In the face of all adversities one must be able to stand upright and say, as Ibrahim Tannuri, a Sufi poet, did,

---

[15] Gülen, *Ümit Burcu*, p. 131; *Çekirdekten Çınara*, p. 187

I may be suffering from misfortunes, or enjoying Your grace;
They're equally pleasant to my soul; Your grace and
wrath are both welcome.

What I mean by standing upright is not panicking, not toppling over, and not abandoning one's duty against all odds. He who becomes a believer is—like the shape of a question mark—always bowing before God; then, complete that shape into a horseshoe and prostrate. This is the state of the greatest proximity to God Almighty. Thus, these two points should not be confused.

Real Chivalry Is Nullifying Oneself

In addition to displaying this kind of performance and attaining such an ideal state, the greatest difference of the volunteers who serve faith is them not considering themselves different and having primacy. Those who see the chivalrous volunteers will probably describe them as "archetype of virtue," but even that would not suffice in describing them. Truly chivalrous people have such spiritual profundity that even if their body is cut into pieces, they will not give up the path to God. In spite of being so brave, what befalls them is to establish the consideration of not having any primacy or superior sides in comparison to others as a deeply ingrained idea in their souls. The idea of having primacy should not even cross their minds, and when it accidentally does, they should turn to God in repentance as if they committed a great sin. As for all the good works realized by their hands, they think that what happens before their eyes is the germination of the seeds others sowed previously—the emergence from the soil and shooting buds, with every bud giving thousands of grains—and they see everything as the outcome of sincere efforts of those who preceded them without taking any personal pride and assuming primacy. Laying claim on this beauty means both violating others' rights and disrespecting God.

Chivalry necessitates forgetting one to be wiser, older, more experienced, etc. These factors or complimentary remarks by others may sometimes evoke a sense of superiority in a person. On the other hand, having manners requires a respectable form of address toward people who started serving faith long before us. Observing a measured code of respect toward seniors is a means of maintaining better coherence between individuals, given that this is done without exaggerating the matter by calling them a saint or a savior and without evoking dislike in other circles with an assumption of superiority for belonging to a certain religious group. However, if people showing respect fail to adopt the idea of inherently being inconspicuous, then they risk danger of feeling flattered. For example, some of them might say, "I am sixty years old now, and so many people treat me with respect, seeing me as their teacher. Therefore, I am a worthy person." This dangerous thought might cause a person to lose balance and be ruined. Utilizing one's experience at work is a responsibility, but that is a different issue. When compliments for one's experience or mental powers turn into a consideration of primacy and domineering behavior toward others, it is nothing but a blatant transgression of one's limits.

The Must of Chivalry: Humility

There is a saying by Ali ibn Abi Talib telling us to live among others as one of them. This gives us a very important criterion. If we wish to be adorned with the virtue of chivalry, we need to go unnoticed like an ordinary person. In my humble opinion, this is a very important depth of true chivalry and a very important discipline. I did not have the chance to meet Bediüzzaman Said Nursi. However, from what I heard from his students, despite the fact that he was the person they were deeply indebted to, he never had an air of primacy. He always referred to himself as "your brother," and explained his approach as follows: "The basis of our way is brotherhood. My relation with you is not like that between a father and children or a Sufi sheikh and his disciples. It is rather a relation between brothers. At the very most, my position of teaching may have some part in it. Our philosophy requires the closest friendship. Close friendship requires being the best, most self-sacrificing friend, the most appreciative companion, and the most magnanimous brother or sister."[16]

The relationship between the noble Prophet and his Companions teach us important lessons as well. As the Companions got to know the Messenger of God, peace and blessings be upon him, better and realized what the dues of being near him is, they behaved so respectably with most refined manners toward him. For example, Abu Bakr, may God be pleased with him, was a person God rendered a paragon of virtue, who gave fascinatingly powerful sermons, who even moved the polytheists when he recited the Qur'an. Still, he entered to the presence of the noble Prophet so humbly and he was so careful near the Messenger of God that you would think he was afraid of startling a bird on his head. I think if the words he uttered in the presence of the beloved Prophet are to be compiled, they will not amount to more than two hundred. Then, who was the person shown so much respect? Even though the relevant *hadith qudsi* is open to criticism in terms of *hadith* authentication methodology; all Muslim saints agree that he is the person for whose sake the universe was created,[17] since he is the unique guide at reading the universe like a divinely authored book, as well as understanding the Qur'an, which teaches the principles of religion. Being respectful toward such a guide was the duty of the Companions, and that respect was his deserve. When the Pride of Humanity set foot somewhere, even rotten bones in the earth stood up. However, when the Companions stood up for him, as Persians did for their authorities, he told them not to.[18] In the same way, he did his own work; perhaps he prepared his own meals when necessary, washed the dishes, and prepared his bed. If he had allowed them, the people in his household would have done everything for him and never let him do a thing. However, the noble Messenger of God, may the most excellent benedictions and the best blessings be upon him, did not let that happen and did his own personal chores; greatness in

---

[16] Nursi, *The Gleams*, p. 229

[17] Aliyyulqari, *Al-Asraru'l-Marfua*, p. 295; Al-Ajluni, *Kashfu'l-Khafa*, 2/214

[18] *Sunan Abu Dawud*, Adab, 152; *Sunan ibn Majah*, Dua, 2; Ahmad ibn Hanbal, *Al-Musnad*, 5/253

great figures lies in their modesty, humility, and humbleness. As for trying to look great, it is a complex of little people. Putting on an air of superiority to demand respect from others is not appreciated. The Messenger of God, millions of peace and blessings be upon him, never adopted anything that would not become him. Everything he did became him so much that even celestial creatures admired his virtues. To conclude, like other virtues, his example represented chivalry in the best way with all its depths and immensities.

The Architects of Thought Who Will Build the Future

Q uestion: *Some educators state that in addition to certain material shortages and difficulties, they are badly affected by students' disinterest and unwillingness to study. What is your stance on this issue?*

Answer: By taking into consideration certain religious principles, we can say that learning and teaching are two exalted duties whose ends extend into the heavens. In so many verses of the Qur'an and sayings of the Prophet, the importance of knowledge (*ilm*) is emphasized and people are encouraged to pursue it. For example, God Almighty points to the fact that those who know are more superior than those who do not, with the verse meaning, *"Are they ever equal, those who know and those who do not know?"* (az-Zumar 39:9). In another verse, He compares those who know to those who can see, and those who do not to blind people, *"Are the blind and the seeing alike? Will you not, then, reflect?"* (al-An'am 6:50).

The Inheritors of the Prophet's Way

As the supremacy of Prophet Adam over the angels is mentioned in the Qur'an, his having a potential for knowledge is also emphasized, which is a meaningful indication of the importance the Qur'an lays on knowledge. After teaching all the names to Adam, God Almighty asked the angels about them, who did not know, whereas Adam told the names taught to him (al-Baqarah 2:31–32). It is understood from here that what gives supremacy to humanity over the angels is the teaching of "names" to them; in other words, their having a potential for sciences.

In a way, the Messenger of God, peace and blessings be upon him, encouraged learning as the Prophets' heritage and stated that "The Prophets do not leave behind money or wealth as their heritage; the heritage they leave is knowledge (*ilm*); whoever attains that knowledge attains a great share indeed."[19] In another statement, the Messenger of God said that he was sent (to humanity) as a teacher.[20] Thus, he both, emphasized the importance of acquiring knowledge and teaching it to others.

So a teacher is a representative of such a lofty mission, a worker, and an architect of ideas. I think a teacher with spiritual concerns can enlighten the minds and souls of his or her students by utilizing the advantages of the contemporary age and reaching into the essential points of sciences, finding ways through every branch of science such as math, biology, physics, chemistry, anatomy, physiology, and geology. Thus, it can be said that the most suitable way of shaping people and making a monument of them is by being a teacher. It is for this reason that the Qur'an lays so much importance on learning, and the Prophet insistently emphasized this matter. In this respect, individuals who wish to be beneficial to their society, people, and all humanity must face all kinds of difficulties and serve in this field against all odds, and definitely make use of such an important tool.

---

[19]   *Sunan at-Tirmidhi*, Ilm, 19; *Sunan Abu Dawud*, Ilm, 1; *Sunan ibn Majah*, Muqaddima, 17
[20]   *Sunan ibn Majah*, Muqaddima, 17

A Field of Influence That Extends from a Student to All of His Relatives

On the other hand, even though children cannot be legal witnesses in religious matters,[21] they actually are the strongest witnesses of the world in terms of human psychology. Everybody believes what a child says. Therefore, the person a teacher addresses is not only the child in sight; students have many relatives who are in contact with them. When the child comes home, he will naturally relate what happened at school and their relations with the teachers. Therefore, when the teacher expresses himself to the child, he will reflect it to his family in the same way. For example, about a teacher who did kindness to him, the student will say, "he did such and such kind act for me. He listened to our troubles. He found a solution for such and such problem. When we felt sad, he dispersed our doom and gloom and consoled us thus..." and statements to that effect. This kind of reports will form a good opinion of the teacher among the family. And if the teacher establishes a sound dialog with them by taking the opportunity of family visits and other similar ones, then you sometimes see that a single student helps establishing a relation with an entire group of relatives. In this respect, a teacher who is caring for a student can be doing the same for a home, even all of the relatives who have some kind of relation with that home. For this reason, a teacher's field of influence is a really wide one.

In my opinion, a profession with so much gaining must definitely be performed no matter how difficult it is. If necessary, one must get by with a minimal earning, and material drawbacks, like low salaries must not be perceived as obstacles. It is not the money everything depends on. Perhaps the Prophets were the most financially disadvantaged people in the world. However, it was the Prophets again who won people's hearts, guided them to righteousness, and offered a fresh life to the world. With these words, I do not mean to say that teachers should seek poverty artificially. The point I am trying to make is

---

[21] As-Sarakhsi, *Al-Mabsut*, 30/153

that money is not everything, and besides that, there are many different riches like gaining hearts, reaching into spirits, and orienting people toward lofty goals. Particularly at a time when the world is globalized through education, teaching has gained a different importance. While some try to carry out this job with coercion and extreme dislike in spite of all positive feedbacks and reactions, you should do it trying to realize journeys to the hearts of people with your gentleness and affection. And the impulsive force behind that kind of approach is teaching. In this respect, I hold the opinion that students of all levels should be motivated in this sense and encouraged to become teachers. Let there be no misunderstanding; all of the professions that make a society stand and survive should be given importance for sure, not leaving gaps in any field of life. However, we should not forget that teaching has an outstanding position of giving life to a society.

Gaining People to Pray for You in Gratitude for a Lifetime

Let us come to the issue of naughty behaviors of students and their indifference to learning. First of all, we need to accept from the very beginning that all students can present such behaviors. An important aspect of teaching is acknowledging these kinds of troubles and putting up with them. Even a sculptor makes so much effort to make a dry body of marble into a work of art. The sculptor sweats, gets tired, and tries to give a certain shape to the marble in the end. A teacher's job is no easier than that! The teacher takes the potential human, and tries to raise them to the level of true humanity by rounding their sharp pointed sides. In other words, by working all of the precious potentialities in them like a jewel-smith, the teacher helps them make a monument of their souls. Like a gifted artist, the teacher almost builds the human anew. Despite all of these, if there are still certain students that pose serious problems and disturb the general harmony, they can seek different solutions such as meeting their parents or applying alternative guidance programs for them, in order to prevent them from harming those around at least. This way, these students will also have been taken under protection in a certain way. For example, if necessary, it is possible to invite the family members of such students and let them watch the situation of their children from afar; then they can seek different methods of solutions in consultation with the teachers. The Messenger of God, peace and blessings be upon him, turned the most bigoted, savage, and uncivilized people into teachers for a civilized world, and thus, he became the beloved one of so many hearts. This was to such a degree that people who once came to the Prophet's presence and shouted, "Who is Abdulmuttalib's son Muhammad?" started to listen to him attentively, as if they were afraid of startling a bird on their heads. So this is the greatest example of teaching and guidance. Given that the Prophets made wildest people into upright figures to be role models for all, this must be possible at all times. Then the teacher will endure pains and suffering if need be, but in the end he or she will gain individuals to pray for them in gratitude for a lifetime. In addition, their students' good deeds will also add to the teachers' as well. For such an outcome, it is worth bearing whatever it takes. A teacher may not be able to bring all of the students under his responsibility to a certain desirable quality and fail to gain all of the students he maintains contact with. Nonetheless, some people abandoned the circles of even the most perfect guides and prepared their own ruin. In this respect, what befalls on the teacher is to show all the effort they can. The one to create the outcome is God Almighty. But it should never be forgotten that if a teacher takes the task he does as the prime goal, and strives to fulfill the due of his job, God Almighty never lets his efforts be wasted, grants him different favors, and inspires him different ways of solution.

There Is No Matter Unsolved with the Message of a Person's Disposition

An important point that should not be neglected by teachers is providing guidance to students with the language of their disposition and with the depth of their representation of values by personal example. Controlling the evil feelings in human beings—with a potential for evils and bad morals, such as wrath, lust, grudge, hatred, and violating others' rights, all of which can make one fall to the lowest of the low—who are doomed to go corrupt when left on their own, and cultivating benevolent feelings, in them can only be realized through a good guide whose attitude and behaviors are envied and who is taken as a role model.

Finally, let me share a feeling of mine, I hope it will not be misinterpreted as pride. I am seventy four now. But still, if they give me a duty in the wooden hut where I used to stay when I was a mentor long years ago, I will gladly run there and try to fulfill that duty. Perhaps, some of our friends can see that task as a simple and trivial one. But I have not underestimated this duty and would never do so. Even today, some people may consider our having lessons with the small circle of young scholars here as a simple and trivial job. However, in my opinion, this is the most important occupation that can take human to the highest levels.

To conclude, one needs to take teaching very dearly, perceive and consider it as the Prophets' way. The truth is that, among the people who serve a nation, it is not possible to show anybody of equal importance to teachers, since service and investment for humanity are more sacred than everything. If you become the gardener of all of the world's gardens, this does not compare much next to teaching something meaningful to a few people. Let alone that, even kingship is not of equal value as a duty in comparison to making people ascend to true humanity. After all, weren't great rulers of the human history apprentices in the hands of excellent teachers? Taking all of these into consideration, we can say that the people closest to God are teachers who devoted themselves to being beneficial to others. For they are the ones who build the human; they are the ones who build the society. The ones to build the present and future, and the ones to put their stamp on the future are teachers.

Lifelong Contentedness

Question: *It has been stated that one of the most important dynamics in the spirit of devotion in regards to serving humanity is "istighna" (contentedness, feeling no need for anyone but God, indifference to and independence from anything, but God). What are the ways to keep up an attitude of istighna for a lifetime in all aspects of life?*

Answer: Firstly, let me state that *istighna* is such a treasure, that one who has internalized it can challenge the entire universe. Since a person who takes wing with *istighna* closes up all doors of material and spiritual expectations, he does not feel obliged to bow down to anybody but God.

However, it should not be forgotten that the concept isn't merely an attitude against seeking material gain; *istighna* is the term for taking a resolved and upright stance against every kind of position, status, appreciation, praises, and all other kinds of temptations of the carnal soul. For example, if ten people insist that you become a manager, consultant general, or senator, you need to ask yourself whether you can keep up the spirit of *istighna* in the position mentioned. In other words, you need to make a self-critique, questioning yourself whether initiating such a process stems from any egoistic wishes or from an intention to serve people for the sake of God. If egoistic concerns seem dominant, then you should strive to resist against that wish. One may wonder whether things will be left unattended if we become indifferent to certain positions. If there are any competent people due for that position, then your stepping forth will cause rivalry, jealousy, and conflict. For example, if there are ten people in a place of worship who are eligible to lead a prayer, expressing your wish to lead the prayer will bring more harm than benefit with respect to that duty. One of those ten people will end up carrying out the task regardless. As Bediüzzaman also underlined in *The Gleams*, we better "prefer being a follower to leadership, which brings responsibility and therefore is risky."[22] Being an imam is tricky business, since he bears the responsibility of all the people he leads in prayer. A mistake made by the imam is not an individual one. The same goes for a governor. Such a person takes on the responsibility of all the people in his jurisdiction in a case that he makes a mistake. Similarly, when a person leading the state makes a mistake that affects the entire nation, he bears the responsibility of all those people before God. In result of this, instead of wishing to be elected, it is wiser to prefer to remain as a voter. Regarding those that are ambitious to get elected, there is no single individual who does not make serious mistakes. On the other hand, few people make mistakes among who say, "It does not matter who holds office, as long as they are competent."

The Most Difficult Form of *Istighna*

The top level of *istighna* is becoming a self-effacing person, who feels discomforted by praise from others. Even though the carnal soul enjoys being praised, the conscience of ideal believers must take compliments as if they were insults. When they receive praises, they should ask themselves, "Why are they offering me a reward in this world that is to be received in the afterlife? Is it me who made them think this way?" Then they should take the humble path of acknowledging their impotence and poverty before God and pray, "My Lord, allow me to forget about my own self and help me dislike talking about myself." A person may be indifferent to wealth and not care about

---

[22] Nursi, *The Gleams*, p. 215

holding office. However, *istighna* in the face of recognition and praise, is most difficult. Therefore taking a firm stance against applause and praise from the very beginning, not cherishing any instances of this kind whatsoever, and even interrupting people, who are about to praise us, bear great significance.

The Unsung Heroes

I see the contributing teachers of the Turkish Olympiad competition as the most self-sacrificing people of our time, because they went to different corners of the world to raise students in order to serve on the path of love and humanity. However, as their students were applauded by millions of people, they humbly remained anonymous. May God not prove us wrong in our good opinion of them. May God let them keep up their work with heartfelt modesty. They present exemplary behavior. After sowing seeds in the soil and completing our various tasks, we need to be able to walk away without seeking to be noticed. We should not hold on to any expectations about witnessing the harvest. Naturally, all Muslims wish to see that the message of the Prophet Muhammad, peace and blessings be upon him, to humanity reaches everywhere and that the truths he taught are welcomed by the people. Even a simple man like me is no exception. In spite of such a wish, if you had a little bit of contribution to this ideal, you need to say, "My Lord, you know how I wish to see those days, but I do not wish to see anyone praising me for any contributions I may have made. I wish to see that after I pass away." They should also target attaining a genuine feeling of *istighna* to make them sincerely say, "If I am also included in this process, who knows what troubles I will cause. It is better for me to watch the blessings of God in the other world."

Indifferent to the World, Turned toward God

Actually, the most important means to keep up the spirit of *istighna* is leading one's life with an ethics of altruism (*ithar*), preferring others to one's own self. The devoted ones should make altruism a part of their nature and be able to prefer others to their own selves not only at material benefits, but even in spiritual blessings and inspirations. They should think that saintly wonders—such as viewing the Ka'ba during prayer—are happening to others, and become indifferent to everything else but God Almighty. This is the spirit of altruism and the stance of *istighna* in the true sense. Above all, we need to adopt such an outlook in our time.

To conclude, we should be indifferent to material gains, praise, and their worldly benefits. We need to strive not to cherish even otherworldly expectations, but expect possible rewards to come in the afterlife as extra blessings out of God's infinite grace. People can obtain nothing valuable if God does not grant it. They can neither enter Paradise, nor be saved from Hell. All of these can only be maintained by Divine mercy, providence, and grace. Also, God opens numerous doors to somebody who turns away from everything else, but Him. Try closing your doors to worldliness and you will see a thousand others opened by God Almighty, the Opener of Doors. That is, He is the only one who opens doors. Thus, if you wish His door of providence, good pleasure, and appreciation to open to you, then you must keep your doors closed to all worldly expectations for a lifetime.

Not Inclining Towards Those
Who Do Wrong

Question: *After the verse meaning, "Pursue what is exactly right, as you are commanded..." (Hud 11:112), believers are told not to incline towards the wrongdoers in the least. What are the lessons to be drawn from these verses?*

Answer: God Almighty commands all believers to pursue that which is right in the character of the Prophet. Therefore, we are supposed to understand this verse as, "*O believers, pursue what is right as you are commanded...*"

The Wisdom in Singular and Plural Forms

The meaning of this verse contains a compliment and praise for the noble Prophet at the same time. It is as if God Almighty strokes the head of His Messenger and commands him to be perfectly upright. This resembles a situation of a good child being complimented by his teacher, who wishes for him to keep up the good behavior he always displays. Otherwise, it would definitely be a mistake to think that there was something wrong with the beloved Prophet and that God called him to strive towards what is right. In my opinion, the verse holds no implications in this sense whatsoever, because all feelings, thoughts, and actions of the Messenger of God were perfectly upright at all times. Therefore, the verse in question suggests the meaning, "Keep on pursuing what is right, as you have always done." The decree to strive towards the righteous path is used in the singular imperative form in Arabic. The next command meaning, "...and do not rebel against the bounds of the Straight Path" is used in the plural imperative form and this also seems to support our point. When this verse and several similar verses are studied, one can derive from them, that the commands about being good are used as singular imperative sentences directly addressing the noble Prophet, whereas those forbidding transgression are in plural form. Based on this notion, we can infer that the real command is to all the believers, but is addressed to the Messenger of God, for he is the best example for all.

In addition, there appears to be a fine point presented about the warning against inclining toward the wrongdoers, right after the command to pursue what is right; it is a warning against a gradual shift toward transgression and misguidance.

Keeping Away from Every Kind of Wrongdoing

As it is mentioned in the question, the next verse (Hud 11:113) gives a command meaning:

> "...do not incline towards those who do wrong (against God by associating partners with Him or transgressing against His commands, or against people by violating their rights), or the Fire will touch you. For you have no guardians and true friends apart from God; (but if you should incline towards those who do wrong,) you will not be helped (by Him)."

A person who leans by a slightest degree toward those who do wrong runs the risk of gradually being included in the same evil. As a matter of fact, wrongdoing (*zulm*) is extensively covered in the Qur'an. As this word is used to express the transgressions of unbelievers and hypocrites, it is also used to describe specific mistakes of Muslims, as in: "*Those who have believed and not obscured their faith with any wrongdoing—they are the ones for whom there is true security, and they are rightly guided"* (al-An'am 6:82). When this verse was revealed, the Companions felt great distress. Seeing their situation, the Messenger of God consoled them with the verse meaning, *"Associating partners with God is a tremendous wrong"* (Luqman 31:13), and stated that the wrongdoing mentioned in the other verse refers to associating partners with God, also known as *shirk*.[23] This being the worst transgression, there are other various forms of wrongdoing from persecution to abusing bureaucratic powers. Considering the verse mentioned in the initial question, the Divine command warns against all kinds of wrongdoing; furthermore, believers are also forbidden from inclining toward those who commit the acts of wrongdoing. An important point that should not be missed is that wrongdoing should not be solely associated with obvious injustice and transgressions. As it is a misdeed for a bureaucrat of any level to favor certain people over others, allocating even a gram of what belongs to the people is also a violation. Relatively speaking, the verse indicates that inclining toward someone who commits any level of wrongdoing is a reason for being touched by Hellfire. In other words, spending time with wrongdoers as a normal order of affairs, being fond of them, or being like them are all included in the meaning of showing inclination. Nevertheless there is another decree meaning, *"When you meet such that indulge in (blasphemous or derisive) talk about Our Revelations, turn away from them until they engage in some other talk"* (al-An'am 6:68).

As a matter of fact, a person who always displays righteousness in their intention, way of living, words, attitudes, and behaviors will naturally stand against misdeeds and injustice. Another verse gives glad tidings to such people, *"As for those who say, 'Our Lord is God,' and then follow the Straight Path (in their belief, thought, and actions) without deviation, the angels descend upon them from time to time (in the world as protecting comrades, and in the Hereafter with the message): 'Do not fear or grieve, but rejoice in the glad tidings of Paradise, which you have been promised'"* (Fussilat 41:30).

---

[23] *Sahih al-Bukhari*, Anbiya, 8, 41; Tafsir as-Surah (31), 1; Istitaba, 1, 8; *Sahih Muslim*, Iman, 197

Question: Why are people inclined to wrongdoers?

There can be different reasons for this. Sometimes, one may feel obliged to side with wrongdoers out of fear. Throughout the history of humanity, so many unfortunate people did just that by fearing to lose their rank and position. In the present as well, many people flatter wrongdoers in order to retain their status and enjoy its advantages. Love of position is one example of the presence of such a virus. In addition, love for being applauded, hedonism, addiction to comfort and one's family are weaknesses of the same kind. A person concerned with making his children enjoy wealth will be doomed to salute wrongdoers along the way. In fact, even though such people perceive themselves as walking on the righteous path, they are actually on a slippery slope and have a great possibility to fall at any time.

It is possible to list many other similar causes or viruses within this issue. Each one of them is like a door to keep away from, which is opening to misdeeds. Keeping away from anything that might pave the way for sins, *sadd al-zarai,* is a principle of Islamic Jurisprudence. Relatively speaking, one must close and bolt up all the doors, such as love of status, passion for applause, fear and the like.

As we keep away from infectious environments in the material sense, we need to do the same with spiritual diseases. Otherwise one can shift towards committing misdeeds unintentionally. It is stated at the end of the verse, that such people receive no help, for their acts cut their connection with Him. As a final point, let me draw attention to the verse that follows the ones mentioned above, *"Establish the Prayer at the beginning and at the end of the day, and in the watches of the night near to the day. Surely, good deeds wipe out evil deeds"* (Hud 11:14). In terms of the coherence between verses, the command to establish prayer is very meaningful. Accordingly, if one can go beyond apparent forms of faith and establish prayer thoroughly with not only its outward, but also its inward dimensions, then he will have protected himself against accepting wrongdoing.

Becoming the Soil for Roses

Question: *People holding certain posts or having attained particular statuses would, in time, develop an assumption of superiority. What are the essential principles to help believers avoid arrogance?*

Answer: As the blessings of God Almighty come showering down, what befalls the children of Adam, who were created from a mere drop of liquid, are feelings of gratitude, thanksgiving, humility, and—whatever position they are in—seeing themselves (not above but) below others. What really matters is being able to say, as Muhammed Lütfi Efendi stated,

> *Everybody is refined but I am rough;*
> *Everybody is wheat but I am chaff.*

You can call this consideration modesty, self-effacement, or reducing oneself to zero if you like, but it is a definite fact that true existence flourishes in the bosom of this consideration.

A Meteor Could Fall!

How beautiful one poet's expression is:

> *Without dropping down to the earth a seed cannot attain blessings,*
> *Those who are truly modest flourish by Divine Providence.*

Meaning, if a seed does not drop and let itself decompose to germinate, it cannot sprout its shoot and produce crops. The process of having fruitful crops depends on being crushed under the soil, becoming soil, and being no one; only then a second existence becomes possible. So whatever status one has in society, true wisdom requires one to see oneself this way. Individuals with such considerations are already prepared for self-effacement and will therefore not lose in the face of even the hardest tests by God's grace. Such people do not feel dizzy before victories, and do not give up in the face of pressures, attacks, and insults, because a man who sees himself as a seed under the soil does not mind others walking on him. As for those who pay tribute to their ego, they would draw negative meaning from the looks, gestures, and innocent smiles of others and would feel discomfort even with trifle and very irrelevant things when they cannot receive the treatment they expect from others.

However, those who get themselves in a cocoon of humility, assuming a modest position below ground level, will neither be disturbed by any insults nor by being walked on. Not only will they not be disturbed, they will deem that all of those negative situations are their just deserts, taking it as a chance for a new self-criticism. For example, if a walnut falls on their heads, they say, "It serves me right. Considering my present state, it could have been a meteor." They believe that there is definitely much wisdom behind every event, since God Almighty would never ordain futile, unreasonable things to happen but decrees everything with infinite wisdom.

Particularly in our time when arrogance has grown out of control, modesty, humility, and self-effacement bear even more importance in terms of being able to provide guidance to others. Think about it; roses do not grow on emerald, ruby, coral, gold, or silver. Although these substances are among the most precious materials that are formed with the permission of God in the earth or sea, no roses grow on them. Roses grow in soil. Even the Pride of Humanity was created from soil. His blessed ancestors were also created from soil. In this respect, if we wish to cultivate beautiful roses, we have to be modest like the soil.

Liberating Oneself from Selfishness

Acting in compliance with the manners taught by the tradition of the Prophet is very important in our relations with others, in terms of not being seized by considerations of superiority and establishing the idea of humility as an ingrained depth of our character. For example, the noble Prophet once said, "Wish for others, what you wish for yourself, so that you become a believer (in the true sense)."[24]

Accordingly, one who is so immensely thoughtful, sensitive, and magnanimous to the degree of wishing for others what they wish for themselves possess the character of a true believer. Let us consider the opposite: If people do not wish for others what they wish for themselves and if what they wish for others is what they do not wish for themselves, then such individuals are distant from the protective atmosphere of true faith and stand on a slippery ground where they can stumble and fall any time.

Moreover, we are supposed to have a good opinion of others' attitude and behaviors even if these do not seem quite right. We need to think that they may have behaved that way for a reason that is not clear to us. To put it differently, we had better try to give a good meaning to others' behaviors which might seem wrong outwardly but is possible to explain with a plausible base and reason. As having such an approach towards others is an important shield against having baseless negative perceptions about them, it is a similarly powerful incentive for keeping a good opinion of others. In addition, not taking any personal pride depends on having such considerations.

Making Modesty into an Ingrained Character Trait

Everybody should know that they need a good rehabilitation through education and training in terms of making modesty into an ingrained

---

[24] *Sunan at-Tirmidhi*, Zuhd, 2; *Sunan ibn Majah*, Zuhd, 24

character trait in them. For this reason, by taking refuge in the Divine name *Rabb* ("Lord" as the Creator, Trainer, Upbringer, and Director of all creatures), we need to carry on our lives under the protection of our Lord and be resolved to acquire an ideal morality in conformity with the Divine training and instruction; we need to make a self-supervision every day with respect to religious criteria.

Naturally, being steadfast and consistent is of great importance. As the Messenger of God stated, "Most lovable of deeds in the sight of God is the continuous one, even though it is of little amount."[25] As is known, steady water drops have the ability to form a hole even on a marble surface. In this respect, rehabilitating the carnal self, spiritual training, and continuous attendance to religious talks are among the most important points of the issue.

At a certain period in history, the traditional madrasa schools and Sufi lodges embraced all areas of life and jointly fulfilled this mission. People who surrendered themselves fully to their education and guidance ascended to the level of true humanity by undergoing serious spiritual training and letting the faculties of their mind, heart, and spirit thrive. Along with keeping the mind ready to welcome scientific matters in their own circumstances, those blessed places showed their initiates the ways of soaring on the horizons of the heart, spirit, and *sirr* (a spiritual faculty meaning "the secret"). Otherwise, if matters are evaluated merely within the field of reason, then it becomes inevitable to be trapped within the narrow boundaries of rationalist and Mu'tazilah thought. Nevertheless, it is very difficult to say whether those who adopt such schools of thought provided sound guidance to those around them, in spite of these favorable conditions. As for those who achieved to whisper some things into people's hearts in the true sense, they have been the ones who led their lives on the horizons of the heart and spirit.

---

[25] *Sahih al-Bukhari*, Riqaq, 18; *Sahih Muslim*, Salatu'l-Musafirin, 216–218, Salatu'l-Munafiqin, 7

Crying of Those with Sad Hearts

Question: *It is stated that sometimes God grants mercy to an entire world upon the crying of one sad heart.*[26] *Today, it seems that we do not feel deeply troubled and sympathize enough for humanity's suffering, so as to weigh heavily on our consciences and prey on our minds. What can be the possible reasons?*

Answer: The human factor lies at the basis of all individual, familial, and social problems, which people have faced ever since the time of the Prophet Adam, peace be upon him. The same is true for the basis of all the cases of anarchy, oppression, strife, and crises. Given that all problems can be traced back to the human factor, the solution of these problems is possible through approaching it anew, with a system of moral training oriented to Divine truths and appealing to the conscience. Otherwise, people cannot be saved from misguidance, misery, debauchery, and poverty.

Realizing One's Being at the Bottom of the Well

The greatest problem of humanity today is the neglect of the human factor. But how many of us feel deeply troubled by this grave problem and feel due suffering within? Unfortunately, since most of us

---
[26] Al-Kushayri, *Ar-Risalatu'l-Kushayriyya*, p. 139

live within the same sort of environment, the vast majority of people are unable to grasp even the scale and size of the debauchery and poverty, the deviation and fall. Let me clarify my point with an example: After having stayed in the city for a while, I visited my uncle who lived in the village. The moment I poked my head in through the door, I said how bad the smell was. On hearing this, my uncle's grandchildren started laughing at me, because I had stayed in the same house for about a month in my childhood and did not feel disturbed at all. Rumi tells the story of a man who gets accustomed to the stench of a leather tannery workshop. When that man passes near perfumery shops and smells the beautiful fragrances, he cannot tolerate them and faints.[27] This story depicts to us the situation of corrupted human nature. As people of the contemporary age, we take for granted everything to such a degree that we feel no shame or suffering, even before the most shameful sights. We see nearly all wrongs as normal. As a poet stated, "Somebody who is full thinks everybody in the world is full; a hungry one thinks there is no bread in the world." Similarly, since we do not feel suffering and have not come to grips with reality, we do not feel a need to say, "Enough!" as a spontaneous reaction of our conscience and then try to fix it. The reason is that we are inevitably influenced by the atmosphere and conditions in which we live. It diffuses into all of our senses and, in a way, influences the cortex. Thus, individuals perceive and evaluate their surroundings accordingly and cannot overcome this framework.

People fail to realize that there is a very distinguished position that they are supposed to take vis-à-vis their Creator and that they stand far below this position in reality. They think themselves to be in an enjoyable clime in spite of staying at the bottom of a well. For this reason, they make no effort to climb out of the well. Human beings possess the gift of adapting to the conditions in which they live. For example, the ears of a person in a noisy environment adapt themselves to the noise, and they become senseless to sounds of a certain frequen-

---

[27] Mevlâna, *Mesnevî*, 4/204–206

cy that they normally would hear. Similarly, we have always seen people who are content to lead a world-oriented life, seeking only to have good time. And, therefore, we fail to realize our own heart-rending spiritual wretchedness.

However, suffering is a very important invitation for Divine inspirations. It whispers to people very different ways first to realize and then be saved from the troubled state that they are really in. For instance, if a man at the bottom of a well or dungeon is aware of his situation and feels due suffering, he will try to get out in many different ways and will achieve his goal in the end by God's grace. Even if he does not possess any tools, he will try to climb out by using his hands like claws. He strives on and makes two small holes where he can insert his feet. After managing to stand on them, he does the same above the first ones. Continuing like this, he makes his way out of the well after a certain period of time. But a man living contentedly down there, even unaware of his situation, will never make such an effort.

The State of Misery That Invokes Divine Compassion

If people suffer deeply over the fall and deviation that they have undergone and turn to God wholeheartedly, as Bediüzzaman puts it in *The Gleams*, at such a moment when all the apparent causes show no sign of hope, one can witness the secret of *Ahadiyya* being manifest through the light of Divine Oneness and Unity.[28] As it is well-known, when Prophet Jonah, peace be upon him, was swallowed by a whale, the animal's body, waves of the sea, and the dark night enveloped

---

[28] Nursi, *The Gleams*, p. 4. *Ahadiyya* expresses God Almighty's being one, single, and unique. He also has manifestations or blessings (of *Ahadiyya*) particular to each thing and being. When one realizes his or her absolute helplessness, he or she can unfold this secret of *Ahadiyya* manifestly through the light of his conviction of the Oneness of God, Who has absolute control over everything. This is because apparent means and causes have no part of their own in the creation of results. Since Prophet Jonah saw with the eye of certainty that there was no refuge other than the Causer of Causes, and he, through his utmost conviction of God's absolute Oneness and His dominion over the universe, fully perceived that in addition to His overall manifestations that reign supreme over all of creation, God also has manifestations particular to each thing and being as the All-Compassionate.

him with no sign of hope. But that great Prophet prayed in that manifold darkness saying, *"There is no deity but You, All-Glorified are You (in that You are absolutely above having any defect). Surely I have been one of the wrongdoers (who have wronged themselves)"* (al-Anbiya 21:87). By praying thus, he appealed to Divine Mercy and Compassion and was delivered in a miraculous fashion. At this point, the words of Ibrahim Haqqi are also meaningful:

> *When you are in dire need,*
> *Divine Providence opens a door;*
> *For every trouble, He sends a cure.*
> *Whatever the Almighty will do*
> *He will do the best for you.*

Now, consider our spiritual life: Aren't we in a worse condition than Prophet Jonah in the belly of the whale? Bediüzzaman states in *The Gleams* that our carnal soul is like such a whale to us.[29] That is, we are in a way swallowed by our (evil-commanding) carnal souls. We have been taken by worldly considerations and fancies of the carnal soul. But the worst is that we are not even aware of our wretched condition. We act as if we are heartless creatures in the face of severe oppression, misery, and subjection in different lands. Therefore, we first must ask ourselves, "Who were we and who are we now?" The next thing to do is to establish a connection between the age we are currently living in and the Age of Bliss (i.e., the Age of the Prophet), and then make a sound comparison. We should even include the following decades when Islamic civilization flourished and try to find out how competent statesmen dealt with the troubles of their time and how they exerted themselves to find solutions for the problems that confronted them. By comparing those lustrous days with ours, we should try to understand how disastrous our condition is. I think such racking of our brains will lead us to knocking on the door of the Merciful God, and He will show us alternative ways out. To the extent we see our state as normal, we will neither find alternative ways, nor discover new methods in the name of deliverance.

---

[29]   Nursi, *The Gleams*, p. 5

The Seeds of Suffering Sown into Hearts

Consciousness of the (Age of Bliss and the following) golden ages where true Islamic spirituality was practiced and realizing our present miserable state is the key to feeling the suffering that we are supposed to feel. Bediüzzaman voiced his suffering about the grim picture before him by saying, "I even have no time to think about the troubles I am subjected to. I gladly welcome going through a thousand fold greater difficulties if only I saw the faith of people in safety."[30] Similarly, he stated that he would even gladly welcome burning in Hell, given that the faith of his people is secured.[31] These sublime thoughts are an expression of having attained the level of true humanity. Given that humanity is heedlessly heading for Hell before our eyes, and that we consider ourselves as conscientious believers, we cannot help but to be appalled by this picture.

It is a reality that not everybody can sense and feel matters with such magnanimity in their consciences.

In addition, it may not be proper for everybody to know about every trouble and problem, since some people cannot resist even the pettiest viruses. However, when those with strong immune systems face a virus attack, this does not cause them anything more than a temporary stagger. In the same way, even the persons who try to serve for the sake of faith may not have the same strength of immunity. For this reason, telling them all of the grim realities might push them to hopelessness.

I would like to express how I feel: If my parents and grandparents were alive today, and if all of them passed away in one moment, I swear by God that this grief would not equal the suffering I go through for the fate of Islam in half a day. Sometimes, I leave my room in the middle of the night bent in two with this suffering and wander in the corridor as if I were crazy. In spite of this, I am trying not to tell everybody about the monstrous souls lying in wait at every corner,

---

[30] Nursi, *Tarihçe-i Hayat* (Tahliller), p. 615
[31] Ibid., p. 610

each one of them running after a different conspiracy and plot. This can make some people lose courage and give in to hopelessness. Therefore, I prefer not to reveal my concerns about it. But if I knew that they could bear the truth, I would wish to sow the seeds of suffering and pour embers into people's hearts, so that they too would become concerned for humanity's troubles, so that they too would lose sleep and walk around restlessly as if they were insane, exerting themselves to find solutions.

Nevertheless, if one is not called insane for suffering for his religion, it is difficult to say that he has attained perfect faith. That is, others will look at such a person and say, "Instead of enjoying this world with its natural beauties and resorts, why does he busy himself with such concerns?" This is an indication of being seen as insane, as the great Sufi Yunus Emre stated, not caring about losing what you possess after having found the ultimately absolute value. What about those who do not feel so? Are they destined to be losers? Never, I cannot dare say that. Since the Pride of Humanity related that a person who passes away with the smallest amount of faith will, finally, enter Paradise.[32] We cannot blame anyone on this issue, nor try to block anybody's way to Paradise. This is a different issue. However, feeling agonized over humanity's suffering and it preying on your mind, and embracing all of humanity with an attitude that befits the Prophets, is a completely different issue.

---

[32] See al-An'am 6:82; *Sahih al-Bukhari*, Janaiz, 1, Istiqrad, 3, Bad'u'l-Khalq, 6; Istizan, 30, Riqaq, 13; *Sahih Muslim*, Iman, 150, 151, 152, 153; Zakah, 32, 33.

Balance and Moderation

Question: *In almost every area of life today, serious deviations of thought are seen and extremism is credited. What are the points to be careful about for those who wish to avoid extremism?*

Answer: Being balanced and maintaining moderation is very important for being able to practice religion in the way God Almighty meant and to make it become the spirit of our lives. For when balance is lost, one strays to one of the two extreme levels—excessiveness or apathy (insufficiency). As these two extremes evoke one another in a reactive pattern, they give way to a vicious cycle. In fact, freedom from the two extremes is through adherence to the Practice of the Pride of Humanity, who always counseled moderation to his community.

The Middle Way

The Qur'anic concept of the *Sirat al-Mustaqim* (Straight Path) has usually been defined with reference to following the "middle way," or moderation, at the three main human faculties of desire, aggression, and reasoning.[33] However, it is possible to evaluate other factors, such

---

[33] The *Sirat al-Mustaqim* is the "middle way" having nothing to do with any extremes. It is the middle way, considering human psychology and the realities of life and creation. In educating people, it disciplines and ennobles the faculty of "reasoning,"

as rivalry, envy, intention, and viewpoint, within the same perspective. Indeed, it is possible to talk about following a middle way for every feeling and thought inherently found in human nature.

For example, if we take "viewpoint" (*nazar*) in terms of gaining insight into phenomena and evaluating them, being an optimist represents the upper extreme, whereas a pessimist represents the lower extreme, and a truthful one represents the middle way. As the first two only tend to see the good or bad side in everything, a truthful person tries to evaluate everything realistically. Nevertheless, (as seeing things and phenomena happening around one through the eye of wisdom make the person think, and thereby act, positively) Bediüzzaman expressed in his *Seeds of Truth*, "Those who attend to the good side of everything contemplate the good. Those who contemplate the good enjoy life."[34] In addition, even with respect to things that do not seem very pleasant, it is better to hold positive considerations as far as it is possible to do so. But this does not mean overlooking the reality and living in a world of fantasy. What needs to be done is to see things as they are without escaping realities or giving into hopelessness, which means having the "middle way," or a "balanced viewpoint."

Actually, when the middle way is taken and moderation is maintained, even the human carnal soul, which seems to be evil, can serve as a positive factor for spiritual progress. Even Satan, who leads people astray with his temptations and deceptions, can be a means for spiritual progress as a factor that makes people turn toward God (as far as the wisdom of his creation and his position is correctly understood). On the other hand—may God forbid—if Satan is assumed as a separate power who is able to exert force, it will lead people to deviation, like the situation of those who think that light and darkness

---

saving it from the extremes of demagogy, cunning and stupidity, and so leads to sound knowledge and wisdom. The disciplining and ennobling of the faculty of "aggression" and impulse of defense saves that faculty from wrongdoing, oppression and cowardice, and leads to justice and valor. The faculty of "desire" is saved through discipline from dissipation and hedonism and grows into chastity.

[34] Nursi, *The Letters*, p. 450

have a force and power on their own. Those who hold this belief think that light and darkness are individual powers, that light brings no harm, but the representatives of darkness have to be pleased. Hence, they commit undreamed-of evils with this deviant consideration. Satanists who act with this philosophy try to please Satan so that they can be saved from its evil. Imagining a powerless creature who has no weapon but deceit and beguilement—God forbid—as a being that possesses a part of the power and force that belongs to the Creator, is the upper extreme, to the degree of insanity. On the other hand, dismissing its deceit and beguilement and turning a blind eye to its goading and whisperings, and thus ignoring the warnings in the Qur'an and Sunnah, is the lower extreme. Satan is a clear enemy of man; if someone does not give his willpower its due and becomes heedless, he risks losing eternal bliss through the hand of his relentless and faithless archenemy.

Victims of Success

As it is very important to strike a balance at the negative factors that can lead one to destruction, it is also very important for people to strike a balance with respect to their feelings concerning the achievements that they are blessed with. That is, it is also necessary to watch one's step concerning the deeds of the heart and body realized in the name of faith, worship, and morality by not straying from the middle way. For example, believers must do their best and seek perfection in observing all their acts of worship such as the daily Prayers, alms, pilgrimage, fasting, supplicating to God, and reflecting on His works. As decreed in the Qur'an, "*Work, and God will see your work, and so will His Messenger and the true believers*" (at-Tawbah 9:105), all the righteous works must be realized in the best way with a consciousness of presenting them to God, His Messenger, and believers. In short, believers must not feel content with what they do but should seek perfection in all of their acts of worship. However, even if they attain a nearly perfect performance, they should never become insolent by

laying claim on the consequent success; it is God Almighty who creates success. If being superficial, slothful, and heedless at worship is
the lower extreme, then the upper extreme is having insolent pride in
one's acts of worship and laying a claim on the blessing which is granted by God after the servant's meticulous efforts. Because, even though
the worshipper exerts oneself and seeks perfection, laying claim on
the consequent success leads to ruin through arrogant sanctimony.

Therefore what becomes a person who attains success are modesty, humbleness, and humility. One must always say, "It is not deserved
of a servant like me; how has this kind favor been granted to me?" As
believers should try to do their best, they should also know to tan their
carnal soul by beating it up, as tanners once did for tanning hides. In
addition, they should never forget that the achievements and success
they are granted might, indeed, be tests for them, which may lead to
their ruin if personal pride is felt.

Imagine that some false prophets—such as Aswad al-Ansi and
Musaylima the Liar—appeared even at a period when the true light
illuminated everywhere. Those poor people became victim to certain
gifts they saw in themselves and perished in the claws of pride and
egotism.

An Inflation of the "Divinely-guided" Saviors, in an Age of Arrogance

Surely such cases of deviation and misguidance are not limited to a
particular period in history. Almost every period witnesses such
events. Today, as well, you can see some people who can talk or write
impressively or have taken a few steps on the spiritual path, who lose
their balance and seek to become an idol and display due arrogance.
When they display themselves and when a circle of naïve ones begins
to form around them, they start seeing themselves like a bright star
immediately. For this reason, there is an inflation of Mahdis—the so-
called "Divinely-guided" people, today. Even a humble servant like
myself knows five or six such "saviors" who have appeared in Muslim
community. Three of them even tried to contact me—in fact, one of

them came here recently. He said he was twenty-two years old. He then told me, "I thought that I was from the lineage of the Prophet's grandson Husayn, but after extensive research I learned that I was also from the lineage of the Prophet's other grandson Hasan." I tried to remind him of some points about humbleness and modesty. I tried to tell him that the sign of worthlessness in worthless ones is their assuming greatness, virtually standing on their toes to look greater than they really are; and the sign of worth in truly worthy ones is their humbly curved stature, in order to look lesser than they really are. After I spoke to him, I thought that he was convinced. To my surprise, the last thing he said before leaving was: "All right sir, but what can I do if I have [been divinely chosen and appointed and thereby] not been given a right to choose at this issue?" However, there is no spiritual rank or title in Islam—including the imamates of the Sunni schools of thought (Hanafi, Shafii, Maliki, and Hanbali) or being the Mahdi—that puts one under obligation of proclaiming it to others, except for Prophethood.[35] However, it is very difficult to tell anything to those who are obsessed with such a thought. May God guide all of the egotist and arrogant ones obsessed with a claim of being Mahdi to the Straight Path.

Let me add one final point here. It should never be overlooked that people with similar claims might surface even in an auspicious circle that is based on an understanding of humbleness, modesty, sincerity, and making no claims whatsoever. Since such people base their arrogance on their affiliation with a certain group, it can be much more difficult to bring them to their senses. For example, one of them might say, "Until recently, I had been a disciple of such and such guide, who was supported by a thousand angels or spirit beings. But now, nine hundred of them have left him and come to support me." As different examples are seen in every period, people can become a slave to their carnal soul and Satan through various delusions.

---

[35] The Prophets who were Divinely chosen and appointed with the mission of Prophethood were required to declare their Prophethood and convey the Revelations they received to their people.

Thus it should not be forgotten that even at the time when the seeds sown have begun to flourish and gardens are filled with roses, an invasion of thorns is always possible. Believers should always be vigilant on the path on which they walk. There will always appear some people to misguide naïve ones. As thorns can exist near roses, ravens might begin to crow near nightingales. Thus, those who have not heard the nightingale, who are not accustomed to its beautiful singing, can be enthralled by the crowing of the raven. For this reason, believers must be alert against such deceptions and constantly maintain vigilance with a good insight—like that of the Caliphs Abu Bakr and Umar, may God be pleased with them—and act sensibly.

Exaggerated Compliments

Question: *When a person achieves something that deserves praise, we express our appreciation to motivate them further. However, such praise and recognition may sometimes lead to arrogance, pride and boasting. What are your considerations on this issue?*

Answer: It is a reality that we are weak to strike a balance after receiving praise and recognition for our achievements. If you exaggerate a matter and praise someone above their worth, which is a behavior God dislikes, Divine Justice might teach you a lesson about it. In this respect, you need to act in a balanced manner on this issue, so that no disrespect is made against God Almighty. When you exaggerate your comments about certain people, telling them how they worked wonders like the greatest saints, God Almighty may give you a worldly punishment and make you see the truth about these people.

Those Who Become Objects of Envy

In addition to the above mentioned points, praises towards someone have another potential side to it. When we sing praises about a person, this admiration might invoke envy in others, who might wish to belittle that person in consequence. Thus, we might provoke other people with what we say, and we need to be careful about that. For example, a person who learned the truths of faith and religion through the works of Bediüzzaman may love him very much. They can be full of admiration and gratitude toward him for helping them broaden their horizons about faith and understand the noble Prophet's teachings correctly. However, this love should never lead them to exaggerate their admiration and perceive him like a Prophet; this is something Bediüzzaman would never dream about. In addition, if highly positive opinions about that great figure are voiced near people who follow another Islamic figure, it might trigger a reaction and feelings of rivalry and envy.

Furthermore, we need to be extra careful when talking about the Pride of Humanity, peace and blessings be upon him, for whose sake we would give anything. That blessed person is the means of happiness for humanity in both worlds. He is the one who unearths mysteries of creation and turns this world, which seems to be a chaos and confusion, into a corridor to Paradise. If we are able to feel peace and contentment within the magical atmosphere of belief, in accordance with the depth of our faith, it has become possible through him. In spite of all of the above mentioned however, we can never attribute anything to the Prophet that can be interpreted as deifying him.

All Praise Belongs to God

In regards to praising God Almighty, there is never a limit for that. As there is nothing comparable to Him, there can be no rival to Him whatsoever. Therefore, nobody is ever heard saying, "Why are they praising God, but not the spiritual master I follow?" As God is the Master of all of us, He is the absolute Master of all masters, including the Prophet. As the noble Prophet also stated, our real Master is God;[36] He is the Master of everybody and everything. You can even fade away like a firefly that has lost its light, before the Eternal Sun of all suns. There is no other way to feel Him anyway. Seeing and knowing God, and His manifestation with true understanding, depends on a person's complete effacement of himself, becoming nearly non-existent. How beautifully a poet expresses this concept:

---

[36] *Sunan Abu Dawud*, Adab, 9; Ahmad ibn Hanbal, *Al-Musnad*, 4/24, 25

You are not manifested while I exist on the screen,
My becoming non-existent, is the condition for Your manifestation...

Given that two sights cannot exist on one screen at the same time, one needs to get non-existent, to feel the Truly Existent, so that he can reflect on and witness Him. We need to accept that our existence is like a shade, so that we can see the Original. So many servants of God, like the Great Prophets, the reputable scholars of purity, and the respected saints, acknowledged their existence being like a shade; we can only be a very faint shade far behind them. Who knows, maybe the ones who will be blessed with the honor of seeing God in the afterlife will be the ones who humbly see themselves as mere shade. God Almighty will tell them, "Given that you lived in the world as shades, the time has come to take refuge under My shade, on the day when no other shelter exists." Even though we cherish such thoughts about God Almighty, we should never give up being cautious about other human beings. As a matter of fact, no matter who speaks and towards whom—all praise escaping our lips belong to God only. Nevertheless, all Muslims who observe their daily prayers voice this truth by reciting Surah al-Fatiha, which begins with the words meaning, "All praise is due to God, Lord of the worlds..." since the definite article "*al*" at the beginning of the word "*hamd*" (praise) denotes that all kinds of praise belong to Him only. Therefore, even the praises we express towards people we love essentially belong to Him as well.

A Great Wrongdoer in a Pitiable Condition

In short, just as we need to be very careful while talking about great figures who deserve appreciation, we need to avoid voicing our sublime pride in them near people who might show a negative reaction. Because doing so might provoke feelings of jealousy and rivalry, which will serve nothing, but raising opposition and pushing those innocent people to sin. People who feel jealousy commit sins and destroy their good deeds. The great saint Hasan al-Basri stated that he had not seen any other wrongdoer like the one who becomes jealous, and ironically appears as if he was wronged, in spite of being the wrongdoer.[37] That is, one who becomes jealous commits such a grave sin, that he falls into a pitiful condition. We have no right to put somebody in such a situation. Even though not everybody can observe the same sensitivity towards others, people in particular positions, where this can be encountered, need to be more cautious and careful on this issue.

[37] Ibn Abdi Rabbih, Al-Iqdu'l-Farid, 2/158; Al-Qurtubi, Al-Jami' li Ahkami'l-Qur'an, 5/251

Enemies of a Happy Marriage

Question: *It is mentioned in a saying of the Prophet that driving a wedge between spouses and spoiling a marriage is among Satan's favorite deeds. How would you recommend married couples stay away from this danger and not have their marriage end in divorce, which is known as the ugliest of lawful deeds in the sight of God?*

Answer: Satan is the instigator of all evil deeds and destroyer of good, righteous deeds. We see that negative deeds are ascribed to Satan in the Qur'an, as in: "*...Satan decked out their deeds to be appealing to them*" (an-Nahl 16:63) and "*Then Satan made an evil suggestion to both of them...*" (al-A'raf 7:20).

The Stealthy and Sworn Enemy

Satan is further mentioned in the Qur'an as *gharur* (deluder), as in "*... nor let the deluder delude you (in your conceptions) about God*" (Luqman 31:33). The original word *gharur* (deluder) is inflected in the verb form that denotes extreme degree, so its actual meaning is "extremely delusive one." Thus, Satan has a terrible and dizzying way of deception. He continuously tries to misguide the children of Adam by corrupting their intentions and thoughts with his own twisted ones and intrigues. The term *khannas* (sneaking whisperer) is used for him in the final chapter of the Qur'an. Because Satan is a stealthy creature who tries to tempt people every which way he can, who withdraws and re-attacks them at every suitable chance, who approaches them in the disguise of being helpful and "seemingly righteous," who makes beautiful deeds seem ugly, and who does his best to make people slip and fall. As Bediüzzaman puts it, one of the most significant deceptions of Satan is making people deny his own existence (thereby rejecting his influence and interference over their actions).[38] To such a degree that even though some people completely come under his influence and move with satanic impulses, they see themselves as the thinker, decider, planner, and doer in all of such acts. And the carnal soul, which is an innate aspect of human essence, serves as the central control unit or the agent for Satan. As the Qur'an reveals, the carnal soul does not leave a person alone and continually makes evil suggestions.[39] To clarify this with an example, Satan constantly sends different messages to the carnal self similar to those written in Morse code. The carnal self decodes these messages and prompts the person to act accordingly. In the face of such a situation, the children of Adam might act upon the impulses from Satan and the carnal self, and thus commit many evils. Therefore, ending a marriage, separating children from their family, and subsequent material and spiritual misery is one of such grave sins.

Size of the Damage

As mentioned in the initial question, the noble Prophet stated that Satan rejoices at nothing more than a married couple breaking up. Here is the full version of this Prophetic saying. *The Devil sets his throne on water*: This teaches us about the places frequented by devils and where those creatures are more likely to make people slip and fall. In other words, the Devil resides in places used for immoral pursuits and places—such as beaches—suitable for every kind of evil. *Then he*

---

[38] Nursi, *The Gleams*, p. 111
[39] Yusuf 12:53

sends his forces here and there to do evil: Some of them make people involve usury; some provoke the eye to look at forbidden sights, triggering bohemian feelings and making people act upon their lusts. Some of them control the mouth and make it lie, backbite, or slander others. It can be said that each one of his aides does what they will according to their special ability to tempt. *The nearest to him in rank are those that cause greatest dissension. All of them go to the Devil to tell him what they did. One of them comes and says: "I did this and this." But the Devil tells him, "You have done nothing"*: Actually, the Devil is pleased with every sin committed, for in every sin there is a way leading to unbelief. Every sin brings about a dark spot on the heart. At the same time, a person committing a sin virtually takes a step to distance himself further from God. However, the Devil expects more from his aides. *Then one of them comes and says: "I did not spare such and such man until he broke up with his wife." The Devil calls him to come nearer and compliments him: "You have done well!"*[40] This refers to a very common social problem in our time. Breaking up a family is such an important matter for the Devil. While he does not praise many of his aides who have people commit other evils, he may praise much and even reward those who achieve separating married couples. But why is this so important for the Devil? Because, by destroying a marriage, he not only harms the lives of two people, but also that of the children, parents, relatives, loved ones, and in a way an entire society. Given that families are the molecules of a society, broken up families mean dysfunctional society causing serious societal deformations. In addition, separated spouses pose a negative example to others, and this situation might pass to other homes as if it were a contagious disease. Although it appears to be a small scale problem at first sight, this evil done by the Devil and his aides upsets so many things in reality. In this respect, it should never be forgotten that the Devil will not give up striving to turn a cozy home into a hellish pitfall; he will do everything possible to drive a wedge between

---

[40] *Sahih Muslim*, Munafiqun, 67; Ahmad ibn Hanbal, *Al-Musnad*, 3:314

spouses. Also, he will continually try to damage the family set-up through the acts of devilish people under his control. Undoubtedly, the children of a family caught in such a web of confrontation and conflict will be the ones gravely harmed, since it is not possible for children to grow a sound soul in a family atmosphere of constant unrest. In an environment of constant conflict between a mother and father a child, often stuck in the middle, is put in a difficult situation and every bad word used by the parents against one another will be engraved in the child's memory. Then the child will go through a series of disappointments and in time, the parents will completely lose respect and credit in the eye of the child. Now think about it, why should the Devil, the sworn archenemy of humanity, not be so rejoiced at such a scene?

Divorce is the Final Solution

The Prophet, peace and blessings be upon him, stated that divorce is the most displeasing of lawful deeds in the sight of God.[41] Therefore, it will be very wise for both sides to have the necessary knowledge about marriage in order to avoid initiating a process doomed to failure. If it was up to me, I would not let anybody get married without taking a few seminars and reading a few books on marriage. For one or two months at least, I would educate the spouses-to-be so that they would be knowledgeable of the significance of married life, mutual rights and duties, how their relations with one another should be, how to raise children, and the like. It is very difficult to have a sound marriage between two people unaware of their spousal responsibilities. On the other hand, it will be a wise precaution to set the marriage on reasonable grounds from the very beginning, for marriage has no tolerance for emotionalism. Besides emotional inclinations, reason must definitely be there to the utmost degree. It is very difficult to have a peaceful and long lasting marriage solely based on good looks and attraction—married life may enter a difficult period and

---

[41] *Sunan Abu Dawud*, Talaq, 3; *Sunan ibn Majah*, Talaq, 1; Al-Bayhaqi, *As-Sunanu'l-Kubra*, 7/322

then end when these are lost with time. Therefore, although emotions have a degree of importance, reason, logic, and judgment must absolutely not be ignored; there must be serious thinking before marriage. Let me add that a person considering marriage should not suffice with his or her own thoughts, but should absolutely consult with other people for sound advice. Also, the traditional process of family visits during the engagement period should not be ignored as this will help create an understanding, within acceptable limits, whether there is conformity of character between the two people.

In addition, beginning from the early days of the marriage, the couple must hang on to the religious principles established for the protection of family and show utmost sensitivity at being discreet about confidential family matters. If this can be maintained, the devil's aides and human devils will not have any opportunity to penetrate into the home and damage it from within. In addition to such precautions, taking a spiritual shield by praying and seeking refuge in Divine protection all the time is also very important for the continuity of a happy marriage.

However, although all the necessary measures are taken and no flaw of reason and judgment is left, the couple might still not get on well or experience serious disharmony. Satan can abuse this situation via his aides from among the jinn and human beings, and set spouses up against one another by constantly goading them with evil whisperings. As a result of all of these, the opinion may arise that the marriage will not last in terms of the apparent conditions. So divorce can be resorted to as a final solution for such a marriage, if no hope of getting along together remains and an atmosphere of peace cannot be maintained. The Qur'an spares pages for telling how spouses who enter such a sensitive process should act. There is even a chapter (at-Talaq) named after divorce. The Pride of Humanity, peace and blessings be upon him, clarified the details about the relevant verses through his Tradition. His Companions and the great scholars of later generations also pondered over the issue and they drew different conclusions and gave rulings. All of these reflect that divorce is no simple matter but a very sensitive issue. Thus, divorce can be considered under the guidance of reason, logic, sound judgment, and conscience—free from emotionalism and egotism—and within a lawful frame, only after trying everything in the name of continuing the marriage but still no light of hope is seen.

Self-Criticism and Asking Forgiveness from God

Question: *What are the points to be considered in the face of misfortunes, so that a person can endure different tests in this world as a believer?*

Answer: It is stated in the verse (which means): "*Whatever good happens to you, it is from God; and whatever evil befalls you, it is from yourself*" (an-Nisa 4:79). People who believe in this Divine decree must first of all ascribe every trouble and misfortune that strikes them to their own faults and sins. For example, if they drop a glass or plate and break it, they must wonder what wrong they committed for this to happen, since there is no event that takes place by blind chance in this universe. When flow of life is observed meticulously, it will be noticeable that even very trivial things going wrong are warnings and all that happens gives a signal. If people take notice of that signal, turn to God repentantly, and commits a good deed to serve as a shield against the oncoming greater trouble, they can be saved by God's grace. Lesser misfortunes, such as a broken glass, may prevent the oncoming misfortunes and serve as expiation for sins. As it is stated in a *hadith*,[42] there is no case of tiredness, illness, grief, worry,

---

42   *Sahih al-Bukhari*, Marda, 1; *Sahih Muslim*, Birr, 51; *Sunan at-Tirmidhi*, Janaiz, 1

trouble, gloom, or even pricking one's foot on a thorn but it surely serves as expiation for the sins of a believer. Those who fail to recognize the real causes of the troubles or misfortunes that befell them usually start saying (unacceptable) things which can be interpreted as complaining about God.

On the Way to Finding the Right One to Blame

We may not always clearly see the underlying reasons behind events. However, people with sound faith are supposed to think about the wrongdoings they may have committed, even in the face of seemingly irrelevant adversities. Because being self-critical is a very significant step in the process of finding the one to blame. Otherwise, those who always look for somebody else to put the blame on will not succeed, even if they continue their search their entire lives. Concerning this issue, Bediüzzaman wrote in one of his letters: "Now I have understood the real reason for the wrongdoing and tortures I have been suffering from. Here I say with true remorse that my fault was taking my service in the way the Qur'an as a means to progress spiritually."[43] These words of this great figure show the profundity of his self-criticism. Moreover, we can infer from these words that serving in the way of faith should not be seen as a means of making spiritual progress or being favored with Divine inspirations and blessings—not even of sublime goals like entering Paradise or being saved from Hell. Taking these as real motives means sabotaging our own way. Our primary and sole concern must be sincerity and gaining God's pleasure and approval. Neither love of Paradise nor fear of Hell must have priority over true worship. God Almighty gives generous rewards for deeds sincerely done. The blessings of God are infinite whereas our worship and servitude is limited. Even if you become king of the world and a multi-millionaire in wealth, you still feel shy while giving, since your wealth decreases in proportion with the amount you give. But

---

[43] Nursi, *Tarihçe-i Hayat*, p. 667

the blessings of God are beyond count. Therefore, things you ask for are so minor in comparison to what He grants.

Refraining from all Kinds of Complaint

As we have said, those who fail to recognize the real reason for the troubles and misfortunes that befall them say things which can be taken as complaining about God Almighty. It is acceptable to complain about wrongdoers to the authorities to defend our personal rights. In other words, people who think that they are subjected to wrongdoing would naturally seek justice through petitioning God or the people of justice. However, no person in no form has the right to complain about God to anybody else. Let alone doing that overtly, even the act of puffing and other gestures that show grievance in the face of troubles and misfortunes will be regarded as complaining about God. Therefore, it is commendable to keep away from all kinds of words and attitudes that express complaint in an overt or covert fashion.

Indeed, blaming oneself for troubles and misfortunes depends on a consciousness of serious self-criticism—this in turn depends on a sound faith in God and the Day of Judgment. It is narrated that Umar ibn al-Khattab said, "Call yourselves to account before being called to account."[44] This clearly shows that self-criticism is directly related to one's faith in being called to account on the Day of Judgment. When we study the personal prayers and litanies of great saints, it is understood that each of them lived with a serious consideration of self-criticism out of their concern for the accountability of their deeds. For instance, Abdul Qadir al-Jilani debases himself in one of his litanies to such an extent that we will probably never do ourselves in an entire lifetime. Likewise, after debasing himself with certain negative phrases, Abu'l-Hasan ash-Shadhili implores God with hope and asks for forgiveness by saying, "So many people like me knocked on Your door

---

[44] *Sunan at-Tirmidhi*, Qiyamah, 25; Ibnu'l-Mubarak, *Az-Zuhd*, 1/103; Ibn Abi Shayba, *Al-Musannaf*, 7/96

of mercy, and were not let down."[45] Hasan al-Basri's weekly litany, which is included in *Imploring Hearts*,[46] also sets an important example.[47] This monumental figure who recited a separate habitual prayer for each day of the week virtually makes a mountain out of a molehill at blaming himself. This hero of faith, who was one of the foremost among the second generation after the Prophet, directly benefiting from the Companions of the Prophet, who stood up as a scholar against the misguided schools of thought in the Basra region, and from whom Imam Azam Abu Hanifa greatly benefited, was a person who kept away from sin even in his dreams. This great man expresses his wrongdoings in such a way that he virtually sees himself as the worst of sinners. He turns to God as if he were an ultimate loser in the spiritual sense, as if he had been one who incessantly committed sins. He would criticize himself every single day.

The Feeling of Self-Criticism That Results in Asking Forgiveness

Individuals who are aware of their wrongdoings with a consciousness of self-criticism consequently resort to repentance and ask forgiveness. After God Almighty mentions different wrongdoings and states that the one who commits them deserves punishment, He gives tidings about the truly repentant: "... *except he who gives up his way in repentance and believes, and does good, righteous deeds—such are those whose (past) evil deeds God will efface and record virtuous deeds in their place. God is the Forgiving, the Compassionate*" (al-Furqan 25:70).

According to this verse, if the ones undergoing spiritual deformation with sins and wrongdoings immediately turn to God in repentance and ask forgiveness, then God will replace their wrongdoings with good deeds. Bediüzzaman approaches this verse differently and says

---

[45] Gülen, *El-Kulûbu'd-Dâria*, pp. 297–353

[46] *Imploring Hearts (Al-Qulub ad-Dari'a)* is a collection of prayers and supplications selected and compiled into a volume by Fethullah Gülen from various Islamic sources.

[47] Gülen, *El-Kulûbu'd-Dâria*, pp. 138–156

that the unlimited human potential for evil turns into a potential for goodness.[48] Then turning to God in sincere repentance becomes a means for them to undergo such a great transformation.

Asking Forgiveness: A Life Spring for Personal Revival

The Messenger of God, most perfect blessings and peace be upon him, stated the importance of asking forgiveness from God by saying, "Whoever wishes to be rejoiced at the book of his deeds (on the Day of Judgment), let him increase the amount of asking forgiveness (*istighfar*) in it."[49] Being a hero at asking forgiveness, the Messenger of God also stated that he made *istighfar* one hundred times a day.[50] We can interpret this situation as a sign of his continuous progress at spiritual journeying, while regarding it as a presentation of the ideal example for all other people to follow. A person with a leading position in a community presents a role model with all of his attitudes and behaviors for the entire community. For example, a corrupt leader of an organization will most probably drift his subordinates to corruption as well. In the same way, the presence of a guide who constantly strives for goodness is a very important incentive in terms of guiding people toward goodness. In this respect, it can be said that the Messenger of God, who was such an ideal role model and who elevated his followers to the horizons where angels hover, made *istighfar* one hundred times a day. In fact, no matter what level, believers who question their lives in retrospect can find lots of wrongdoings to make them ask forgiveness from God. They might have cast lustful looks at forbidden sights while going somewhere or they might have backbitten somebody in another case, without even realizing this grave sin. Thus, people must realize that even one such sin can bring them to

[48] Nursi, *The Words*, p. 337
[49] At-Tabarani, *Al-Mu'jamu'l-Awsat*, 1/256; Al-Bayhaqi, *Shuabu'l-Iman*, 1/441; Al-Haythami, *Majmau'z-Zawaid*, 10/208
[50] *Sahih Muslim*, Dhikr, 41; *Sunan at-Tirmidhi*, Tafsir as-Surah (47), 1; *Sunan ibn Majah*, Adab, 57; Ahmad ibn Hanbal, *Al-Musnad*, 4/211, 260

eternal ruin, so they must immediately seek refuge in asking forgiveness. In *The Gleams*, Bediüzzaman drew attention to the fact that seemingly little things might cause someone to be lost for good: "So be alert and careful, always act with caution and in fear of sinking. Do not drown in a morsel, a word, a grain, a glance, a beckoning, or a kiss! Do not cause your faculties—that are so extensive that they can contain the whole world—to drown in such a thing."[51] People make very serious plans even about worldly matters. For example, before starting a new business, they conduct in-depth feasibility studies and invest accordingly. Then they make monthly analyses to monitor progress and profitability. If even business in this passing world takes so much planning and evaluation, should we not take much more of eternal life into consideration?

I think it will be useful to mention another point related to this issue. Bediüzzaman says, "Prayer and trusting God greatly strengthen our inclination to do good, and repentance and seeking God's forgiveness defeat our inclination to evil and break its transgressions."[52] That is, as repentance and seeking God's forgiveness (*tawba* and *istighfar*) serve as a barrier against human inclination for evil and neutralize sins by slamming them with a sledgehammer, supplicating to God similarly strengthens our inclination for goodness. Accordingly, people moving with the wing of repentance and asking forgiveness on the one hand and supplication on the other, by God's grace, may ascend to the peak of human perfection and find themselves below the feet of the Pride of Humanity, upon him be peace and blessings.

On the other hand, let me express how I wish that—instead of struggling to restore their hearts and spiritual lives—people could build up barriers against their destruction from the very beginning, for it is very difficult to restore something after it has been destroyed. As I have mentioned in different talks, when I was assigned as a young imam to the Selimiye Mosque in Edirne, restoration work had begun.

---

[51]   Nursi, *The Gleams*, p. 188
[52]   Nursi, *The Words*, p. 487

During my stay of six to seven years in Edirne, the restoration of the mosque, which had been built at the time of Sultan Selim III in six years, was still not completed. Because restoring something ruined into its original condition is far more difficult than constructing it anew. So, spiritual restoration of a person who underwent sinful deformation is not as easy as thought. Then one must try to be cautious of destruction from the very beginning and remain vigilant of sins.

Key Concepts for Interpreting Existence

Question: *Bediüzzaman states that in his forty years of life he learned four words and four phrases, and "viewpoint" (nazar) is one of these words. Would you please tell us the meaning to be inferred from the word "viewpoint", and how do you describe a "viewpoint" that becomes believers?*

Answer: In his work: *Al-Mathnawi al-Nuri* (Seedbed of the Light), Bediüzzaman draws attention to the importance of four key phrases: *mana-i ismi* (self-referential meaning), *mana-i harfi* (other-indicative meaning), intention, and viewpoint.[53]

Since these are closely interrelated, let us briefly introduce the first three phrases before we expound on the fourth.

Mana-i İsmi and Mana-i Harfi

These two phrases essentially belong to Arabic grammar. An *ism* (noun) has a meaning on its own. That is, when you say it as a word, the person addressed understands its meaning. However, a *harf* (letter) cannot be understood on its own, since it does not bear an individual

---

[53] Nursi, *Al-Mathnawi al-Nuri*, p. 67

meaning. For example, prepositions such as "with, from, to, in" do not give a meaning on their own. In order to understand their meaning, they need to relate with other words. Just as Bediüzzaman attaches special meanings to the phrases *cüz* (part) and *küll* (whole), here he similarly gives new meanings to the concepts of *mana-i harfi* and *mana-i ismi*. Specifically, he uses these as key concepts for interpreting existence. He believes it is a mistaken perspective to view the universe with *mana-i ismi*, that is, simply seeing things as beings on their own or products of causes. Instead, he states that things in the universe should be viewed with respect to what they point to. Accordingly, blessings should bring to mind the Giver of blessings; the beauty and art in creation should bring to mind the Artist, and causes should bring to mind the True Causer who creates them.

Intention, Which Changes the Nature of Deeds

As for intention, Bediüzzaman states that intention resembles an elixir that turns daily habits and acts into worship, and a spirit that enlivens dead conditions, bringing life to them with a meaning of worship. He also posits that even some wrong acts can turn into good deeds due to the intention behind them.[54] It can be said that making a wrong decision can be a means for spiritual rewards if the intention is sincere. There are certain points in religion that are left to the flow of time. When time and conjuncture generate some gaps in them, they need to be "filled" with certain disciplines and principles in conformity with the spirit of religion; this is called *ijtihad* (the process of deriving legal judgments from the established principles of the Qur'an and Sunnah to meet new circumstances). The *mujtahid* (a scholar authorized to deduce new laws) is the person who strives to fill such a gap. Therefore, he will gain a reward for his sincere intention even if his decisions are not correct. On the other hand, the deeds of a person who does not aim to seek the good pleasure of God but instead to gain fame, or to demonstrate his courage, generosity, and knowledge,

---

[54] Ibid., p. 68

will gain him sins instead of rewards. At this point, you can think of a *hadith* related in *Sahih Muslim*: Three unfortunate men were called to account in the presence of God. The first one fought in the world so that others appreciated his bravery. The second one donated to charity so that others appreciated his generosity. And the third one tried to make people admire him as a great scholar.[55] Thus, if a man writes articles and books, if he pretends to give great sermons and tries to present examples of eloquent speech, it means that such a person closes his eyes to the good pleasure of God, in return for appreciation from people. One who acts on such a simple and contemptible consideration resembles an ignorant one who sells the priceless jewel in his hands for the price of a piece of rough iron. However, if he had sought an infinite reward such as the good pleasure of God, what he obtained through his efforts would have been completely different.

Viewpoint and Being Able to See

As for the word "viewpoint", above all else, a person needs to know how to see. As it is known, looking and seeing are different things. If a person with open eyes does not look consciously with an intention to see, it will not be possible for him or her to tell the difference between things. For example, if a man turns his eyes absentmindedly to the bookshelf in front of him, the books, writings, colors, and patterns there will not register with him. Seeing is something beyond looking. It means realizing the objects in sight and having a perspective of them.

Another dimension of viewpoint is about determining what to look at and how. For example, if people view everything according to the criteria of the three-dimensional realm, they will not be able to see, sense, and feel so many things. In the past, a comment by a cosmonaut appeared in the media. He made a remark that he had toured around the world but did not see God. The famous poet Necip Fazıl responded to this mistaken point of view as follows: "You fool, who told you that God was a balloon in space!" If one tries to see God

---

[55] *Sahih Muslim*, Imara, 152; *Sunan at-Tirmidhi*, Zuhd, 48 ; *Sunan an-Nasa'i*, Jihad, 22

Almighty, who cannot be contained by time and space whatsoever, like a physical object in the sky, then he can never see the truth and can never be saved from making such mistakes. For this reason, let us state once more that not being able to adopt a correct viewpoint is one of the obstacles to faith, along with other factors such as arrogance, wrongdoing, and imitating ancestors. On the other hand, the entire existence bears witness in every way to the existence and oneness of God. Bediüzzaman voices this truth in his *Al-Mathnawi al-Nuri* as follows:

> *Reflect upon the lines of the [Book of the] Universe,*
> *for they are letters to you from the Highest Realm.*[56]

However, a materialistic, naturalistic, and positivistic viewpoint of the universe makes it impossible to hear the voice of creation, which proclaims the Creator through millions of tongues. Even if people with such an outlook study the universe meticulously—since they cannot see in spite of looking, since they cannot pass beyond the apparent reality—they will conclude every issue with naturalism again. In other words, since they do not know what to look at and how, they will fail to attribute the things and phenomena that they study to their true Divine source.

The viewpoint Bediüzzaman presents through an imaginary debate with Satan about the Qur'an is important for our subject here. There, Bediüzzaman draws attention to the fact that a person who considers the Qur'an needs to see it as the Word of God.[57] The reason is that, if the Qur'an is assumed to be a body of human words, it will have been degraded from the heavens to the level of a simple text. It is a reality that the Qur'an is Divine speech revealed in a comprehensible form for humanity as a blessing. Still, one first needs to look at it with a correct viewpoint in order to feel this Divine message coming from beyond, with its true depth and immensity.

---

[56] Nursi, *Al-Mathnawi al-Nuri*, p. 177
[57] Nursi, *The Words*, pp. 199–205

A Comprehensive Look

Another point to be mentioned concerning the issue of viewpoint is having a comprehensive view of creation. This can also be called a perfected viewpoint. Nevertheless, let me note that it is not easy to obtain such a comprehensive viewpoint, particularly while pondering the outside world, and everybody may not be able to achieve such a viewpoint. For this reason, Bediüzzaman suggests the principle of "thinking deeply with respect to one's inner world, and having a comprehensive look with respect to the outer world,"[58] during reflection (*tafakkur*). That is to say, one may recognize his or her own being, by looking at one's own anatomy and physiology under the light of medicine (rather than looking at other beings) and can delve into it more easily. For example, when a person monitors the systems working in his or her body with a conscious view, it is possible to see the absolute power and infinite knowledge beyond that splendid order and dizzying harmony. In the same way, when individuals look at the depths of their inner world such as the heart, soul, and other mysterious human subtle faculties—*sirr* (the secret), *khafi* (the hidden), *akhfa* (the most hidden)—that make up their spiritual structure, they can hear the voice of their heart, understand the meaning of their feelings, comprehend what consciousness truly means, and realize their willpower. Thus, individuals can reflect upon, contemplate, and ponder their own self with respect to both their physical and metaphysical (*mulk* and *malakut*) dimensions and thus attain great profundities and immensities. As for the universe, one is supposed to adopt a comprehensive look. According to Bediüzzaman, knowledge gained from the outer world cannot be free from apprehensions and groundless fears. However, knowledge from one's own inner world is free from delusions and suspicions. Thus, it is more sensible to look from the center to the periphery, from the inside to the outside.

Individuals can more easily look at the universe through the scope of their inner world, using it like a field glass, because it is possible to

---

[58] Nursi, *Al-Mathnawi al-Nuri*, p. 176

see the laws prevalent inside in the outer world as well. If one follows these patterns, it becomes possible to gain profundity in the inner world first, then to witness that all of the systems in the outer world take place with His infinite power, then to see that the same laws operate in the great book called universe, and then it will be possible to read the outside world with a comprehensive look.

Horizons of Spiritual Knowledge

Question: *The poet Niyazi Mısri states,*
With fasting, Prayers, and pilgrimage / It's not over O
ascetic! / Spiritual knowledge is what is needed / in
order to be a perfected soul (insan al-kamil)," and thus draws
attention to the importance of spiritual knowledge. In addi-
tion to fulfilling the essential religious duties, what other
ways are there in order to gain spiritual knowledge?

Answer: Although different religious responsibilities constitute the foundations of worship, the secret key to opening the door to essentials of faith and worship is the proclamation of faith. In this respect, it is a blessed phrase which holds both the beginning and the end. In other words, the proclamation of faith is both the start and the ultimate point. Without that, neither belief in angels, Divine books, and Prophets, nor belief in the Hereafter and Divine Destiny and Decree bear any meaning. In the same way, acts of worship gain value and meaning by entering through the door they open. As it is related in the famous *hadith* about Gabriel, faith (*iman*) comes first. Then comes Islam, and in the end the believer reaches *ihsan* (perfect goodness, acting and praying as if seeing God, and knowing that He sees you though you do not see Him).[59] Namely, faith is the essence and starting point of religion, its consequence and ultimate fruit is perfect goodness.

---

[59]   *Sahih al-Bukhari*, Iman, 37; Tafsir as-Surah (31), 2; *Sahih Muslim*, Iman, 5, 7

Acts of Worship Crowned with Consciousness

As for spiritual knowledge, it is a concept to be contemplated within considerations of perfect goodness. For this reason, a person who wishes to reach horizons of spiritual knowledge must have sound faith first, then do good deeds, and then make it into a "culture of conscience" in the long run. The most important way to attain spiritual knowledge is to observe worship in a meticulous and conscious way. If there is no consciousness in worship, it will not be possible to attain spiritual knowledge. And for a person who fails to attain spiritual knowledge, it is not possible to attain love of God and the Prophet in the true sense. It should not be forgotten that since these are concentric depths, one is reached only by passing from the other. When the issue is seen from this perspective, the poem cited at the beginning makes very good sense:

> With fasting, Prayers, and pilgrimage
> It's not over O ascetic!
> Spiritual knowledge is what is needed
> In order to be a perfected soul.

Because, for individuals devoid of consciousness of being seen by God (*ihsan*) and the light of spiritual knowledge, acts of worship they do may not amount to anything beyond a repeated formality and practice of culture. They observe the fast because everybody does; they perform the Prayers because their parents did; they go to Hajj because others do. Therefore, since such acts of worship do not go beyond the physical act, one fails to capture their spirit and meaning. In order to express this situation, the Most Noble Messenger of God stated that there are many people who fast but they have no share of the fast except for hunger, and there are many people who get up for the Prayer, but they have no share of the Prayer except for drowsiness.[60] Thus, the value of worship depends on the spiritual depth it holds. For example, the Prayer can be offered with such a deep spiritual conscious-

---

[60] *Sunan ibn Majah*, Siyam, 21; Ahmad ibn Hanbal, *Al-Musnad*, 2/373

ness that the worshipper feels to be in the Divine presence. This can be to such a degree that even while moving the hands and feet, it is as if he or she is touching the covers of the Divine Throne. Such worshippers shake with the idea that any unmannerly move of the hands and legs can be disrespectful in the Divine presence. Nevertheless, God Almighty relates the situation of the Glorious Messenger of God at the Prayers: "*He Who sees you when you rise (in the Prayer, and in readiness to carry out Our commands), as well as your strenuous efforts in prostration among those who prostrate.*" (ash-Shu'ara, 26:218–219). Believers who cannot attain such a level of worship must at least willfully believe that God Almighty always sees them and try to fulfill every movement during the Prayer with such consciousness. Acts such as keeping hands and feet in the proper position, knowing where to turn one's gaze at the Prayer, and knowing what considerations to have at prostration are indications that the consciousness of being in Divine presence is reflected in the worshipper's manners.

In order to attain spiritual knowledge, acts of worship must definitely be crowned with consciousness. For example, a person at the Prayer must be in full consciousness of worship from the beginning to end. As for making the intention for the Prayer, it is not correct to reduce it to uttering certain words ceremonially, "Here, I intend to perform the Prayer..." True intention is felt in the worshipper's heart. That is, erasing everything other than God from one's entire soul and thoughts, having a deep feeling of being in the Divine presence in complete obedience, and even forgetting one's own self to the degree of completely being erased. Indeed, one should not even be aware of that self-erasing, and he or she should try to keep up this mood throughout the Prayer. From time to time, one might be exposed to certain negative breezes during the Prayers. But at each time, he should use his willpower effectively in order to overcome them. In addition, one must know the meaning of the verses and prayers recited during the Prayer, be aware of the truths that they should evoke in one's heart, and keep these truths up consciously until the end of the Prayer. These efforts made for the sake of conscious worship are important and reliable references for spiritual knowledge.

Wonders Worked by Keeping a Steady Course

In addition to having a serious, resolved, and conscious relationship with God Almighty, keeping a steady course in this regard is of utmost significance in terms of spiritual knowledge. God's treatment of you will be in proportion with the quality and continuity of your relationship with Him. As the Prophet, who was at the peak of horizons of spiritual knowledge stated, the most lovable of deeds to God is the one constantly observed, even if it is of little amount.[61] It should not be forgotten that what pierces marbles is not drops of water, but the constancy of the drops. Even though water is a liquid, it is this constancy that makes a hole through marble. In this respect, a person's constant observance of worship in patience, steadfastness, determination, and resolution is very important in terms of opening up to knowledge of God (*marifa*). Therefore, I think that the consideration of Imam Abu Hanifa that the blessed Night of Qadr could be hidden in all nights of the year, reflects a very fine understanding of this fact.[62] God Almighty could have hidden it among any night of the year. Of course, it is laudable to spend the final nights of Ramadan in worship, with an intention to benefit from this blessed night, but that is a different issue.

What really matters is taking every night as such a blessed one to spend in worship, in accordance with the approach of this great imam. With this intention and consideration, one must get up every night and offer the *Tahajjud* (Late Night) Prayer, at least as an effort of having a blessed light in the grave, and thereby revealing one being true hearted to God Almighty. What value can be found in being a guest of one's bed, while it is possible to be a guest of God! Ibrahim Haqqi voices this idea beautifully:

---

[61] *Sahih al-Bukhari*, Riqaq, 18; *Sahih Muslim*, Salatu'l-Musafirin, 218
[62] Ibn Abdilbarr, *At-Tamhid*, 2/208; An-Nawavi, *Sharh Sahih Muslim*, 8/57

O eyes! What is sleep? Come, wake at nights!
Watch comets lighting up the sky at nights
Look and watch those wonders in the sky of the world;
Find your Maker and host Him at nights.

The Mysterious Key to All Kinds of Goodness: Modesty

As a way to reach spiritual knowledge, it is also possible to follow the steps of spiritual journeying. In the same way, it is possible to take the alternative path of "impotence, poverty, joyful zeal, and thankfulness" that Bediüzzaman derived from the Qur'an as a remarkable discipline to reach the horizons of spiritual knowledge.[63] In other words, individuals can attain a state of spiritual alertness and relevant enthusiasm by constantly reminding themselves that they cannot really do anything without the help of God, that they live like kings although nothing really belongs to them in essence, and thus everything that they own comes from the Absolute Owner of everything.

Reading the Qur'an with reflection is also one of the important means on the path to knowledge of God. Setting sail to the special profundities of the Qur'an from the perspectives of great scholars such as Hamdi Yazır of Elmalı, Qadi al-Baydawi, Ebussuud Efendi, or Al-Alusi and feeling the revelation as it is freshly being revealed are factors making a person take wing toward the horizons of spiritual knowledge and helping him to maintain his spiritual alertness.

In order to experience in one's conscience the opening of mysteries with respect to knowledge of God, it is essential to live in modesty, humility, and self-nullification. As one of great figures of spirituality Yusuf ibn al-Husayn al-Razi expressed, the mysterious key to all kinds of goodness is modesty, and the key to all kinds of evil is arrogance and selfishness. Even if arrogant and selfish people prostrate for a lifetime, they still will not reach the point they expect. Indeed, as decreed in a *hadith qudsi*, greatness absolutely belongs to God Almighty and if

---

[63] Nursi, *The Words*, p. 494

someone attempts to compete with Him in this respect, He seizes that person and throws him into Hell.[64]

As this discussion shows, so many means can be tried in terms of attaining to the horizons of spiritual knowledge, as the paths leading to God are as many as the breaths of creatures.

---

[64] *Sahih Muslim*, Birr, 136; *Sunan Abu Dawud*, Libas, 26

Those Who Become Dizzy with Worldly Pleasures and Remain Behind

Q **uestion:** *What are the messages to be drawn from the verse (which means), "Those who were left behind in opposition to God's Messenger rejoiced at staying at home, and abhorred striving with their wealth and persons in God's cause. And they said: 'Do not go forth to war in this heat.' Say (O Messenger): 'The fire of Hell is fiercer in heat.' If only they had been able to ponder and penetrate the essence of matters to grasp the truth!" (at-Tawbah 9:81) by those devoted to serving humanity?*

Answer: According to the books of Qur'anic exegesis that provide the context of the verses, this verse criticizes the hypocrites' attitudes and behaviors against striving for the cause of God.[65] This verse also holds a very significant warning and lessons for any believer who presents laziness in terms of serving in the Name of God and indulges in a life of ease. Relatively speaking, so many great figures— Aisha, Abu Dharr, Umar ibn Abdulaziz being the foremost—even saw the verses revealed about the hypocrites as somehow relating to

---

[65] At-Tabari, *Jamiu'l-Bayan*, 10/204–205; Al-Baghawi, *Ma'alimu't-Tanzil*, 2/317; Ibn Kathir, *Tafsiru'l-Qur'an*, 2/379

themselves and drew so many lessons for themselves from the issues related in them. One must be careful, though, because with respect to religious belief, it is definitely not correct for believers to see themselves as hypocrites, since being a hypocrite in the real sense means unbelief. It is not possible for a Muslim to accept that. Therefore, as Bediüzzaman expresses in *The Gleams*, a believer must always say, "All praise and thanks are for God for every state, save unbelief and misguidance."[66] Thus, accepting unbelief makes a person an unbeliever. For this reason, a Muslim is supposed to keep away from hypocrisy and unbelief as if they were poisonous creatures.

Children of Adam Can Turn to Any Direction

Human beings, however, do have certain weaknesses and faults. Satan saw in Adam's mold—not in his essence—many human weaknesses and faults, such as pursuing fancies of the carnal self, seeking fame, greed for laudation, seeking comfort, addiction to home, fearing beings other than God, and misappropriation. Then he said: "*Now that You have allowed me to rebel and go astray, I will surely lie in wait for them on Your Straight Path (to lure them from it). Then I will come upon them from before them and from behind them, and from their right and from their left*" (al-A'raf 7:16–17). All of these latent faults in human beings allow Satan to operate. In this respect, we can say that a human being is potentially susceptible to misguidance, hypocrisy, and unbelief. We can also paraphrase this fact as follows: Even if a person is a believer, he or she can possess some qualities associated with misguidance, hypocrisy, and unbelief. But as it is not correct to see that person as misguided, it is definitely wrong to label him as a "hypocrite" or "unbeliever." What befalls on individuals is for them to continuously watch their inner worlds and to evaluate in themselves whether they possess contemptible qualities, as well as to try to rid themselves of these as soon as possible if they detect any.

---

[66] Nursi, *The Gleams*, p. 15

The Misfortunate Ones Who Cheered
at Their Own Loss

Returning back to the initial question, it is stated in the relevant verse that the hypocrites rejoiced at staying at home. Who knows, perhaps they thought themselves to be very smart and said to themselves: "Look at them! They are going to confront the great empire of Rome. They will not only be scorched in the desert heat, but also will be struck by a great power and come running back." With similar expressions, they made fun of the Muslims who joined the expedition and rejoiced. As it is known, the Tabuk Expedition was made during July and August when the desert heat was as high as 50–60°C (122–140°F). At home in Medina, the trees yielded fruit in that season and their pleasant shade was a real temptation. Thus, it was extremely difficult to leave spring waters, the shade, and ripened fruits to set out under intense heat. Also, this expedition was against the powerful Romans, who had come as near as Jordan. By launching a campaign against the Romans in a period of adverse conditions, the Sultan of Prophets wanted to make everybody realize that there was an independent power centered in Medina and to maintain security and peace in the desert. Thus, against all odds the Pride of Humanity set out with his army in order to stop the Roman advance and parried the danger with the consent and grace of God. In such a situation, where the conditions were very hard, a few hundred hypocrites did not want to join the expedition, preferring to stay at home and using various pretexts to avoid going. In addition to the hypocrites, three people from the Muslims failed to show due sensitivity at responding to the order and did not join the expedition, remaining behind. Who knows, perhaps they misjudged the situation that not everybody was responsible for joining this expedition. However, God Almighty described their case as they well-nigh "swerved" (*takhalluf*). Since swerving was a behavior associated with the hypocrites, they also received a Divine punishment through a temporary boycott. However, those chivalrous souls passed their test in the best way and attained Divine forgiveness in the end.[67]

Concerning the verse in the question, God Almighty states that the hypocrites' behavior was realized "in opposition to the Messenger of God." It can then be inferred that straying from the way of the Prophet is a very serious mistake, which leads to destruction. For this reason, one needs to keep following his way no matter what happens.

Passing the Virus to Those Around

The hypocrites whose attributes are related in this verse not only stayed back from striving with their wealth and persons in God's cause, but they also influenced other people by telling them, "Do not join an expedition under such heat!" There are certain people that their horizons always possess a potential for sedition and discord. They send arrows of discord all around. They continuously try to prevent righteous acts. So these people programmed to sedition and discord wondered among the Muslims and tried to change their mind about forming a counterforce against the Romans, by emphasizing the heat and likely troubles. In response to this verse, God Almighty revealed the words which mean, "*Say (O Messenger): 'The fire of Hell is fiercer in heat.' If only they had been able to ponder and penetrate the essence of matters to grasp the truth!*" The Arabic verb used in the verse is not a commonly used word like "*ya'lamun*" (they know) or "*ya'qilun*," (they reason) but "*yafqahun*," which denotes to ponder deeply, to approach the issue within a consideration of a cause-and-effect relationship, or to evaluate the issue on a priori and a posteriori grounds; thus, this word choice is very meaningful. The meaning sensed from this wording is: "If only they had some horizons of *fiqh* (Islamic Jurisprudence, penetrating to the essence of matters), so that they could grasp the relationship between the cause and effect. Unfortunately, they failed to do so despite all of the warnings."

---

[67] *Sahih Muslim*, Tawbah, 53; Abdurrazzak, *Al-Musannaf*, 5/400; At-Tabarani, *Al-Mu'jamu'l-Kabir*, 6/31

Would the Mistakes Ever Recur If They Had Learned a Lesson?

When we compare these past events with the events of today, we see that nothing has changed much. As the hypocrites of those times failed to recognize the importance and necessity of walking on the path of God, multitudes today do not comprehend this fact. As in the past, today as well, some people underestimate migrating for a lofty cause and serving for the sake of God, caring nothing at all about introducing the example of the Prophet and the essence of his message to others. Indeed, any place where the truth of his message has not germinated is no different than a prison. Hence, realizing that so many people are condemned to live in prisons in this sense and standing up against every kind of difficulty in order to take them to serene immensities are matters of deep insight—and not to be understood with a superficial view.

In conclusion, it is necessary in our time to undertake every kind of difficulty and troubles for the sake of helping people to remember and recognize their Creator and eliminating the obstacles between people's hearts and God. For the sake of conveying the inspirations of our soul to others' hearts and letting others know about a spiritual heritage of more than a thousand years, we must run incessantly and never fall into lethargy concerning this issue. Also, it should never be forgotten that the way to being saved from hellfire in the next world depends upon enduring the heat in this one. And the suffering experienced in this world is a means of attaining bliss in the next, just as the difficulties faced in this one are a means of attaining eternal ease in the next.

The Qur'an and
Scientific Discoveries

Question: *Right after any scientific discovery or invention, it is expressed that there are certain allusions to it in the Qur'an. From this perspective, what should be researchers' general attitude toward the scientific truths in the Qur'an? What is the message such verses convey particularly to those who study natural sciences?*

Answer: The Qur'an and the universe are two different books of God Almighty. Therefore, it is inconceivable for them to contradict one another. The Qur'an, the Miraculous Exposition, is a manifestation of Divine Speech; it is an eternal interpreter, an expounder, and a lucid proof of this Great Book of the Universe, which is a manifestation of Divine Power. The Qur'an expounds the Book of Universe, and thus the universe gains light with it. In other words, the Qur'an proclaims the principles prevalent in creation, Divine mysteries, and Divine disposals.

Since the Qur'an expounds and interprets the universe as the word of the Almighty, it contains allusions to certain sciences exploring the creation. For this reason, from very early on scholars have studied the verses alluding to scientific truths, along with those on faith, worship, and morality, and have expressed different considerations on their

meanings and implications. For example, when you consider the interpretation of certain verses by Ibn Jarir at-Tabari, who lived in the
fourth century of Hijra, it will be seen that his commentaries are very
close to scientific findings in our time, in spite of living eleven hundred years ago. The conclusions drawn and commentaries made by
this great interpreter of the Qur'an are far beyond the scientific level of
his age. For example, with respect to verse 22 of Surah al-Hijr which
means, "*And We send the winds to fertilize...,*" Ibn Jarir expounds upon
the role of winds at fertilizing seeds. The interesting fact here is that,
at a very early time when nobody knew about positive and negative
charges of clouds, he points to the fact that this verse alludes to the
fertilization of clouds by winds, which paves the way for rainfall.[68]

It was not only Ibn Jarir, but other scholars as well, who made
many remarkable commentaries and conclusions about the verses
concerning the "creative commands" (the laws of God's creation and
maintenance of the universe and the laws He has established for life).
However, until the last century or two, this issue was not taken as a
separate branch of study. Toward the contemporary age—in a way
with the influence of the positivist understanding of the time—more
emphasis began to be laid on this issue. For example, Muhammad
Abduh, who interpreted the Qur'an until the Surah Yusuf in fifteen
volumes, also made some modern commentaries about verses related to scientific facts. And Rashid Rida, one of his foremost students,
corrected some points in his teacher's work and completed the remaining chapters himself. However, there are certain mistaken commentaries that contradict the general acceptances of former Sunni scholars. For example, the final verse at the end of the Surah al-Fil (105:5)
meaning, "*And so He rendered them like a field of grain devoured,*" is
explained with a commentary that the relevant army was destroyed
by the smallpox virus brought by the birds.[69] In fact, the metaphor of
devoured grains here describes how the bodies of the soldiers were

---

[68]   At-Tabari, *Jamiu'l-Bayan*, 14/20
[69]   Muhammad Abduh, *Al-A'malu'l-Kamila*, 5/504

pierced like leaves eaten by insects. Shortly after this interpretation was published, the scholar Tantawi wrote an interpretation entitled, *Al-Jawahir*, in which he explained Qur'anic verses from the perspective of developments in science. Even though the desired profundity is not maintained throughout this work, he tried to explain many verses under the light of the findings of modern science. However, other interpreters of the Qur'an saw his work more as an encyclopedia than an exegesis. The late Said Hawwa also made efforts in this direction. As a result, studies and efforts by many scholars led to a new era in the name of scientific interpretation of the Qur'an, and a great deal of studies have been carried out in Turkey and several Arab countries.

For example, Zaghloul al-Naggar, who I followed on a Saudi television channel for a long time, is a person with important studies in this field. This valuable scholar is both deeply knowledgeable about the Qur'an and is an academic with high scientific achievements; he knows his field well and is able to explain scientific matters after scrutinizing them in meticulous detail. As for Bediüzzaman, he did not go into great detail on this subject in his works, but sufficed with explaining certain verses that were challenged, such as how Moses struck a rock and made water gush from it[70] and how Prophet Solomon had the Queen of Sheba's throne teleported.[71] But one thing that he highlighted was that the miracles of the Prophets mark the furthest horizons sciences can reach and encourage people to explore. In my opinion, this is an extremely significant remark and an approach to be considered seriously.

The Place of Scientific Inventions within the General Purposes of the Qur'an

As for how often scientific discoveries and inventions are mentioned in the Qur'an, Bediüzzaman's approach tells us that the verses of the Qur'an mention everything in accordance with their ranking among

---

[70] Nursi, *The Words*, p. 263
[71] Ibid., p. 269

the general purposes of the Qur'an.[72] When the Qur'an, the Miraculous Exposition, is viewed with a holistic perspective, it will be seen that it shows humanity the ways to eternal bliss by primarily expounding on the pillars of faith and religion. At the same time, it provides happiness in this world by making the necessary regulations about the individual and society. Namely, the Qur'an gives priority to the crucial matters that are necessary for humanity's happiness in both worlds. When the issue is seen from this perspective, it will be clear that the matters related to scientific discoveries and inventions are of a secondary importance in comparison to these crucial issues raised in the Qur'an. Furthermore, the Qur'an is not a scripture that is addressed to scientists exclusively. On the contrary, it addresses the whole of humanity. Therefore, as its contents are addressed to everyone, the style it uses allows everyone to receive a message. If the Qur'an had explained matters in accordance with the horizons of scientific experts, whose number do not even amount to five percent of humanity, ninety-five percent of humanity would not be able to benefit from it.

Inferiority Complex and Overstated Commentaries

On the other hand, while commenting on verses related to scientific truths, it is a mistaken attitude to blow things out of proportion and seek fantasy, attaching irrelevant things to the Qur'an with an ambition to make scientific commentaries. Additionally, attempting to test the Qur'an through knowledge presented by natural sciences is a great disrespect against the Word of God. Pretending that issues of science and technology are essential and trying to fit the explanation of the Qur'an to them in some way, and taking every scientific discovery and development as a base and trying to support them with Qur'anic verses by pushing the limits of obvious religious truths is an approach of great disrespect toward God's Word. Moreover, the Qur'an alludes to different scientific matters in its own style. It

---

[72]   Ibid., p. 277

uses a style that addresses both the understandings of its contemporaries and the people of our age, when science has made a great deal of progress. In other words, although the verses of the Qur'an made perfect sense to the people of the Prophetic period, they do not contradict at all the scientific truths of our time. To give an example, chapters in the Qur'an such as al-Hajj, al-Mu'minun, and al-Mursalat openly tell about the phases an embryo passes through in the womb. As the people of those days read these verses and benefited from them as far as their horizons allowed, the gynecologists of our time cannot help but be fascinated by the truths revealed about embryonic development in the Qur'an.

There is another issue that requires us to be careful about: While interpreting verses of the Qur'an and sayings of the noble Prophet under the light of scientific developments, we need to present matters with alternatives, or at least keep in mind that there can be other meanings pointed out or alluded to by these verses, leaving the door open for other possibilities and never sealing the issue. Particularly, if research is being conducted in a new field and on a different subject, making decisive judgments about the interpretation of verses before matters gain clarity can lead to serious mistakes. In addition, it is absolutely necessary to refer to earlier studies and know about the commentaries about the issue in basic reference sources of Qur'anic interpretation from past to present.

Underlining one more issue can be beneficial here: Scholars that deal with Qur'anic interpretation must be experts in several different fields. For example, they need to know the Arabic language very well, together with disciplines of *Tafsir* (the Qur'anic Exegesis), *Hadith* studies, *Fiqh* (Islamic Jurisprudence), *Usul at-Tafsir* (the Methodology of the Qur'anic Exegesis), and *Usul ad-Din* (Theology). In addition to knowing these, they must have sufficient knowledge to understand the scientific explanations. Likewise, a researcher must have adequate knowledge of religious disciplines in addition to knowing his own scientific field profoundly, if truth is to be reached. Unfortunately in our time, these two fields advance along separate paths. We see that an expert of natural sciences knows the depths of his own field but does not know very much about religion. I would like to clarify the point I am trying to make by saying, "does not know": Knowing basic facts about religious practices does not mean knowing religion. Even if a person learns by heart Imam Bukhari's collection of the Prophet's sayings, this does not mean that he knows religion. Memorizing the entire Qur'an is not sufficient to have a saying in this field either, because, in addition to committing the sayings of the Prophet and verses of the Qur'an to one's memory, it is necessary to know the disciplines of religious methodology in order to understand Divine purposes correctly.

Believing Hearts Burning to Discover

Today, Western scientists are meticulously studying the existence with the researches they conduct. One cannot help admire their boldness and efforts in exploring. However, since most of them have not discovered the true identity of the Prophet and his teachings, they interpret everything within the narrow dimensions of material objects and happenings. For this reason, the systems they establish are bound by materialism, positivism, or naturalism. In other words, the extent allowed by these systems—which see matter as everything—restricts the horizons of a researcher from the West. As researchers on the history of science and philosophy insistently emphasize, until the fifth century of Hegira when Muslims lived their renaissance, Muslim scientists made staggering scientific advancements. At a time when many such matters were not even discussed in the West, they conducted serious research, leading to discoveries in medicine, geometry, astronomy, and more bitter fact is that after the fifth century of Hijra, Muslims gave up their scientific pursuits for about ten centuries and the West took the flag, carrying it further. When this happened, the Western scientists were the ones who set the framework of the present system. Since they established the system in their own way, they evaluated the existence through their own understandings. However, reason alone has its limits with respect to perceiving the truth. Reason can only take one to a certain extent and can only explain the issues of research to a certain degree. There are such matters that cannot be understood without using Divine revelation as the touchstone; revelation must have the final say in all fields, including science."

To reiterate, in the fields of science and research the spirit and the metaphysical must be considered along with the physical. Only with such a balance can you correctly see and evaluate the things that you study by telescopes, microscopes, and x-rays. These expressions should not be misunderstood. We do not adopt an approach that condemns everything discovered by the West. Since the power of reasoning also given to humanity is a wisdom, there are many correct things stated by basing them on reason but all of the theories that have been developed by only taking physical matter into consideration must undergo a critical revision, distinguishing what is right with them and what is wrong. And this necessarily depends on considering natural and social sciences from the perspective of the Qur'an and Islamic faith. And only those who understand the Qur'an correctly will achieve this.

At this point, some Muslims talk about transferring or "Islamizing" knowledge. I think this is a defective approach that cannot lead to the proper conclusion; it is like putting on a borrowed shirt. Instead, we must evaluate issues together with their fundamental principles and re-examine the present sciences with the united perspective of sound reason, reliable senses, as well as authenticated knowledge from Divine sources. Using this criterion, Muslims must then come up with their own truths. Success in this regard depends upon raising individuals thirsty for truth, knowledge, and discovery. If we are to write a real Qur'anic interpretation that appeals to the understanding of people of our time, we must first form a council of scholars with encyclopedic knowledge on all fields of sciences. This council must initially consider matters among themselves and then decide what is right or wrong by using the well-established methodologies of the Qur'anic Exegesis and Theology. The interpretations and commentaries made only after the affirmation of such a collective consciousness must be included in religious literature. If such a council comprised of both experts on Islamic disciplines and natural and social sciences can be formed, then with the help of God, the consequent study of interpretation should be free from artificial commentaries seeking fantasy. It is our hope and expectation that the contemporary scientists whose hearts are firm in and content with faith come together and collaborate in order to form a Qur'anic interpretation of the desired level, so that Muslims will have, to some extent, paid part of the tribute they owe toward the Noble Qur'an.

Transforming Knowledge into Practice

Question: *When we study the life of the Companions, we see that as soon as a Qur'anic verse was revealed, they would immediately begin to act upon the Divine command. We are, however, unable to put forth the same attitude. What would be the reasons for our inefficiency at putting our knowledge into practice, and how can this ideal be realized?*

Answer: In order to implement what we know in practical life, first of all, knowledge must be saved from being rough and simple information; it needs to be transformed into *"ilm,"* in the sense of knowing a matter with its true nature and grasping that matter through consciousness and systematic thinking. Otherwise, if what we know does not amount to anything beyond superficial information, it will not yield any practical behavior, for it does not make an impression on the heart. In this respect, the first thing to do to turn knowledge into practical behavior is to try to reach true knowledge and, from there, to certainty in faith, with an insatiable and fervent desire to learn. In the Qur'an (Ta-Ha 20:114), God Almighty gives the command to His Noble Messenger (which can be interpreted as follows): *"...say, 'My Lord, increase me in knowledge.'"* Each and every one of us as the follower of the Prophet is then supposed be a fervent seeker of knowledge always trying to grow deeper in knowledge. For example, it is a religious obligation to recite the Qur'an. However, even if we commit the entire Qur'an into memory, if we do not make efforts to understand and delve deeper into it, we will fail to benefit from the treasures of the Qur'an, the eternal source of light. There are such meanings and inspirations to be derived through full concentration and sincere efforts that they cannot be attained in any other way.

Offering Gratitude for Knowledge

After the first phase of transforming information into true knowledge (*ilm*), there are other points to be taken into consideration. You may attain a magnificent profundity in theoretical knowledge and gain the certainty of knowledge (*ilm al-yaqin*), even to the degree of the certainty of vision (*ayn al-yaqin*). However, if you fail to implement such theoretical knowledge in practical life, then you will fail to recognize the truth of Divinity with the Divine Names, Attributes, and Qualities, and fail to be a loyal servant at God's door. In addition, there is a glad tiding about the issue by the beloved Prophet, "Whoever acts upon what he knows, God lets him acquire what he does not know."[73] Accordingly, having a share from true knowledge requires acting upon what one knows. If God Almighty grants you a certain level of knowledge, you should strive to give gratitude for this blessing, without taking any personal pride in it. For example, if others perform forty units of Prayer a day, together with the Sunnah Prayers, you should think, "Having been honored with abundant Divine blessings, I should do as much as eighty units a day," and thus ascend to the immensities of subjective responsibility.

Incidentally, I would like to relate a memory that is especially significant for me. In one of my visits to my late mother, she told me, "I read the *Jawshan al-Kabir*[74] every day from beginning to end. Is there

---

[73] Abu Nuaym, *Hilyat*, 10/15; Al-Munawi, *Fayzu'l-Qadir*, 4/388

[74] A voluminous prayer book compiled by Bediüzzaman, including the "Jawshan" prayer, which consists of one hundred parts, transmitted from the Prophet.

anything additional you would recommend for me to read?" This is a reflection of the spirit of someone asking for evermore and thus making continuous progress. A person honored with Divine blessings must turn to Him in due gratitude. The Prophet would pray until his blessed feet were swollen as narrated by his wife Aisha. Imam Al-Busiri expressed this in a poem, "I failed to follow the Practice of the Prophet who kept vigil until his feet were swollen at the Prayer."[75] On witnessing that, Aisha asked the Prophet, "O Messenger of God, although God has forgiven your (possible) past and future sins, why are you praying to the degree of tormenting yourself?" The Pride of Humanity gave the following answer to her, "Should I not be a thankful servant (in the face of such blessings of my Lord)?"[76] There is a very important message here in terms of consciousness of being a servant: Every servant of God is obliged to offer thanksgivings to Him and praise the Almighty to the degree of the Divine blessings and favors bestowed upon him, and thus put his knowledge into practice in proportion to the profundity of his knowledge.

Practical Reason

At this point, it is possible to mention a consideration in Kant's *Critique of Pure Reason*. Kant states that God cannot be known through theoretical reason and that knowledge of God can only be attained through practical deeds. If this can be realized, in other words, if theoretical knowledge is efficiently put into practice, believers can feel a profound knowledge of God inside of them and consequently feel a deep love for Him—to such a degree that they will be saved from the gloom of this world and be seized by an intense yearning for reunion with God, craving, "Reunion with You O God, reunion!" Bediüzzaman mentions faith in God as the essence of worship. Knowledge of God comes after this faith in God, then comes love of God, and then spiritual pleasure, which is granted as an extra Divine favor.[77] When such a

---

75 Altuntaş, 2009, p. 23
76 *Sahih al-Bukhari*, Tahajjud, 16; *Sahih Muslim*, Sifatu'l-Munafiqin, 79–81
77 Nursi, *The Letters*, p. 239

spiritual pleasure is experienced, we will naturally feel an irresistible flood of eagerness to see the true source of beauties, given that all beauties are merely faint shadows of the Divine Essence. If we do not feel such eagerness in our inner worlds, then we have not passed through this process and are still wandering outside. I do not mean to push anyone to hopelessness; however, we need to know that this is the result of the course we have taken. In this respect, let me reiterate that no matter how much you delve in theory, you are doomed to not make any progress but stay where you are as long as you fail to further rise to the level of practice. If you start practicing, but this time fail to deepen in the meaning of that practice and to acquire knowledge of God, you will not make further progress, unable to go beyond mechanical forms—to such a degree that you will view worship as if it were a daily chore; you do the relevant acts but fail to attain knowledge of God, and unable to feel love for Him, and savor spiritual pleasure. Those who do not implement their theoretical knowledge in practical life are likened to "*a donkey carrying a load of books*" in the Qur'an (al-Jumu'a 62:5). One needs to avoid from falling into such a situation, so that knowledge does not become a burden on the back. Otherwise, his or her knowledge will be useless. At this point, we can benefit from the power of prayer at putting knowledge into practice, as the beloved Prophet did by saying, "O God, I seek refuge in You from the knowledge that is not beneficial..."[78]

Broader Horizons through Reading Circles

Although it is commendable for individual believers to carry out reading, thinking, research, to scrutinize things and phenomena, to reflect upon the relationship between human, universe, and God, it will be a means for much different blessings to attend a gathering of faithful ones who cherish considerations and thoughts in this direction and benefit from that blessed atmosphere. Somebody who steps into such an atmosphere will unite with the other individuals in the group togeth-

---

[78] *Sahih Muslim*, Dhikr, 73; *Sunan Abu Dawud*, Witr, 32; *Sunan at-Tirmidhi*, Da'awat, 68

er and they will journey toward different horizons with this special connection among them, pervaded by the same spiritual hue (*insibagh*). As it is revealed in the Qur'anic verse, *"God's Hand is over their hands"* (al-Fath 48:10). Also, the Messenger of God stated, "God's hand (of support) is with the community,"[79] and drew attention to importance of being included in a group. In another case, the Prophet emphasized the danger of being alone by stating that a stray sheep is to be devoured by wolves.[80] Accordingly, one who acts against collective consciousness, who leaves the circle, and who does not fall into step with the group is doomed to be devoured by wolves. Therefore, we must try to be included in a righteous circle against all odds, support one another at that, and avoid acting individually. However, a very important point to be careful about here is to keep our gatherings or circles free from useless talk and amusements, and to benefit from them in the name of deepening in knowledge and spirituality, without even wasting a second. Unfortunately, we do not present the required sensitivity to do this. It is such a pity that even when we come together in the name of religion, faith, and serving for God, we sometimes talk about irrelevant matters that are of no benefit to our worldly or otherworldly life, or we adopt lighthearted attitudes, which lead people to heedlessness. In my opinion, a true believer must try to lead a disciplined life as was once lived truly in Sufi lodges. In an authenticated narration, it is reported that the Pride of Humanity laughed to the degree of chuckling only three times in his entire lifetime.[81] As it is known, his blessed face was always smiling, but he never gave up being serious. That blessed person had such a manner that His consciousness of the omnipresence of God was reflected in his entire being. And one

---

[79] *Sunan at-Tirmidhi*, Fitan, 7; Ibn Hibban, *As-Sahih*, 10/438; At-Tabarani, *Al-Mu'jamu'l-Awsat*, 6/277

[80] *Sunan Abu Dawud*, Salah, 46; *Sunan an-Nasa'i*, Imamah, 48; Ahmad ibn Hanbal, *Al-Musnad*, 5/196

[81] *Sahih al-Bukhari*, Tafsir as-Surah (39), 2; Tawhid, 19, 36; Riqaq, 44, 51; *Sahih Muslim*, Iman, 308–310; Sifatu'l-Munafiqin, 19, 30

could not help but remember God Almighty upon seeing the Prophet's state, manners, and even the depth of his looks.

In a nutshell, we must try to benefit efficiently from all the assemblies, all of our gatherings and the circles we attend in the name of reviving the horizons of our heart and spirit, in order to be well-equipped in knowledge and then implement it in our lives, thus making it very spirit and way of our lives in the true sense. If we wish to walk on the straight path, without any collisions and straying, all of our feelings, thoughts, senses, conversations, and discussions need to be straight; they need to be oriented toward becoming deeper and richer on the horizons of the heart and spirit.

Rights of Neighbors

Question: *Rights of neighbors are commonly ignored in our time, just like many other rights. What is the importance of observing neighbors' rights in Islam? What are the benefits of such observance at the formation of a healthy society?*

Answer: Observing neighbors' rights is an issue that the Qur'an emphasizes, along with treating one's parents kindly, being faithful to relatives, and caring for orphans. It is commanded in a verse (which can be interpreted as): *"...worship God and do not associate anything as a partner with Him; do good to your parents in the best way possible, and to the relatives, orphans, the destitute, the neighbor who is near (in kinship, location, and faith), the neighbor who is distant (in kinship and faith), the companion by your side (on the way, in the family, in the workplace, etc.), the wayfarer, and those who are in your service. (Treat them well and bring yourself up to this end, for) God does not love those who are conceited and boastful"* (an-Nisa 4:36).

Here, directly following the command to worship God and not to associate any partners with Him, doing good to parents is commanded. In principle, when love, respect, and yearning to meet someone are concerned, what comes after God's right is His Messenger's: We recognize our Lord thanks to him; we learn the way to perceive and interpret creation correctly thanks to him, and we understand that we are created and meant for eternity thanks to the messages he brought. In these respects, we are greatly indebted to him. However, as the verse in discussion addresses this issue, not in terms of fundamental principles but in terms of practical deeds, parents' rights, not the Prophet's, are mentioned second. The fact that the beginning of the Divine command is not related to faith in God but to worship Him also indicates this practical side.

After mentioning parents, the verse commands doing good to relatives, orphans, and the destitute, respectively. Then, the verse draws attention to the rights due to neighbors by commanding the doing of good to both near and distant neighbors. Accordingly, all people living around us are included in this meaning, and they deserve to be treated well.

A Way to Attain Perfect Faith

An authenticated saying of the Prophet, confirmed by great scholars including Imam Bukhari and Imam Muslim,[82] stresses the importance of neighborliness. Indeed, Archangel Gabriel gave such insistent advice to the Prophet about neighbors that he thought Gabriel would nearly declare neighbors as inheritors to one another.

Given that a person's inheritors are their closest relatives, we can imagine how important neighbors' rights are in the sight of God. Actually, we do not know all of the advice concerning neighbors' rights that Gabriel gave to the Prophet as the Messenger of God did not relate the details of the case. However, the fact that the Prophet nearly thought neighbors would become inheritors to one another indicates how much emphasis Gabriel placed on this issue.

Another saying of the Prophet relates this issue to faith: "Whoever believes in God and the Day of Judgment, let him be good to his neighbor. Whoever believes in God and the Judgment Day, let him treat his guest. Whoever believes in God and the Judgment Day, let him speak goodness or be silent."[83] As it is seen, being good to neighbors

---

[82]   *Sahih al-Bukhari*, Adab, 28; *Sahih Muslim*, Birr, 141

[83]   *Sahih Muslim*, Iman, 74; Adahi, 19; *Sahih al-Bukhari*, Adab, 31, 85; Riqaq, 23

is mentioned as a requirement of having belief in the true sense. There is another point to note here: Faith in God naturally requires belief in other essentials of faith, including belief in the Judgment Day. It is additionally mentioned in this context, since goodness done here for the sake of God will be rewarded generously when the Judgment Day comes.

Good Neighbors Who Offer the Key to Eternal Bliss

The Messenger of God also gave warnings that a person who comfortably sleeps with a full stomach while his neighbor is hungry cannot be a believer in the true sense,[84] and that a person whose neighbors are not safe from his harm cannot enter Paradise.[85] If the rights of neighbors are stressed so much in the verses of the Qur'an and in the sayings of the Prophet, it is an issue of great importance. In this respect, a Muslim should embrace—near or distant—all of their neighbors magnanimously. People with sound faith should know how to share all of the beauties they possess with their neighbors; it is a requirement of Muslim ethics. When rights of neighbors are mentioned, the first thing that comes to mind is the material kind of aid, such as offering them food, clothes, and the like. As it is known, zakah—the prescribed alms—is given to Muslims only; however, other kinds of alms can be given to non-Muslims. For example, one can provide financial aid to near or distant neighbors whether they are Muslims or not, because these are basic human needs. Particularly in circumstances of poverty, Muslims should never let their neighbors starve, no matter who they are, and should absolutely provide them with support. Helping a neighbor find a job is also a very important means of doing good.

However, it is not a correct approach to reduce neighbors' rights to material aid alone. Greeting neighbors and asking about their wellbeing, getting acquainted better through mutual visits, paving the way to friendly relations between people, and making efforts to eliminate negative feelings—if there are any—are also very important

84 Al-Hakim, *Al-Mustadrak*, 2/15
85 *Sahih al-Bukhari*, Iman, 4, 5; *Sahih Muslim*, Iman, 64–65

points. It is essential to establish a relationship with one's neighbors, particularly for Muslims living in a foreign country. For example, they can take the opportunity on special days to make their neighbors happy with presents and visits. In this way, they can find chances to warm hearts, eliminate biased opinions about Muslims, and introduce their values to others. When the issue is seen from this perspective it is more easily understood that rights of neighbors should not be reduced to a notion of material aid.

Grounds of Sin That Grow into a Disaster

There is another matter worthy of attention concerning neighbors that the Prophet mentioned. Adultery is many times over a graver sin if it is committed with a neighbor.[86] As it is well known, forbidden and disliked acts have a certain ranking. For example, attributing certain things to God Almighty is such a grave sin that, as related in the following verse , it would nearly bring a great destruction: "*The heavens are all but almost rent, and the earth split asunder, and the mountains fall down in ruins...*" (Maryam 19:90). Similarly, there are certain kinds of sins that nearly shatter the heavens and earth asunder. As fornication between relatives fall into this category, such a sin between neighbors is evaluated by the noble Prophet in the same way—as an evil made worse many times over because the predominant feelings between relatives and neighbors must be trust and safety. Therefore, an evil committed by the people whom you trust will not be an ordinary evil; rather it will grow into an evil of manifold ramifications.

Bridges of Friendship Build through a Bowl of Pudding

Unfortunately, it is a bitter reality that there exists a serious void in terms of neighborly relations, as a result of neglecting our own values. To such a degree that even in Muslim countries, an entire society lives

---

[86] *Sahih al-Bukhari*, Tafsir as-Surah (2), 3, (25) 2; Adab, 20; Diyat, 1; Hudud, 30; Tawhid, 40; *Sahih Muslim*, Iman, 141, 142; *Sunan Abu Dawud*, Talaq, 50; *Sunan at-Tirmidhi*, Tafsir as-Surah (25), 1, 2

in their own worlds, retreated in their apartments. Neighbors knock on one another's door only when there is a disturbing noise, in order to warn the latter. Therefore, we need to do our best to make use of every possible means in order to eliminate this chronic problem.

However, it should not be forgotten that changing the established notions and understandings in people's minds is not something easily done like taking off a suit. This issue requires persistence and resolved efforts. Sometimes, you take this chance through the tradition of cooking Noah's pudding and offering your neighbor upstairs a bowl of pudding. Sometimes, you contact them while celebrating the birth of the Messenger of God, or sometimes, you show your good intentions on some other day that is important to your neighbor. Let us not forget, benevolence is a part of human nature and we do appreciate kindness. Therefore, acts of kindness will definitely make their effect one day, sooner or later. Maybe your neighbors will try you for a long time but once they see that you seek no personal benefit, they will gradually open their doors and mutual visits will go on. The Messenger of God, peace and blessings be upon him, compared the situation of believers with respect to one another to a good building whose bricks are soundly integrated.[87] Naturally, all the factors—observing parents' rights, strengthening bonds of kinship, caring for the needy, and observing neighbors' rights—mentioned in the verse in discussion play an important role at building such a society.

Since neighborly relations undergo serious destruction in modern life, the first attempts to enhance relations may not be welcomed at the beginning. However, acts of kindness—even an individual gesture of goodwill—continued in a resolved and steady way will melt the icebergs between people. After a while, they will stimulate good feelings in hearts and, over time, turn into such a strong connection that they will become solid bonds between individuals. Thereafter, individuals will support one another without any expectations in return.

---

[87] *Sahih al-Bukhari*, Salah, 88; Mazalim, 5, Adab, 36; *Sahih Muslim*, Birr, 65; *Sunan at-Tirmidhi*, Birr, 18; *Sunan an-Nasa'i*, Zakah, 67

When one falls, the other will lend a hand, and they will set about a race of goodness toward one another. An ideal society, without clash and conflict, can only be built from individuals such as these.

Finally, in the words of Bediüzzaman, a society whose elements and building blocks are made up of sins cannot be a healthy one.[88] Thus, in order to become a healthy society, it is an important duty for individuals to support one another at protecting against sins and getting rid of vices. God Almighty reminds believers of their responsibilities toward one another with the command (which can be interpreted as): "*...help one another in virtue and goodness, and righteousness and piety, and do not help one another in sinful, iniquitous acts and hostility*" (al-Maedah 5:2). In the name of maintaining such a feeling of help and solidarity, relationships between neighbors provide a very significant ground and opportunity, in my opinion, and is a responsibility that should never be ignored.

---

[88] Nursi, *Münazarât*, p. 52

A Social Disease That Paralyzes
Sound Reason: Bigotry

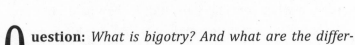

Question: *What is bigotry? And what are the differences between being steadfast in faith and being bigoted?*

Answer: The term *"taassub"* (used for "bigotry" in the English language) means evaluating matters only according to one's own understanding without considering it from different aspects and being pertinacious even in matters that contradict reason and the essence of religion. This very fact is expressed in the sayings of the Messenger of God with the word *"asabiyya,"* which literally means "nervousness,"[89] because a bigoted attitude (*taassub*) is completely based on nervousness and emotionalism; it is an outward reflection of animalistic feelings in human beings. The term *taassub* in this inflected form denotes forcing. In this respect, it conveys meanings such as insisting on a certain issue to the degree of excess, continuing to be headstrong with a complete disregard for others, refusing to see or hear, and considering one's own self as the very focus or basis for everything. As will be seen, *"taassub"* has nothing to do with reason, sound judgment, or sensibility. For this reason, as bigoted ones cannot act with common

---

sense, it is not possible for them to have true spiritual experiences, which are felt through a certain faculty of the conscience.

A Barrier against Faith

Those who persecute believers have always been bigoted. For example, the polytheists and hypocrites at the time of the Prophet, peace and blessings be upon him, were bigoted against Islam and Muslims. They were deaf and blind to the message of the Pride of Humanity. However, if they viewed the noble Prophet in a neutral way, they would also see what sensible ones did; if they paid attention to his words of wisdom even a little bit, they would also hear what sensible ones did. If his adversaries turned over the truths he conveyed in their minds and pondered over them, they would see, understand, and appreciate. Unfortunately, they were blind to these beauties by bigotry, grudge, and hatred, and they drifted to unbelief.

Along with arrogance, wrongdoing, and the deviations from the sound point of view, one other factor that prevents a person from accepting faith is blind imitation of their forefathers, without questioning whether they had been right or not. Actually, such blind imitation is a different form of bigotry. The polytheist people of the Age of Ignorance, therefore, opposed Islam with the arguments that they inherited from their forefathers. Their preventing Muslims from visiting the Ka'ba prior to the Treaty of Hudaybiya was an outcome of the same bigotry. The Qur'an names this attitude of theirs as *"hamiyyat al-jahiliyya"*—zealotry particular to the Age of Ignorance. They adopted this zealotry to such a degree that they kept on blindly sticking to their traditions and practices as before, so that their pride was not broken in the sight of other Arab tribes. Thus, they even prevented Muslims from entering Mecca.

Indeed, such events are experienced in today's world as well. For example, when you wish to express yourself with reference to your faith and heavenly values, certain people immediately take action and try to deprive you of this freedom with a harsh and reactionary attitude you cannot understand. You may come up with different plans and projects in order to contribute to the welfare of the society and elevate it to a better status; but in spite of that, some circles will try to prevent you, since your attempts will mean altering their accustomed ways and claim, "These people actually want to harm our values under the pretext of improvement and welfare." Even though you say nothing wrong about their Marxist, Leninist, and similar understandings and do not say anything against the figures they esteem, when your understanding and values are accepted by society, they feel neglected and claim that your activities are against them, purposefully intending to push them and their values into oblivion. Moreover, even if you somehow find a way and show them a staircase leading directly to Paradise, certain people will still remark, "By doing that, they are trying to make us forget our ideology." All of these attitudes and behaviors are based on "zealotry," as in the Age of Ignorance.

A Dangerous Disease

Such an example of zealotry can be seen in any society or country. There is no particular homeland for bigotry. This negative attribute can pass to any people with different understandings and thoughts. Seemingly religious people can also be under the influence of such bigotry in such a way that some evaluate everything from their own narrow perspective, by solely taking their primitive knowledge as absolutely true. Therefore, they can present a very strict and intolerant attitude toward matters of secondary importance. In our time, suicide attacks—so called "in the name of religion"—are results of such bigotry, given that the attackers are not under the effect of any drug or illusion, that they are not brain-controlled or robotized to commit these attacks. This is such a terrible disease that people ruin their own spiritual lives, for the sake of such delusion of their understanding of righteousness. Those who commit suicide attacks and thus casually take the lives of innocent people, including children, elderly ones, and women, do not become eligible for Paradise but for Hell with such a deed. How grievous an ending it is, when somebody falls into Hell instead of taking the path to Paradise and guiding others toward it!

Being Steadfast in Faith

Since a true believer is a righteous person, they already have nothing to do with bigotry. It is unthinkable for those who have taken the righteous path to stand against what is right and become indifferent to the truth. Otherwise, they will have shown disrespect to the truth. For this reason, what becomes believers is steadfastness in faith and not being bigoted.

"Steadfastness in faith" relates to the words, behaviors, and state of a believer. It does not mean being strict, harsh, and intolerant. Being steadfast in faith means presenting a complete resolution and sincerity in practicing all aspects of the Islamic teachings, against all odds. In other words, it is continually seeking the good pleasure of God in all of one's attitudes and behaviors, even if everybody else gives into worldly temptations; it means not being slothful in any religious practices and being resolved to preserve one's identity in every situation. In order to maintain such steadfastness, a believer must strive to attain true faith based on inquiry, then constantly delve into the truths of faith, and then base all matters on reliable knowledge after having assessed them with sound reason and judgment. Such a journeyer, with knowledge of God, relies on Him in the face of every event, holds onto piety, fulfills what causes require, takes every step with precaution, is not deluded, and never acts emotionally, because the honeycomb formed in that journeyer's soul by wisdom, love, and yearning for God shows the way at every instance. For this reason, bigotry is found in the attitude and behaviors of those whose practices are mostly based on hearsay and imitation. For believers to attain steadfastness in faith free from bigotry, they first need to know thoroughly and digest the main essentials in the Qur'an and Sunnah; then, they filter and check their knowledge with these two sources, and then, they test what they have learned from the Qur'an and Sunnah, according to the pure understanding and common agreement of the distinguished scholars. After all of these, believers must entreat God in all of their decisions saying: *"Our Lord, do not let our hearts swerve after You have guided us, and bestow upon us mercy from Your Presence. Surely You are the All-Bestowing"* (Al Imran 3:8).

As much as bigotry is a contemptible trait, steadfastness in faith is a laudable one in the same degree, as steadfastness denotes an unshakable stance like an upright monument. In fact, it is very difficult for a bigoted person to maintain an unwavering course and be steadfast in faith, since he does not act under the light of reason and judgment but upon emotional motives. For this reason, those who become bigoted in the name of a certain ideology will do the same for another ideology in the future. You see that they are bigoted defenders of a certain ideology that sees the material and animal aspect as everything; when they come under the influence of spiritualism, this time they become zealots furiously propagating it. On the other hand, wherever true believers stood at the time of the Prophet with respect to their essential values, they keep the same upright stance fourteen centuries later.

As for making new judgments according to the requirement of new conditions, it is a different issue that does not contradict steadfastness in faith. The importance of referring to the opinion of competent scholars is related in the Qur'an (an-Nisa 4:83). Answering to newly emerging situations with the methodology of the reliable scholars is a kind of progress. Undoubtedly, such progress is completely different from degeneration, making exaggerated rulings in order to become popular, or showing bigotry at a certain issue without reasoning over it; it is the name of reaching into infinity with a finite body of principles, of the universality of Islam and its encompassing nature.

Vigilance against Transgression

Question: *What does "fisq" (transgression) mean? What are the factors to be careful against it in order not to bear any characteristics of this kind?*

Answer: In terms of the meanings it holds, *fisq* is a comprehensive word. If we make a brief definition, *fisq* means transgressing the limits set by religion; it means stepping out of the sphere of obedience to God by committing major sins or insisting on lesser sins. The Messenger of God, peace and blessings be upon him, stated: "That which is lawful is explicit and that which is forbidden is explicit. But, between the two are doubtful matters about which many people do not know. Thus, he who avoids doubtful matters clears himself with regard to his religion and honor..."[90]

That is, as there are forbidden zones surrounded with mine fields and barbed wire in this world, there are divinely forbidden zones in order to protect people from ruining their lives in the next life. Thus, those who disregard the limits and stray from the main road to forbidden trails commit transgression. This is the situation of those who go astray by indulging in certain weaknesses after having found guidance, as stated in the verse (which means), *"whoever does not judge by what God has sent down, those are indeed the transgressors"* (al-Maedah 5:47).

---

[90]   *Sahih al-Bukhari*, Iman 39; *Sahih Muslim*, Musaqat, 107

In Arabic language, vermin such as rats, scorpions, and snakes that come out of their "holes" and harm people in their homes are termed as "*fawasiq al-buyut*" (transgressors of houses), because they transgress out of the area where they are supposed to remain. The noble Prophet named five animals that are allowed to be killed, even within the boundaries of the sacred areas in Mecca: rat, scorpion, snake, raven, and mad dog.[91] This *hadith* should not be taken as a command to kill these animals wherever they are found. It is a permission to kill the creatures that are likely to harm people. Indeed, it is forbidden to kill animals within the sacred zone of the *Haram*, or Sanctuary, in Mecca.[92] Even killing a single locust there necessitates giving alms for atonement. However, as the vermin mentioned above recognize no limits and harm people, they are considered transgressors and can be eliminated. In other words, people are given permission and the opportunity to protect themselves against these creatures, which transgress out of their nature.

Characteristics of *Fisq* in Believers

Rather than referring to individual persons, the Qur'an describes the negative qualities of those without faith; guidance requires directing the criticism to the qualities not to individuals, so that they can correct themselves. In addition, this method conveys a very important warning to believers. As Bediüzzaman stated, just as an unbeliever does not possess solely negative qualities, every quality of a believer may not be befitting for a believer.[93] Sometimes, you see that some believers assume certain qualities of unbelief or transgression in a cer-

---

[91] *Sahih al-Bukhari*, Bad'u'l-Khalq, 16; *Sahih Muslim*, Hajj, 67, 68, 69, 60

[92] The *Haram* (Sanctuary) is the region of security and safety that covers the Ka'ba and the surroundings, where any act of violence, like killing a human being, or cutting any green grass or trees, disturbing the natural environment, harming animals, or interfering with the lives of beings is *haram*, or prohibited, in conformity with the command of not violating the sanctity of this place. Its borders were defined by Prophet Abraham under the instructions of Archangel Gabriel, and later redefined by the noble Prophet.

[93] Nursi, *İşârâtü'l-İ'câz*, p. 166; *The Words*, p. 749

tain period of their lives. For this reason, believers have a lot to learn from verses referring to hypocrites or unbelievers.

Sometimes, believers who observe the basic acts of worship might transgress into forbidden areas without knowing it by lying, backbiting, or slander; they stray from the main road and cause traffic problems in different alleys. Even if such people claim to have very strong faith, such acts indicate their bearing a certain quality of transgressors. As far as they keep living with that quality, it is not possible for them to guide others with the Divine teaching; God Almighty grants success in this respect only to those who adorn themselves with laudable virtues. An ideal believer's character is in keeping with accepting faith, gaining insight into faith, elevating it to the horizons of spiritual knowledge, crowning the attained spiritual knowledge with love of God, and then crowning that love with a yearning and zeal for God; and, at the same time, deepening such faith through worship, and adorning worship with *ihsan*, or a consciousness of the omnipresence of God. When somebody possesses these laudable virtues, they can succeed at conveying the Divine message to others. Even if they cannot, God Almighty rewards them generously with His blessings as if they have succeeded. What really matters is having fulfilled one's responsibility. There are certain Prophets that had no followers at all, while only a few people followed some others. However, even the worth of all other human beings cannot be equal to a single Prophet's worth in God's sight. In other words, if it were possible to extract human values from all people and make them into a statue, it would still not amount to a Prophetic one, because those blessed people are chosen ones, specially adorned with refined virtues of the highest kind. In spite of that, some of them only reached two or three people, some even none. Even so, they were never discouraged and continued their mission in a resolved fashion.

At this point, one may wonder the wisdom of sending a Prophet who would be followed by only a few people. First, let me state that since a Prophet in such a situation carries out his duty thoroughly, he still gains the reward for the Prophetic mission and becomes eligible for God's special favors. On the other hand, if a Prophet becomes a reference for future guides with the beautiful example he presented to a handful of believers, and if those new guides achieve a moral reform by following his traces, the wisdom of that Prophet's coming is fulfilled. In addition, pioneering ones will be granted blessings for the goodness realized by those who come later, having paved the way for them. Actually, this fact is not limited to the Prophets. For example, if it was not for Bediüzzaman Said Nursi, who exerted himself for making hearts awakened to the truths of faith and who blazed a trail of faith through the heart of Anatolia with the two or three hundred people behind him, the people of Anatolia would probably have not welcomed the idea of serving faith as much as they do now, and they would not go voluntarily to the far corners of the world in order to share this beauty. For this reason, let me reiterate that what really matters is a person's walking toward sublime ideals adorned with laudable virtues, seeking the good pleasure of God with pure intention, that becomes a believer, without narrowing the issue to the achievement of certain results.

The Blind Alley before the Transgressor

As for transgressors, even if their lifeline somehow intersects with an auspicious circle of volunteers serving for the sake of God, they mostly dislike things that do not comply with the expectations based on their fancies and desires, and they set about different quests of their own. Even though they do not openly state it, such people have unending expectations of this kind. Mostly, they fail to meet these requirements and sulk. It is as if such a person expects those around him to read his mind, and he feels disappointed as an unappreciated genius that has been let down with respect to his wishes when they do not. On the pretext of trivial matters, such people leave their friends with whom they shared certain feelings and thoughts and, for a while, believed in the same ideal. They then try to start personal initiatives. This is a different type of *fisq*. Surely, such a renunciation does not mean forsaking one's faith. However, their position in a circle of righteous ones is a blessing by Divine Providence. By leaving the circle out of personal fancies, such people put themselves in a perilous situation as mentioned by the Noble Prophet. At one instance, one man did not make any effort to find a place in the circle formed around the Prophet by his Companions. Instead, he turned away and left. The Messenger of God drew importance to the gravity of the matter by stating that as the man turned away, God Almighty turned away from him as well.[94] In short, it is a type of *fisq* for people to hold different expectations, to think that their true worth is not appreciated, and to believe that they deserve a higher reward and payment than others with the abilities and capacities that they possess, not satisfied with the blessings in hand and then setting about new quests. This kind of *fisq* mostly leads one to a very different end than the one intended. And when such individuals are brought to account in the Afterlife, they will be asked why they left a righteous circle and strayed to a dangerous zone that might make them devoured by wolves.[95] Along with this, if somebody backbites others in an arrogant manner and raises discord and strife, in a way it means that they are marring the beautiful activities realized by the efforts of so many volunteers.

Love of Status and Doors Opening to Transgression

The greatest test to pass in such slippery ground is overcoming the love of status in human nature. Sometimes, destiny brings someone— maybe someone twenty years younger than you— to a higher position. For example, this can happen between an experienced teacher and an administrator of younger age. What befalls on the administrator is to benefit from more experienced staff members and not make them feel ignored. What befalls on the staff, however, is to comply with the person in charge of them. Otherwise, they commit transgression. Even imagining to do such things is a kind of transgression in the mind. For this reason, individuals need to rehabilitate themselves continuously and do not leave any room for transgression, even in their imagination.

---

[94] *Sahih al-Bukhari*, Ilim, 8; Salah, 84; *Sahih Muslim*, Salam, 26
[95] An allusion to the *hadith* stating that wolves eat the one who strays from the flock.

At this point, we can remember the example of Usama ibn Zayd. Shortly before the Pride of Humanity, peace and blessings be upon him, departed from this world, he prepared an army to stop the Roman advance under way and appointed Usama as the commander, who was about eighteen years of age. Imagine that the greatest figures among the Companions, such as Abu Bakr and Umar, were soldiers in that army. After the army reached the first stopover after Medina, the news came that the Messenger of God had passed away and Usama ibn Zayd returned to Medina, thrust the flag into the ground outside the door of the Prophet, and waited. Right after this news, Abu Bakr had become the caliph after the electoral meeting in the land of Bani Saida tribe. As soon as Abu Bakr became caliph, the first thing he did was to carry out what the noble Prophet's initiative, and he accompanied the army until they were outside Medina. In the meantime, Caliph Abu Bakr approached Usama, who was only the age of his grandson, held his arm and humbly asked, "Could you let Umar ibn al-Khattab remain in Medina to assist me?"[96] This is the ideal level of mannerliness to be targeted by every believer. No matter who they are, if a person is charged with a certain duty, what becomes believers—with the exception of the right and responsibility of mannerly warning in case of mistaken practices—is avoiding to question others' eligibility and not raising strife by adopting negative attitudes. Otherwise, social harmony will be damaged. Nevertheless, the Messenger of God stated that believers are supposed to obey the person appointed as their leader, even if he is a black slave.[97] This is where true triumph lies. Indeed, if everybody cherishes expectations out of their own desires and fancies, discord and rout will be inevitable. Therefore, in the name of inhibiting transgression and strife, one must virtually declare war against the love of status inside them and learn to be satisfied with whatever position and duty appointed for them.

---

[96] At-Tabari, *Tarikhu'l-Umam wa'l-Muluk*, 2/246; Ibn Asakir, *Tarikh Dimashq*, 2/50; Ali al-Muttaqi, *Kanzu'l-Ummal*, 10/258

[97] *Sahih al-Bukhari*, Ahkam, 4; *Sahih Muslim*, Imara, 37

Offhanded Attitudes
toward the Sunnah

Question: *Some people in order to justify their personal wishes say, "If the Prophet were alive today, he would act in the same way." And when they come up with some religious matter that they do not like, they make an offhanded remark with a similar claim saying, "My Prophet would not say so." How do you evaluate such remarks? And if new interpretations can be made, what are the necessary qualifications for someone to be eligible to do that?*

Answer: Such words can be evaluated differently with respect to the situation of the individuals and on which considerations they made such remarks. The noble Prophet, peace and blessings be upon him, did not solely convey messages from God, but he was a *mujtahid*[98] who clarified and established religious matters with his Sunnah (Tradition) through words, practices, or silent approval. We can consider his identity as a *mujtahid* and say, in the name of finding solutions to such and such problems, according to the changing conditions of the time that the Messenger of God would most probably act in this way

---

[98] A practitioner of *ijtihad* who is authorized to deduce new rules through juristic reasoning from original sources—the Qur'an and Sunnah—if these two sources present no decisive ruling on a particular matter.

with respect to this issue and fill this gap thus. This could be an agreeable approach, and it is possible to find a reasonable basis for it.

Time is an important interpreter. It serves like a pointer at making judgments about certain issues that depend on conditions and conjuncture. In other words, the Qur'an and the Sunnah leave certain issues to the requirements of changing conditions; to the "time" which can be regarded (and thus be referred to) as the *mufti* giving legal opinions and rulings on religious matters. However, the people qualified to make such interpretations and rulings according to the time and conditions must know whether there is a clear statement about the issue in the Qur'an and the Sunnah, and they must make a thorough inquiry into it, as it is not acceptable to say anything contradicting the essentials in the Qur'an and the Practice of the Prophet. Similarly, if the great *mujtahid*s, or expounders of the Islamic law (like the founders of the various Sunni schools of thought) who established matters with their verified evidences and agreed on a certain judgment, contradictory comments are unacceptable. Even though some refuse to take *ijma* (consensus of scholars) as substantiation, it is very sound substantiation in accordance with the statements of the Prophet: "My community does not agree upon misguidance;"[99] "God's support and power is with the collectivity;"[100] and "I petitioned God so that my community would not agree upon deviation, and He accepted this petition."[101] As it is seen in these lustrous statements, *ijma* is rather sound substantiation. In addition, it is a very important proof for *ijma* being substantiated that people who are so pure with respect to their heart, soul, reason, conscience, and inward and outward senses agree on a certain issue with no dispute or ill will. Thus, as it is not possible to contradict the Qur'an and the Sunnah under the title of *ijtihad*, the same is true for *ijma*, which tells us how to understand the essentials in the Qur'an and the Sunnah and how to interpret them. For this rea-

---

[99] *Sunan ibn Majah*, Fitan, 8; Al-Humaydi, *Al-Musnad*, 367
[100] *Sunan at-Tirmidhi*, Fitan, 7; Ibn Hibban, *As-Sahih,* 10/4
[101] Ahmad ibn Hanbal, *Al-Musnad*, 6/396; At-Tabarani, *Al-Mu'jamu'l-Kabir*, 2/280

son, we need to make a distinction between these two conditions: making offhanded remarks out of one's desires and fancies by ignoring the essential sources is one issue, but on the other hand, stating scholarly opinion on a certain matter, with reliable knowledge and insight about the subject in conformity with the essential sources and established judgments is a totally different issue. Therefore, when seeking solutions to familial, political, social, or economic problems, the established sources come first. If no clear solution is found in these, it is important to be careful so that the new ideas suggested in the name of filling a certain gap do not contradict the essential disciplines.

Hearts Must Shiver While Giving a Legal Opinion

It should be emphasized, however, that in order to arrive at reliable scholarly solutions for problems arising in different areas of life, the person giving legal opinions must be sensitive enough to fear saying something against the Divine will and must shiver with this concern. Otherwise, people who are lax in their religious practices, who continually make indulgent remarks about religion, and who seek recognition with sensational remarks can say, "The Prophet would also do the same in this issue," or they can say with respect to matters that they feel lazy about, "The Prophet would not act this way." Their asserting the name of the Prophet as so-called evidence is surely not an acceptable approach whatsoever. Indeed, when people make such remarks at issues that do not suit their fancies, they are making an imaginary Prophet speak in accordance with their personal desires and whims, causing him give rulings that suit their fancies. However, the matters that concern people's happiness in both this world and the next have no tolerance for such offhandedness. The righteous scholars of the early period acted with great caution concerning matters of *ijtihad*, such that when they tried to find an answer to a particular question, they searched through the entire Qur'an, solely for an answer to that question. In addition, great figures such as Imam Azam Abu Hanifa would discuss a certain matter with their disciples for several days. But this scholarly discussion should not be confused with today's debates on TV programs. Such kind of scholarly discussion does not mean trying to refute one another's opinions; rather, it means to discuss matters by comparing them with similar and established issues. That is, scholarly discussion on a religious issue aims to find a solution by making an evaluation according to the meanings of essential commandments and comparing it with similarly established issues. Sometimes, the disciples of Abu Hanifa would accept their teacher's opinion on a certain issue, but that great Imam would ponder upon the essential commandments through the night, and in the morning he would say: "You accepted my view on that issue, but I failed to take certain commandments into consideration. Your opinion is better placed." This was their degree of righteousness. Another example was the great imam Abu Hasan al-Ash'ari, who had a profound knowledge of the Qur'an and Sunnah, excellent command of language, and powerful oratory. For a while, he favored the rationalist approach of the people of *i'tizal*, who accorded creative effect to human will and agency. Later, he suddenly—most probably on hearing compelling scholarly evidence from someone else—relinquished that view, which sees everybody as the creator of their own actions, as commonly asserted by many people today. As a great scholar who had gained a deserved fame with his peak scholarly level, Imam Ash'ari gathered everyone he could find and proclaimed his acceptance of the opinions of the majority of Muslims[102] by declaring, "Whatever I said on this issue was wrong. And the correct opinion is thus..."[103]

Those Who Take Their Lusts and Fancies for Their Deity

Unfortunately, we witness today such offhanded approaches to religion that some try to deny obvious Divine commandments such as

---

[102] *Ahl as-Sunnah wa'l Jama'ah*, or those who follow one of the four Sunni schools of thought.

[103] Al-Husayn, *Imam Ahli'l-Haq Abu'l-Hasan al-Ash'ari*, p. 35

modest dress, which is an issue directly referred to in various verses of the Qur'an,[104] and one explicitly established by the detailed clarifications and practices of the Companions of the Prophet and the great figures of the following period. Even if we have adopted a measured manner (without reacting in a counter-attitudinal way) about those who deny such explicit principles in religion, the ruling of the Islamic law about the people who deny their existence is crystal clear.

To reiterate, if a ruling (*ijtihad*) is to be made in the face of personal, familial, social, political, and administrational issues, first the Qur'an and the Traditions of the Prophet must be known well and the judgments and considerations of the righteous scholars of the early period must be referred to. Then, possible equivalent matters in the essential sources must be searched for. After completing these, a solution to the problem in question must take into consideration the era and the present conditions. For example, the Qur'an advises to assign a person to mediate between a couple with bitter feelings toward one another and states that peaceful settlement is better (an-Nisa 4:28), thus presenting such a discipline to ponder over the issue. In the same way, the ninth verse of Surah al-Hujurat commands making peace between two parties fighting against one another. These essential principles can be generalized for matters between greater parties and can even be taken as basis for matters on an international scale. Given that peaceful settlement is better for a married couple, the smallest unit of the society, then peace between different sections, cultures, currencies, or nations will obviously be good. The significance of peace will increase directly proportional with the scale of the matter in question. When a married couple is at odds, the situation of their children will resemble orphans. When two societies clash, however, the consequent damage will be far greater if the issue is not settled by peaceful means. In this respect, the volunteering believers of our time must seek ways for peace in the name of solving social problems of any scale and by taking possible means and present needs into

---

[104] An-Nur 24:31, 60; al-Ahzab 33:59

consideration. They must establish grounds for dialogue, form platforms of agreement, and even assemble mediatory councils, if necessary.

As a matter of fact, this point that we have tried to make can be seen from the perspective of the discipline of *qiyas* (logical deduction by analogy) in Islamic Jurisprudence. In Islamic methodology, *qiyas* means giving a judgment on a certain issue by comparing it with similar ones.[105] When done in the name of righteousness and faith, God Almighty will reward it even if the personal judgment is mistaken; those who give a correct judgment at *ijtihad* can gain, in accordance with their depth of intention and significance of the issue, from two to one hundred blessings, or even more. If they make a mistake, they will still be rewarded for the effort that they made. As for those who evaluate matters according to their own fancies, the Qur'an refers to them in the verse, as translated, "*Do you ever consider him who has taken his lusts and fancies for his deity...*" (al-Jathiyah 45:23).

To conclude, from believers' perspective, in all of personal, familial, or social matters, God Almighty and then His Messenger have the final word. When they have made a clear judgment on something, what befalls on people is to keep silent. For this reason, if somebody asserts a personal wish against a clear commandment by God or His Messenger, they should know that they will be among those who have taken their desires and fancies as their deity.

---

[105] Al-Jurjani, *At-Ta'rifat*, p. 230

The Role of the Spiritual Guide

Question: *Some see it as an obligation to follow a certain "murshid" (spiritual master) and assert that it is not possible to be saved without pledging allegiance to such a master. Could you state your opinions on this?*

Answer: There are two meanings for the word *murshid*, the first being a general term and the second being associated with a Sufi context. In its general sense, *murshid* denotes a guide who averts people from straying to ominous trails and shows them the righteous path, who awakens hearts to the Divine, who opens minds, feelings, eyes, and ears to certain truths, and thus who guides them to the horizons of the heart and spirit. In this respect, it is possible to see a person giving a sermon in a mosque or giving a religious talk in a circle as *murshid*. In the same way, a shopkeeper who pours the inspirations of his heart into another's by talking with a visitor to his shop about the truths of faith can, in a way, be seen as a *murshid*, or spiritual guide, as well.

As for the more specific meaning of *murshid* in a Sufi context, it refers to a person who had initially become the disciple of another *murshid*, who went through rounds of forty-day retreats (*chila*), who ate and drank little, who slept little, and who passed different levels at spiritual journeying. That is, *murshid* is a person who experienced astonishment before the Divine (*hayra*) and annihilated his carnal soul in God (*fana*), who attained a certain spiritual rank on the path to find

Him, and who in the end was entitled as a new spiritual master by his own master to guide others to the Truth and convey the Divine messages to them. This entitlement is named *khilafa* (vicegerency) and the person who is entitled is named a *khalifa* (successor or vicegerent). I think the initial question was related to this Sufi sense of the word *murshid*; therefore, I would like to elaborate on it a bit further.

Perspicacity of the *Murshid* and the Potential of the Initiate

From past to present, there have been so many great figures who were raised by following one of the Sufi paths that lead to truth—Naqshbandi, Qadiri, Shadhili, Rifai, Badawi, and the like. Particularly, when some people with potential and ability find a perfected master, they experience a metanoia and become radiant light sources. For example, when Muhammed Lütfi Efendi of Alvar and his father Hüseyin Kındığı Efendi, who were from the lineage of the Prophet, arrived at Sheikh Kufrawi's Sufi lodge in the province of Bitlis, the sheikh paid attention to them and treated them as special guests, probably since he discovered their potential. Eventually, he entitled both of them as spiritual masters. On witnessing this, the disciples who had served the sheikh until then accosted the two newcomers at night. Suddenly the door burst open; Sheikh Kufrawi came in and brought them to their senses: "You disciples! Hüseyin and Muhammed Lütfi Efendis did not need me. It was their perfection that led them here." Some people have such a God-given potential that they are ready to give light without a touch of fire, as it is referred to in the verse (translated as), "...*The oil almost gives light of itself though no fire touches it*," they can rocket to certain spiritual ranks by a single puff. And there are certain initiates who, in spite of having potentials to thrive elsewhere, prefer to serve loyally to their sheikh. For example, in spite of having completed his education at Islamic disciplines, Mawlana Khalid al-Baghdadi served as a sweeper at Abdullah Dahlawi's lodge for twenty years, and then returned to Baghdad. As it is known, Khalid al-Baghdadi is accepted as the reviver (*mujaddid*[106]) of his time. With respect to his character and way of guidance, he resembles Bediüzzaman Said Nursi very much. When we study his letters, we see that he invited his students to sincerity, brotherhood, and dignified contentment (*ghina*): "Never ask for posts and positions for which you would most certainly pay a price and refrain from becoming obliged to anyone, do not establish relations with authorities (in order to gain material benefit from them), do not covet what somebody else possesses, and be indifferent to anything inviting you to worldliness..." In terms of their main approach, these pieces of advice coincide with the points Bediüzzaman makes in his epistles on *Sincerity*[107] and on *Brotherhood*.[108] Such a great figure humbly served as a sweeper at a Sufi lodge for twenty years.

Even if the *Murshid* is a Perfected One

Getting back to our main topic, in Sufi tradition there is a rank of being *murshid* in its true sense. The important figures who attained this rank appraised the people who became their followers very perspicaciously—sometimes from their faces, looks, and even from the irises of their eyes—and discovered their aptitudes and capacity. Accordingly, they guided their disciples to realize their spiritual potentials and commissioned them to guide others in different places when the time came. In this respect, if there are any guides like Abdul Qadir al-Jilani, Mawlana Khalid al-Baghdadi, Muhammad Bahauddin Shah an-Naqshband, Alaaddin Attar, and Abu'l Hasan ash-Shadhili, who are truly profound in every aspect, then it is very important to benefit from their guidance in order to realize one's spiritual potentials. But it should not be forgotten that God Almighty appointed different persons to guide others through different methods according to the con-

---

[106] God Almighty sends a distinguished spiritual guide (*mujaddid*) in every century to realize a revival in religion.

[107] Nursi, *The Gleams*, pp. 225–235

[108] See Nursi, *The Letters*, pp. 281–294

ditions and needs of their time. In this respect, it can be said that had the great guide Abdul Qadir al-Jilani been alive today and used the same methods he used for guiding people in his time, which was inspired from the original teachings of the Prophet, it probably would not help much for curing the troubles of our time. In the same way, if a great figure like Imam Al-Ghazali, who was honorably referred as the Proof of Islam, were to suggest the same arguments he used against the anti-Islamic discourses of his time as a prescription to cure today's troubles, it would not suffice against today's complicated problems. I am not trying to make any comments with negative connotations about those great masters, let me not be misunderstood; those exalted figures complied perfectly with the requirements of their age and even transcended it.

However, the point I wish to highlight is that the Divine message always comes in accordance with the addressees' level of cognition, comprehension, and needs. For this reason, I only tried to express a reality. Surely, today's people have a lot to learn from those great guides and their very valuable works in terms of broadening their horizons of spiritual knowledge. However, struggling against the contemporary form of hypocrisy and antagonism toward faith under the guise of science and philosophy requires relevant background knowledge and arguments. There must be a *murshid* who can see and read our era correctly, who uses his means accordingly, who distills facts as he should, and who can write appropriate prescriptions so that he can derive appropriate cures for the troubles of our day. When such a guide is found, following him is very significant in the name of taking wing toward the horizons of the heart and spirit. If people remain loyal to such a perfected guide, he can broaden their horizons, clear up the way before them, and thus they can travel in a faster and safer way in their journey toward God. But in my opinion, even if they find a perfected guide who comprehends his age perspicaciously and suggests important solutions for the troubles of the time, people should refrain from reducing and narrowing the issue down only to this person. If you adopt a pressurizing attitude toward other believers and dare to say, "If you do not take a pledge of allegiance to that guide, obey what he says, and read what he writes, then you are misguided," you will have reduced the issue to bigotry and subscribed to a horrible view about other believers. This is because another person who does not exactly think like you and who has adopted a different line of spiritual journeying can, by God's grace, walk behind the Messenger of God—the ultimate *murshid* and the most perfected guide—and can enter Paradise. For this reason, even though it is important to love the circle one is affiliated with, taking the matter to the degree of being unable to stand others and even becoming antagonistic toward them is absolutely wrong.

The Blow on the Spirit of Unity

Since this humble servant also spent his childhood in different Sufi lodges, I occasionally witnessed some people make such remarks. For example, some people quote out of context a saying ascribed to Bayazid al-Bastami, "the *murshid* of someone without *murshid* is Satan."[109] They misinterpret this saying with a narrow understanding and assert that it is obligatory to follow a sheikh from a particular Sufi tradition. In my opinion, this saying of that perfected master stresses the significance and necessity of the issue, but interpreting it in such a narrow frame will mean reducing this statement to a disagreeable one that conflicts with the universal and encompassing nature of Islam, which can give way to subscribing to negative opinions and partisanship. We have the essential disciplines of the Qur'an and the Sunnah in our hands; they possess the immensity and inclusiveness to embrace all of the hearts that believe in them.

Bediüzzaman stated that narrow-mindedness stems from loving one's own carnal soul[110]—in other words, a person's attempt to orient everything toward his or her own ideas is a kind of egotism. A different form of this is partisanship of a religious circle, which means see-

---

109 Al-Maqdisi, *Al-Uqudu'd-Durriyya*, p. 76
110 Nursi, *The Words*, p. 737

ing the absolute truth as limited to the particular Sufi order, religious group or movement that one belongs to and believing that others are striving in vain. Again, it should be noted that such an approach means subscribing to a horrible view of other believers, which can lead one to a total downfall.

If a person's arrogance is based on taking pride in being affiliated with a certain religious group, it grows stronger. Those who are affiliated with a certain Sufi tradition, a religious group, or a movement will naturally think they have chosen the right guide and love that person profoundly. On the other hand, they must shun from being unfair about others and condemning them to fallacy. Otherwise, they will have strayed to a devilish path while trying to walk on the righteous one. This danger is possible for everyone. If one of the great figures I admire—such as Imam Al-Ghazali, Izz ibn Abdis-Salam, Fakhruddin ar-Razi, Najmaddin al-Kubra—were alive today and gave such a mistaken counsel to the people around them, I would humbly put my head under their feet, kiss their soles, and say, "Sir, you are mistaken on this subject."

In sum, believing that salvation can only be possible through affiliation with a certain Sufi order, religious group or movement, seeing it as compulsory to follow a certain traditional Sufi master, and seeing those who do not follow that person as misguided is absolutely wrong; it denotes losing in a zone of winning. May God protect believers from such deviations and disasters in these days when we are in such dire need of solidarity and unity.

Our Era and the Ways
Leading to God

Question: *What are the points of consideration for the people of the contemporary age striving to remove the barriers between people and God and thus let their hearts meet the Truth, particularly in terms of a spirit of unity and togetherness?*

Answer: Until our time, different ways, methods, and means have been tried in the name of reflecting the very spirit and essence of the perspicuous religion of Islam through various paths and practices. For example, the path followed by the Naqshbandi order is formulated as follows:

One must renounce four things: the world, the Hereafter, "becoming," and the idea of renunciation.[111]

This means that four things must be renounced to take the Naqshbandi path. The first two are renouncing this world and the next. That is, initiates of this path must first push aside the temptations of this world; second, they should never attach their worship to a consideration such as, "Let me observe worship, so that I can go to Paradise." This is because the real reason for worship is the Divine

---

[111] Nursi, *The Letters*, p. 24

commandment and its outcome is the good pleasure of God.[112] In this respect, believers must move their shuttle between the command-ment and good pleasure of God and weave their lives accordingly; they must work such a beautiful pattern that even the angels would admire it.

Third, a traveler on this path must also renounce himself, or more precisely, his carnal soul, taking a stance against its never-end-ing demands and fancies, in addition to adopting an absolute attitude of dignified contentment (*ghina*) towards everyone but God. Finally, the journeyer must renounce even the very idea of having renounced all of these, in order to avoid feelings of pride and self-appreciation. When a thought such as, "I am a hero of such and such renunciation" passes their mind or even imagination, they must seek purification by asking forgiveness from God.

The Characteristics of an Era of Arrogance

In our time, however, arrogance has become widespread and people act upon egotistic motives. Therefore, it might be difficult to maintain such an advanced degree of renunciation; it is probably with this con-cern that Bediüzzaman presented an alternative approach in "The Fourth Letter" where he says: "In our way, depending on one's per-ception of his [or her] nothingness, four things are necessary: per-ception and admission of one's absolute poverty vis-à-vis the Divine Riches, of absolute helplessness vis-à-vis the Divine Power, of abso-lute gratitude or thankfulness to God, and of absolute enthusiasm in His cause."[113]

Thus, Bediüzzaman stresses the importance of adhering to these four essentials in our time. That is, one must first perceive and admit their helplessness and adopt the understanding: "I cannot do any-thing unless God wills." In the same way, believers on this path must see themselves essentially so poor that they become aware that what-

[112] Nursi, *The Gleams*, p. 181
[113] Nursi, *The Letters*, p. 24

ever they possess is granted by God Almighty. In spite of their help-lessness and poverty, they must be filled with gratitude before the Divine blessings and favors so generously granted, and they must strive to let everyone's hearts feel God Almighty with never-ending ardor, energy, and enthusiasm. In the "Addendum of the Twenty-sixth Word," Bediüzzaman lists the essentials of his path (by switching the last two) as "helplessness, poverty, compassion (or affection), and reflection,"[114] which indicates that the system he put forth has six different depths. In my opinion, these considerations of that great master, which con-vince the reason and satisfy the hearts of contemporary people, are very important points that need to be pondered. Nevertheless, so many people who benefited from his works feel obliged to him for having let their hearts feel the truth of Divinity, setting a throne for the Prophet in them, and for having presented the truth of resurrec-tion and afterlife to cognitions nearly with the certainty of eye witness-ing, by God's permission and grace. Actually, expressing this indebt-edness to such people is a duty. It is stated by the Messenger of God that one who does not thank people, does not thank God either.[115] Then one must possess a character of offering thanks and a feeling of grati-tude. Therefore, people who attained the blessing of knowing God, the Prophet, and life after death through the works of that person will naturally have deeper respect for him. However, this respect should not give way to taking pride in being affiliated with a certain religious group and growing arrogant; it should not lead to excessive approach-es about him. There are so many people walking on other lanes of the great highway of Islam who attain true faith, salvation, and good plea-sure of God by means of the lane on which they proceed. For this rea-son, expressing gratitude should not be turned into an advertisement and show of the achievements of a certain group; narrow-mindedness, which stems from self-admiration, should be avoided. Means and ends (or goals) should not be confused, and it should not be forgotten that,

114 Nursi, *The Words*, p. 494
115 *Sunan at-Tirmidhi*, Birr, 35; *Sunan Abu Dawud*, Adab, 11

no matter on which lane one travels, the ultimate goal is to gain the good pleasure of God.

The Souls that Found Reunion through Migration

Those who move to different lands for the sake of helping people know God and sharing their values with them are also on a separate line to attain the good pleasure of God. As a spiritual confirmation of being on a righteous path, let me relate that in hundreds, maybe thousands of instances, people saw the Messenger of God, peace and blessings be upon him, in their dreams, or sometimes in wakeful state, and received glad tidings from him. For example, one man related that they kept vigil on a blessed night and invoked blessings on the Prophet for a few thousand times. And then a vision of the noble Prophet appeared and said that he stood behind their services on the way of God. And another one saw that cobras were attacking his friends, who could not protect themselves from them. Suddenly, the door opened and people with radiant faces came in; the Prophet was leading them with his blessed staff in his hand. After dealing a blow on the cobras with his staff, he said to them, "Do not fear, we are behind you." Actually, I feel embarrassed to relate subjective things of this kind. But since the issue has nothing to do with me, I see benefit in relating such visions from time to time. To tell the truth, with respect to the circle of serving faith in which we are included, thanks to Divine guidance and Providence, I have always held the following thought: "If I could give the due of my position and make good use of the favors and opportunities granted by God Almighty, the services would run faster reaching more people all over the world. More important achievements could have been made had it been for more sincere people instead of me." In addition, one should compare the glad tidings given in these visions to candies given to children in order to spur them on and keep up their hope. Otherwise, a true seeker of Truth must not expect any of these. As the one with the most faults in this movement, even I say in my prayers: "My God! Do not let us consume the blessings You will grant in the Hereafter by giving us some good things in this world! Do not let us be among the ones to be reprimanded on the Day of Judgment as described in the verse (translated as): "...*you consumed in your worldly life your (share of) pure, wholesome things, and enjoyed them fully (without considering the due of the Hereafter, and so have taken in the world the reward of all your good deeds)*" (al-Ahqaf 46:20)." But in spite of everything, if some people see such visions as important for boosting morale in times of trouble and take them as a reference from the Prophet, there should not be anything wrong in telling them.

On the other hand, in spite of so many antagonistic circles trying to prevent people from benefitting from the perspicuous Religion, the volunteers who migrate for lofty ideals are welcomed everywhere they go; this is obvious support by Divine Providence. In the same way, although these people did not have enough opportunity to receive professional seminars on peaceful coexistence with others from different cultures in a globalizing world, they did not experience failures in the very different regions but rather gained acceptance there. This can be considered a different indication of their gaining acceptance from God and His Messenger and that they act in compliance with the Divine Will, as it is difficult to talk about an opening of this scale, after the time of the Companions.

The volunteers inspired by the essential principles of helplessness, poverty, thankfulness, enthusiasm, reflection, and compassion set out on the road in modesty, humility, and self-effacement. These people join hands and serve as a port of guidance for journeyers destined for the Truth. In short, for all believing hearts, God is the ultimate goal (to be sought), human beings are the travelers on the way to Him, and the ways leading to Him are as many as the breaths of all creatures. In this respect, what befalls on us is to applaud those trying to serve by seeking the good pleasure of God and implore to Him for their success.

Worldly Means and the Criteria
for Planning the Future

Question: *The Messenger of God enjoined being like a stranger or traveler in this fleeting world. Some Muslims of the early period regarded even planning what to eat the following day as a form of cherishing long-term worldly objectives and delusion of eternity. Considering the conditions of our time, however, making certain plans about the future is deemed as necessary, particularly at issues such as choosing which schools to attend and what profession to learn. How can we strike the balance at making plans for the future?*

Answer: As it has been mentioned in the question as well, the noble Prophet, peace and blessings be upon him, did enjoin being like a stranger (*gharib*) or traveler (*abiru sabil*) in this world.[116] The term "*gharib*" used in the Prophetic saying denotes a person who somehow leaves his or her hometown and migrates to somewhere else, thereby staying there for a while as a guest, and who has thus no deep relation with the things and people around. And the other term or phrase is "*abiru sabil*." The root of the first word is *ubur*, which denotes *journeying* or *crossing* a road. As a matter of fact, every individual is a

---

116 *Sahih al-Bukhari*, Riqaq, 3; *Sunan at-Tirmidhi*, Zuhd, 25

"traveler" journeying from the mother's womb to childhood, from there to youth, maturity, to old age... from there to the grave—an intermediate realm between this world and the next, and finally (rise up from the grave to go) to the Plain of Great Gathering for judgment. Thus, the beloved Prophet counsels taking the journey of worldly life as if passing from one side of the road to the other.

The noble Prophet pointed to this same fact another time when he rested on a plain rough mat, which made marks on his body. With eyes full of tears, Umar ibn al-Khattab mentioned how the Sassanid and Roman kings lived (in luxury) and implied that the Prophet could benefit from worldly blessings. It is reported that the Messenger of God replied that he did not have anything to do with this world. The noble Prophet, peace and blessings be upon him, compared his position in this guesthouse of the world to a traveler who takes shade under a tree for a while and then continues on his way.[117] All of us know that had he wished so, the Companions would have brought anything they could find to make him feel comfortable. However, the Pride of Humanity, peace and blessings be upon him, likened himself to someone who stops temporarily under a tree for a rest and then goes on his journey, and this was the scope of his relation to the worldly life. He maintained this understanding until his blessed soul passed to the next world.

Fortunes Spent for the Sake of God

When the issue is seen with a holistic view and the commands of religion are taken as a whole, we understand that the noble Prophet does not tell us to absolutely neglect the world, but rather to refrain from indulging in worldliness in pursuit of lowly pleasures and delights. The following verse, for example, decrees that the Messenger of God, peace and blessings be upon him, is authorized to handle one-fifth of war gains: "*And know that whatever you take as gains of war, to God*

---

[117] *Sunan at-Tirmidhi*, Zuhd, 44; *Sunan ibn Majah*, Zuhd, 3; Ahmad ibn Hanbal, *Al-Musnad*, 1/301, 391

belongs one fifth of it, and to the Messenger, and the near kinsfolk, and orphans, and the destitute, and the wayfarer (one devoid of sufficient means of journeying)" (al-Anfal 8:41). Even if the noble Prophet chose to take only one tenth out of the one fifth of the war gains for himself, he could have led a very prosperous life and lived in palaces. However, he preferred to lead his blessed life in a little cell instead. It was so little that, as his wife Aisha reported, when the Messenger of God stood in the Prayer at night and before prostration, he would touch his hand to the feet of Aisha, and only after our blessed mother receded her feet did he have enough space to prostrate.[118] Imagine, he could not even find sufficient room for prostrating in his cell—let our souls be sacrificed for that cell. However, as we take into consideration the riches allocated to his use we see that he had the means to equip an entire army. He spent them for the sake of God and preferred to live an austere life. In terms of his personal life and abstention from worldly pleasures, he acted in such a careful, cautious, and measured way that he fulfilled the due of the virtuous conduct God Almighty demanded from him: *"Pursue, then, what is exactly right (in every matter of the Religion) as you are commanded (by God)"* (Hud 11:112).

The Representatives of Dignified Contentment (*Istighna*)

Undoubtedly, the Messenger of God, peace and blessings be upon him, was a transcendent person with respect to his relation with God, his position, state, profundity, and immensity. He had such a lofty and different nature that he expressed how he felt delight in worship, as other people take delight in physical pleasures. To relieve his aching for worshipping his Lord, the Prophet would frequently ask his wives to be excused and get up in the middle of the night to be nourished from the fount of worship and devotion. In this respect, let alone comparing him to ourselves, even comparing him with the Companions is not right: no other person can be compared to him. And I dare say

---

[118] *Sahih al-Bukhari*, Salah, 22, 104; Al-Amal fi's-Salah, 10; *Sahih Muslim*, Salah, 272

that even comparing the Archangel Gabriel with him is a mistake. As an angel, Gabriel did not bear any burdens related to carnal desires and physicality. In spite of bearing the burdensome side of human nature, the Prophet was far beyond angels in spiritual progress. It is for this reason that as the Prophet, millions of blessings and peace be upon him, returned from the Ascension back to live among us, he descended from his high horizons to the level of ours to convey objective truths for our understanding and spiritual life. When we look into the matter within these criteria, although nobody can be compared to him, we can say that believers should lead their personal lives in dignified contentment, in compliance with his teaching. Indeed, all the great figures who were true to his path preferred to live this way. For example, if you study the life of Bediüzzaman, you see that dignified contentment is one of the important principles he held throughout his life. He would sometimes spend his days on his little platform on a tree; sometimes he would stay in the mountains for months, and sometimes he resided in a wood cabin, which was not really suitable for habitation. In short, he preferred to live a very austere life until the end of his life. Actually, not only people from the Muslim tradition, but also followers of others teachings who changed the fate of the societies to which they belonged, similarly lived a life of dignified contentment. In this respect, we can say that such virtues, which can be taken as a sign of greatness with respect to universal human values, are the same in almost everyone, but with one difference—in believing hearts, this virtue is more soundly established and it promises permanence, because they have Divine approval behind them. For some others, even though they temporarily possess virtues becoming of believers such as dignified contentment, self-sacrifice, and altruism, they do not necessarily promise continuity and permanence. And one thing that needs to be known is that God Almighty grants success in this world to anyone who possesses characteristics and qualities becoming of believers, because He treats His servants according to their good character and conduct. Therefore, even if someone is a saint flying miraculously in the air, God

Almighty will not treat him in a way that becomes true believers, given that he acts in a lethargic or lazy way, or becomes a selfish one who runs after personal benefits; those who act thus fail to fulfill the meaning of being human in the true sense. Indulging in worldliness, leading a physical-oriented life, and acting upon animal desires are unacceptable for a believer, who should be proceeding toward realizing the God-given spiritual potential for human perfection. Obviously, such a lifestyle is not the way of the Prophet.

The Way to Eternalize Transient Means

Surely, today's believers need not push aside everything about the world and live like ascetic dervishes in retreat. This is contradictory to the ideal of becoming a powerful community upholding justice; Muslims must try to have worldly means as much as they can. However, they must make use of the means they acquire in a benevolent way to eternalize them. At this point, I would like to express a feeling of mine: Sometimes I imagine and wish that when I step into the room I find a great amount of money, out of nowhere, and distribute it to the people volunteering for benevolent services for humanity so that they can establish schools and cultural centers in different corners of the world and thus conquer hearts of people. This is just a dream of course. Since it is a dream, I realize no practical goodness with it. But let me point out that if such a dream did not belong to me but to a friend of mine, and if he shared this consideration with me, I would tell him that even such an imaginary action can bring you manifold rewards and blessings to be gained at worship. Sharing the inspirations of our heart with others, illuminating worlds with the torch in our hand, taking the beauties we learn from the Prophet to everywhere the sun shines upon,[119] exerting ourselves with this thought, and becoming oriented to such a lofty goal even in our dreams are all very important.

---

[119] *Sahih Muslim*, Fitan, 19; *Sunan at-Tirmidhi*, Fitan, 14; *Sunan Abu Dawud*, Fitan, 1

Returning back to our main subject, though, let us reiterate that as far as worldly means are used correctly, there is nothing wrong with having them. However, adoration for one's worldly goods, status, home, children, or carnal pleasures as if one worships them, leads a person toward worldly and otherworldly disaster. A person must adore and worship God Almighty only and love anything else solely for His sake. He must be the One to be remembered at the beginning and end of something and everything must be attached to Him. Otherwise, when we act in the name of physicality and our carnal side, everything will be condemned to our own narrowness and it will mean wasting ourselves and our God-given spiritual potential. A human being, who is as worthy as all the worlds and who is endowed with a vast potential to ascend to otherworldly ranks as great as the earth and sky, should not be condemned to such narrowness I think. One the contrary, he or she must run after eternity and seek His good pleasure all the time—so much so that a title of "conqueror" should not be anything desirable as far as it does not take one to God, as such a thing does not bear any meaning on its own. What makes an action valuable is the depth of a person's sincere intention. An accomplishment will be truly valuable as far as it is meant to gain the rewards heralded by the noble Prophet, to hold Islam in esteem, and to share the values we learn from the Prophet with the entire world.

Intention as a Determining Factor

The same point holds true for the efforts directed to graduating from certain schools and performing certain jobs. In other words, if a person wishes to do something for the sake of their lofty ideals and pass through certain stages, they will naturally carry out what they need to do. For example, a student who wishes to have a good education must say, "I cannot go to the university without finishing high school. I cannot reach a good position to serve my people without finishing the university. I cannot be welcomed and respected without having such means to serve others. And if I do not become worthy of respect, I cannot do anything serious for the sake of my people and lofty ideals." And a student must make such an intention from the very beginning.

We cannot stop ourselves from questioning previous generations and blaming them for having failed to see certain things, leaving gaps in certain fields, and losing continuously. But if we do not wish the next generation to question us in the same way, we must exert ourselves to fill the gaps left by the earlier ones and not let new gaps appear. We have to take certain pains in order not to receive righteous criticism from our children and grandchildren. What needs to be done first is to have a strong faith and to try not having any flaws in our worship, and then to attach everything we do to a sincere and sound intention. If this can be realized, a person's studying at high school, finishing the university, and every other achievement they plan to do will be counted as worship and gain them blessings; because, whatever is the intention of attaining a goal, the means used to obtain it will assume the hue of that very intention. In this respect, everything that is done must be woven according to the pattern of a sound intention.

In conclusion, true believers never do—and must not do—anything in order to receive praise from others or for worldly concerns. They always strive for conveying the heavenly values distilled from their spiritual roots to others and make continuous efforts so that the representatives of these high values gain an esteemed status in the world. For this sake, they sometimes face difficulties, experience pain, and bend in two with suffering. But they know that their troubles and suffering for the sake of a sublime ideal will gain them so many blessings that such progress could not be attained even through a process of spiritual journeying.

Chastity of Thoughts

Question: *Could you please elucidate the phrases "purity of ideas" or "chastity of thoughts" which you draw upon from time to time?*

Answer: Thought and action are the two most important dynamics that show us the way to truly exist, help us stay as ourselves in the face of fierce storms, and help us change ourselves in the progressive sense. Although thought in its general meaning comes before actions, a certain thought with its intricate and detailed meanings develops within the very process of (putting it into) action. That is, a person can concentrate on a certain subject first, give much thought to it, and try to fathom it correctly. However, only after putting the issue into real life practice will one gain further insight into it, accept and accommodate themselves to it, and found it on a sound basis. This is because implementing what one has thought about will make one face some new situations which will, in turn, lead to deeper thoughts on the issue, and thus the general ideas at the beginning will rest upon unshakable grounds. So be it in a general context or a specific one with lots of details, the most important essential we need to pursue in all of our intentions and thoughts is "purity of ideas." In this respect, we need to remain faithful to the purity of ideas, seeing it as part of our very character, and protect it under our wings against all odds.

Sound Thoughts Produce Sound Conduct

It is possible that some people may adopt negative opinion and attitudes toward us, but others' wrong attitudes should never lead us to
reflect back a similar sort of attitude. Wherever we stand with respect
to our essential values, we need to stand our ground against all odds.
Otherwise, once our thoughts and feelings begin to waver according
to others' attitudes and behaviors, the wavering will continue and
eventually take us off the righteous course. What we need to do, however, is not even let others distract and keep us busy—let alone taking us off course—and try to keep away from every kind of influence
that might serve as a provocative factor against our course and our
stream of thought. We should know that the real purpose of provoca-
tions is to avert the volunteers devoted to high ideals from their path
and make them change course, not with the purpose of achieving something else but for achieving this very end.

For this reason, representatives of sound thinking should never
change in the face of the inconsistent and baseless claims made by
others—of course with the exception of making legal claims by appealing and refuting in order to protect one's reputation against defama-
tion and using their lawful right to sue them for slander and other
violation of rights—and always try to keep up their purity and inno-
cence. We need to think straight at all the times so that the actions
we are to build on those thoughts are right and straight. Otherwise, if
we move away to one side with every storming wind, we might lose
track, fall to other trails, becoming adrift in the end.

Those Who Think Positively Take Delight in Their Lives

The Messenger of God, peace and blessings be upon him, once stated
that a believer's silence should be reflection (*tafakkur*) and his speaking should be wisdom."[120] Taking this radiant statement into consideration, we can say that thinking, imagining, and shooting for good

---

[120] Ad-Daylami, *Al-Musnad*, 1/421

things will be counted as worship for a believer. Even though busying ourselves with seemingly impossible thoughts normally means wasting our energy, if a person cherishes a wish to transform the color and pattern of the world into a more beautiful and vivid one, I think even the dreams and imaginings of that person will take on a hue of worship. Thus, what befalls on believers is to become oriented to such beautiful considerations and lead their lives accordingly. In one of the epigrams at the end of *The Letters*, Bediüzzaman states: "Those who attend to the good side of everything contemplate the good; those who contemplate the good enjoy life."[121] Therefore, someone's turning his life into a delightful melody and spending his life as if he were walking through the corridors of Paradise depends on his thinking beautifully. However, one's thoughts also could take people to negative ways, such as hedonism and bohemianism, unless he uses it in a positive way. Also, even imaginings and conceptions that are not channeled toward goodness can make one face such negativities. For this reason, believers must continuously be preoccupied with thoughts that take root in their values, overflow with them, continuously read and think, and feed on their essential sources without leaving any voids in their life. At the same time, they must give their willpower its due to such an extent that they always remain close to the feelings and thoughts that are not granted a visa by their pure conscience. If they are prone to negative winds in spite of all their efforts, they should— as advised by the Messenger of God—try to free themselves from that atmosphere immediately. Otherwise, a person who sets sail into dreams that might corrupt the purity of his mind sometimes may go too far and not have the opportunity to return to the shore (of safety). Therefore, if one does not control the feelings of grudge, hatred, vengeance, and lust, they might break down barriers and thereby cause them to take wrong decisions and commit evil acts. One must give their willpower its due on one hand and ask protection from God on the other. Those who can achieve this will lead their lives in a green-

---

[121] Nursi, *The Letters*, p. 450

house of Divine protection. But still one should never forget that even the most upright people might topple over, and thus we must never give up our vigilance. When we stumble and lose our balance, we must turn to our Lord and ardently pray like our forefather Prophet Adam did: *"Our Lord! We have wronged ourselves, and if You do not forgive us and do not have mercy on us, we will surely be among those who have lost,"* (al-A'raf 7:23) then straighten up, and turn toward Him again.

Desires and Fancies in Guise of Ideas

Another point to raise in terms of chastity of thoughts is that there is always the possibility of desires and fancies masquerading as ideas to misguide a person. The touchstone to distinguish desires and fancies from true ideas is the religious criteria. For example, if you feel enraged when someone's words and attitudes bother you, you first need to determine whether there is anything that goes against the Truth. If this is not the case, it means that you are getting angry in the name of your carnal self, which shows that the angered reaction stems from personal desires and fancies. The criterion to use in the face of evil as decreed in the Qur'an is to *"repel evil with what is better (or best)"* (Fussilat 41:34). Accordingly, if someone does evil to you, the primary response towards him or her must be a smiling face intended to defuse the intensity of their strong dislike and malice. But if the evil in question is directly related to sacred values or public interest, as an individual, we do not have the right to forgive his or her act; one can only forgive and show tolerance towards violations against his or her personal rights. God Almighty did not assign anybody as a substitute authorized to forgive violations of His rights. No one should dare make such claims, which are clearly disrespectful of God's rights.

Getting back to our main subject, desires and fancies with no sound base sometimes present themselves in the guise of ideas and try to misguide people, in cooperation with the devil and our carnal soul. One might commit certain wrongs in consequence. You can clearly see this on some debate programs where people try to outwit one another. As if they are fixed on controversy, they always try to say the opposite of what the people before them say, not caring whether it is right or wrong. Let us suppose that one of the people with whom such a person argues says, "Now I am going to show you, by God's grace and permission, a way directly leading to Paradise." If the gates of Paradise miraculously and suddenly appear wide open before him and enable him to see the wonderful blessings beyond imagination, he will still say, "No, we do not want to enter Paradise. We are trying to win here, and you are trying to stop us and push us to inactivity." That is, such a person will try to respond with demagogy even against the most plausible words and thoughts. Such words actually stem from one's desires and fancies and are uttered under the influence of the devil. However, people mistake all of them as stemming from their own thoughts and ideas.

Sometimes, people from among believers can also fall for this trap of the devil and carnal soul. When you ask help from such a person, he might say that he needs to stay where he is so that he can guide many others, attempting to hide his desire for spending more time with his family and enjoying worldly life under the guise of altruism. However, a sincere believer burns with a desire for reunion with God, overflows with a desire for meeting the noble Prophet, and wishes to sit at the table of the Rightly Guided Caliphs and share their atmosphere. In spite of these feelings, a sincere believer watches his step and says: "My God, I do not know whether I served my time in this world or not. Therefore, I am afraid of committing disrespect towards You." The conscience is a very important reference point here. For this reason, one must always judge the words one utters with his or her conscience and seek its righteous counseling at every choice and decision made. If someone can achieve this, he or she will be saved from confusing fancies with guidance and carnal desires with commonsense.

Keeping up Sincerity of Intention and Having a Consciousness of Self-Criticism

Question: *What are the points of consideration in terms of keeping up sincerity in our intentions?*

Answer: In order to gain the good pleasure of God Almighty, it is very important for a person to say what they are saying sincerely and do what they are doing sincerely. Because, if deeds are like a body, sincerity is like the soul; if deeds are like a wing, sincerity is the other wing. Neither can a body live without a soul, nor can a wing function without the other. A word uttered or an action realized sincerely is so precious in the sight of God that angels take that word to their mouths and include it in their habitual prayers; spirit beings keep reciting it as if it were a phrase of glorifying God. If the words coming out of one's mouth are the true voice of his or her heart, then those words make their way from mouth to mouth until they reach the Holy Sphere (*Hazirat al-Quds*). In addition, it needs to be known that as far as such words uttered sincerely remain in memories, the Divine reward for the goodness keeps flowing into the speaker's record of good, righteous deeds, and thus every word uttered gains infinity through their replicas.

Spoiling Good, Righteous Deeds by Revealing Them Sanctimoniously

However, if someone adds a personal emphasis on his or her good act by the tone of voice, facial gestures, and other sanctimonious attitudes, that person becomes a loser on a ground of winning and becomes deprived of the abundant reward in consequence.

For example, the Daily Prayers are an exalted form of worship that takes one's journey through the skies of infinity. It is so wonderful to glorify the greatness of God at bowing and prostration, and to praise the Lord while rising from bowing; the Prayer is such a laudable form of good, righteous deed. However, if a thought such as, "Let others also hear how I am glorifying Allah in the bowing and prostration positions," passes the mind of the person at the Prayer, the glorification will be ruined; the words will become lifeless, and that beautiful act of worship will be turned into a movement devoid of spirit and a title without meaning. If one holds any consideration of showing off to others, even one percent of weight, he or she expels the spirit of those words and let it fly away.

You can evaluate all acts of worship, such as making the (first and second) calls to Prayer, reciting a portion from the Qur'an during the Prayer, and the recitations and prayers made right after the Prayer within this frame. It should be kept in mind, however, that tuning into the inner voice and musicality of the Qur'anic verses recited during the Prayer, thereby letting oneself into that stream naturally, and trying to impress others by showing off with their vocal skills are two completely different things. It should be known that a person who shadows his deeds with his ego, in a way, allocates a share for himself from what belongs to God, proportional with the degree of this shadowing. This resembles breaking the wings of a bird, and thus preventing that good deed to take wing to the realms beyond.

Therefore, a person must consider his or her sincerity in all he or she does. With the condition of not becoming a negative example, one must look simple when viewed from the outside. That is, one must be unpretentious and look like a simple hut, but should be more dazzling and noble than the greatest palaces with respect to his or her inner world.

Self-Criticism as a Shield

Believers need to see themselves so lowly to the degree of saying, "How surprising, when I view my inner world, I consider myself as a person who fell from level of humanity to that of animals. But as a Divine favor, God still lets me continue my life in human form." As for their contribution to the services carried out for the sake of God, they should say, "I could have used these opportunities granted by God Almighty in the best way and exerted myself to tell the truths of faith to others. But I haven't been able to make efficient use of these opportunities for His sake; I wasted them. For this reason, I am a contemptible person who has not been faithful toward Islam and the Qur'an. I feel surprised that I did not turn to stone." They must come to grips with their carnal soul and continuously be at its throat. Seeing oneself in such a low position triggers a wish for spiritual progress as well. If seekers of perfection wish to reach higher levels, they need to see themselves as being in a lower position than they are. Also, journey to the Infinite One is infinite. God Almighty has revealed for us the horizons of perfection and completeness: *This day I have perfected for you your Religion (with all its rules, commandments and universality), completed My favor upon you"* (al-Maedah 5:3). We must become insatiable journeyers on the path to infinity in such a way that, even if God Almighty openly grants us Divine love in a bowl in a miraculous way without or beyond any manner and measure, we would still be asking for more and more of it. Attaining such perfection and completeness depends on constant self-criticism. Otherwise, those who perceive themselves as already perfected individuals and who act as if further progress is not possible will be condemned to remain where they are; it is impossible for such people to taste and thus become acquainted with perfection.

In addition, there is another negative side of not facing oneself: a person who does not make self-criticism begins busying himself with a fruitless concern about others' shortcomings unawares that he is doing so. And if the pride of being affiliated with a certain group adds to one's personal arrogance, that person has a greater risk to become a loser. As Bediüzzaman emphasizes, communal arrogance gives strength to personal arrogance. Therefore, it can be said that communal arrogance is a fatal and destructive calamity of great danger. The way to be saved from all of such dangers is to constantly face oneself and make self-criticism.

For example, God Almighty may grant one man the opportunity to carry out very important services in different parts of the world. Indeed, this man may have conquered the hearts of all people in a place and may have realized a breakthrough in knowledge and spirituality there. But our consideration in the face of such achievements must always be: "Since I have been in charge, so many other things have not been completed. Had it been for another one enlightened in heart and mind, God knows how the services here would have further flourished. I wish the services had not been narrowed down or hindered because of me." This must be the true spirit of self-criticism that journeyers to God must possess.

In fact, avoiding a stumble and fall in the face of praises and flattery depends upon maintaining a practice of self-criticism. That is, a person must criticize himself several times a day, keep himself under self-surveillance, and adjust his relationship with God Almighty, accordingly. Thus, even if others sing his praises and extol his virtues, he still says, "I know myself. This can be an intervention of Satan here," thereby saving himself from giving into pride and arrogance.

May God fill all of our hearts with such a high consciousness of self-criticism. May He enable us to give the due of the duties He granted us as a blessing! Amin!

Temporary Retreats in Serene Corners and Reading Sessions

Question: *People of the modern age who feel suffocated in the hectic flow of daily life feel a need for a quiet corner, a haven of peace they can take refuge in. The believing souls like to organize occasional retreats in serene corners for the sake of a refreshment of their heart and spirituality. What are your suggestions to benefit from these retreats most efficiently?*

Answer: Everybody has certain responsibilities to fulfill in the society. If believers wish to be beneficial for the society, guide the people they address to a certain lofty horizon, and let others feel their values profoundly, then they have to live among other people. A person with sound belief in God and the Day of Judgment must live among other members of the society and become a compass of truth and righteousness. The Pride of Humanity, peace and blessings be upon him, stated that a Muslim who lives in the society and endures the troubles from others is better than one who does not.[122] Accordingly, a permanent retreat will mean escaping from one's responsibilities to be carried out in the society. For this reason, even though it is done for the sake of personal spiritual progress, a person who escapes

---
[122] *Sunan at-Tirmidhi*, Qiyamah, 55; *Sunan ibn Majah*, Fitan, 23

from these responsibilities will commit a sin, because what matters in Islam is maintaining one's connection with the Almighty while living among others and striving to serve humanity.

However, it is a reality that while we are among others for the sake of lofty ideals, sometimes we face certain undesired situations—to such a degree that we might walk on mud unawares and get our skirts spattered with mud. Without even realizing it, our eyes and ears may have been polluted in the societal life; improper situations may have violated the purity of our inner world.

So, those who forbear many negative effects for the sake of their high ideals need purification from pollutant exposures in the societal life; they need to allocate a period of time to spend in a quiet place for the sake of a refreshment of their heart and spirituality, retreat to a clean atmosphere, fill their lungs with fresh air, and thus recharge themselves. In my opinion, all of the discussions and reading sessions oriented toward this goal can be regarded as a kind of worship.

However, there is one point to be careful about: people who retreat to those serene havens, which entail certain troubles and incur certain expenses, should make the most of the retreat without wasting a second. They must organize a program with disciplined reading sessions and bring life to it with remembrance and glorifications of God. Through the spirit of collective consciousness, heartfelt remembrance and glorifications of God must make up such choruses, such symphonies to make the heavens and the earth vibrant that even the inhabitants of heavens should wish to join them.

An Atmosphere Open to Spirituality

During the summer programs that we held many years ago, the recitations of the Qur'an, prayers and litanies recited by our friends, each of whom withdrew to a corner for nocturnal devotions, moved me so much. At the same time, they would read an average of 200-300 pages on truths of faith during the day and discuss different issues. In addition, conditions were so simple. For example, people would sleep on mats made of straw. This humble servant cooked the meal and served it. Once, an important guest witnessed that atmosphere and remarked, "This must be the best place in the world to feel true spirituality." He attended the program the following year as well.

At the same time, in those pure environments we had better face ourselves and look critically at what we have thus far done with the intent of serving for the sake of God. We need to see our mistakes and make a self-criticism about where we stand and where we should stand. We need to make a resolution for journeying in the orbit of the heart and spirit by turning our backs on physicality and the animal side, and try to steer toward spiritual courses. For the sake of clarification, let me relate a consideration at this point: during those summer retreats, I thought of telling our friends to observe a hundred units of supererogatory Prayer every night. But I hesitated, wondering whether it would be too difficult of a task for them. When we view the lives of great spiritual masters, however, it is seen that they observed a hundred units of Prayers each and every night, even at very young ages. In this respect, those who are able to do so should observe a hundred units of Prayer every night, if possible. They should benefit from the mysterious and somber silent hours of the night in the best way with devotions by entreating and asking forgiveness from God, along with certain remembrances and recitations.

The Great Works Victimized by Indifference and Benefits of Comparative Reading

For the sake of making good use of those temporary retreats, one should try to read 300 pages of religious books a day, if possible. If this target can be realized, a person who joins a 15-day retreat program will be able to read 4500 pages in total. If such programs can be held twice a year, it will allow a great deal of reading in terms of being nourished by Islamic sources.

In addition, it will be very beneficial to read the essential books of religion and spirituality by comparing them with other works, which will greatly help breaking the monotony. Realization of this depends on collective acceptance. Therefore, those who try to initiate such activities of comparative reading should know that they will find it a bit difficult at the beginning until they rid themselves from old styles and habits. But there is another thing to keep in mind—people should adjust themselves according to the ones supposed to guide them. If those who walk in front consider this a matter of serious concern and persevere in practicing it, others will follow them in doing the same. Unfortunately, our friends have fallen into the clutches of a narrow minded consideration of reading through those precious works in a shallow fashion—without making an effort of gaining insight into their true depth. Since no method of reflective, pensive and comparative reading had been established, reading that treasure of jewels is being taken for granted and is now seen as an ordinary task. I think that the authors of those works feel heartbroken toward us.

Let me state one final point: Maintaining such purity in a quiet place, be it only temporary, will serve as a protective shield with respect to the participants' later societal life. It is a reality that Muslim society has never been this polluted in history. The streets are dirty; downtown is dirty; courtyards of the mosque are dirty, and educational institutions are dirty... So in terms of leading the rest of one's life in a pure and virtuous line, I believe it is very important to be purified from all of the dirt and become oriented toward purity, feel purity, and invigorate with it once more.

In addition, seeking refuge in the Divine Will through prayers and remembrance is a mysterious source of power that brings one under His protection. God Almighty commands: "... *always remember and make mention of Me (when service to Me is due) so that I may remember and make mention of you (when judgment and recompense are due)*" (al-Baqarah 2:152). Accordingly, if we remember God Almighty with glorifications and praise and proclaim His greatness, He will remember us and see us through hard times. It is also possible to understand this verse thus: "You turn toward Me by acknowledging your impotence and poverty, so that I support you with My Power." This agreement is actually a mode of manifestation of Divine blessings. That is, God Almighty addresses us as if we are one of the parties of an agreement and says, "You do this, and I will do that."

In conclusion, we all need temporary isolations in order to clean our eyes, ears, and tongue from sins, purify our hearts, and recharge our spirituality. However, minds should focus on reading and hearts should be immersed in the remembrance of God at such gatherings; things related to worldly fancies should not be spoken in lieu of sublime issues.

True-Hearted, but Not a Chauvinist

Question: *Would you please explain the points that we need to be careful about while talking about certain spiritual guides who have a special place in our personal spiritual enlightenment, and thus whom we deeply love and respect?*

Answer: As the believers strive to pour the inspirations of their soul into others' hearts, they might sometimes have to express certain good things about the circle they are affiliated with. They must, however, definitely take into consideration the feelings of the people whose spirituality developed in a different lane. Others may tell or write about certain beauties they witnessed as becomes their understanding and style. However, a person with sound belief should never be chauvinistic or zealous and never make exaggerated statements about the people they love profoundly and respect deeply. If the points to be stated are not directly related to the spirit of religion but to secondary issues and details, and if stating them is likely to raise disagreements, then utmost sensitivity must be shown to avoiding talking about such issues.

A person may, for instance, be a very loyal follower of Sheikh Bahauddin Naqshbandi to such a degree that he or she may gladly be ready to sacrifice his or her life a thousand times for the sake of that blessed guide. However, there are different schools among the Naqshbandi order, such as the Mujaddidiyya, Khalidi, Kufrawi, and Taghi orders, and their followers might have some feeling of competing with one another (*tanafus*). Actually, *tanafus* does not mean competing with one another, but striving for more goodness with the consideration of "let me not fall behind the others on my path." In other words, *tanafus* is a way of acting and competing for good, with the idea of not separating from fellow believers on the way to Paradise. But if one fails to hold this feeling in a balanced state, to maintain it, and in a way starts to abuse it, then it might give way to rivalry. Furthermore, the feeling of rivalry can turn into envy and intolerance. Such feelings are very dangerous for believers. For this reason, the believing souls should never narrow down issues to affiliation with certain groups in order to avoid provoking feelings of envy in those who walk on neighboring lanes; they should restrain their feelings for the sake of maintaining unity and concord among the wider circle of believers.

Steadfastness as the Greatest Rank

Indeed, what really matters is not following a certain person but being steadfast and true to the cause one's guide tried to germinate by devoting his or her life to it, as people are mortal but the cause is everlasting. There is no title higher than being truthful. As revealed in a Qur'anic verse (an-Nisa 4:69), the truthful ones (who are loyal to God's cause and truthful in whatever they do and say) come before martyrs and saintly ones. Abu Bakr, may God be pleased with him, is regarded as the greatest person after the Prophets and he was honorably referred by the Prophet as "The Truthful One." In this respect, true wisdom is not to make exaggerated claims about the persons we love and respect by declaring them as Mahdi or Messiah, but to follow their example as much as possible on the path they walk.

Also, a person who claims to feel genuine and a great deal of attachment and love for a certain guide, but is not deeply saddened when remembering him, and does not shed tears after him, and does not open up his hands after performing one hundred cycles of Prayer at night and supplicate "O Lord, resurrect me together with him!", and most importantly, does not sacrifice whatever he has in the path of his guide and in the name of his sublime ideals, I believe he is not sincere in making such a claim. But this is only a criterion to be followed for the people themselves while making individual self-criticism, as we should not, indeed cannot, charge anybody with being insincere.

In addition, it also needs to be known that if you set to extoll the virtues of a certain guide, you might unintentionally provoke others and raise many different oppositions against him. We can even say that your exaggerated words, attitudes, and behaviors do not only provoke anti-religionist circles but also other circles of faithful ones. When you narrow down the issue to certain individuals, you even provoke other circles trying to serve faith and cause their ruin with the sin of envy. In this respect, let me reiterate that what really matters is not the individual himself but perfect loyalty to his cause.

Exaggerated Remarks as Harmful as Betrayal

Attributing good acts and achievements solely to people seeming on the fore, and thus making exaggerated statements about them, is evident injustice and wrongdoing. If there is any success and achievement, it is a Divine bestowal for the sake of the collective spirit. Therefore, ascribing all the services carried out to the ones seeming on the fore is both a grave disrespect toward God—that might lead to associating partners with Him—and unfairness toward the efforts of other people who exert themselves for His sake.

As for seeming on the fore, we should never forget that we are brothers and sisters. Some people may have come earlier and thus have been placed in certain positions in the first ranks as a dictated Divine blessing—that is, Divine destiny may have decreed certain people to come to this world earlier; nobody can determine the time of his or her birth. Therefore, preceding others in time cannot be criterion for absolute value. The noble Prophet, peace and blessings be upon him, stated that those who do not show compassion to the young and those who do not respect the elderly are not one of his followers.[123] Accordingly, we always respect the elderly. However, this does not mean attributing titles to them that they are not eligible to bear and singing their praises near others with exaggerated statements. For example, those who learned truths of faith from the students of Bediüzzaman, such as Hulusi Yahyagil and Tahiri Mutlu, may their abode be Paradise, can view those righteous people as the *qutb*s, or the axes of the spiritual hierarchy. However, if they express their feelings about these people and their master chauvinistically, it will be a betrayal to the cause of those great guides.

In our time as well, there may be certain volunteers who migrated to different parts of the world and made important achievements. Even if it is based on innocent and sincere thoughts, speaking too highly of those persons under different spiritual titles will be a betrayal against the Movement of Volunteers as a whole, because this means forming new opposition groups envious of their achievements. People who are unaware of your sincerity may exceed all bounds of fairness and respond by making unbecoming claims. You cannot hold others' tongues. However, you can willfully save your own tongue from exaggerated and chauvinistic statements. I find this issue extremely significant to the future of the Volunteers' Movement. For this reason, I believe in the importance of constant and overall counseling on this issue. In some respects, this can be seen as one of the requisites of serving on this path.

Seeing Oneself as "Nothing within Nothing"

Additionally, when you come together with the believers who serve on other lanes, it is very important to refer to the people whom they respect by expressing their virtues and appreciating them—if you show respect, you will be shown respect. But if you give in to narrow-mindedness and only speak of love for your own way, you dis-

---

[123] *Sunan at-Tirmidhi*, Birr, 15; *Sunan Abu Dawud*, Adab, 58; Ahmad ibn Hanbal, *Al-Musnad*, 2/185, 222, 4/358

tance others from yourself and raise negative reactions against the circle you are affiliated with. People who cherish deep love for their own path and seek to make others love it must consider whether this can best be accomplished by emphasizing only the people from their own circle or by appreciating others and feeling respect for them.

In conclusion, even though we walk on different lanes for the sake of upholding the truth, as fellow believers we resemble bearers of a lofty treasure, each of who holds it from one side. Making a remark such as, "This person bears the heaviest side of this treasure," is not at all sensible as it might evoke feelings of rivalry. If it really is the truth, God Almighty will already give him the greatest reward. But if we sing the praises of certain people from among us in this world, we will have both committed the sin of associating partners with God—by ascribing Divine works to certain individuals—and sabotage the spirit of concord and unity. In fact, people whose primary concern is upholding the belief in the Unity of God and fighting against the idea of associating partners with God should avoid the slightest trace of what they fight against. God Almighty is the One who brings everything to existence. In the Qur'an, He declares that it is He who created us and our actions (see as-Saffat 37:96). Therefore, the notion of "I did it! I made it!" is an anathema that Greek philosophy inflicted upon Muslims. We need to rid ourselves completely from all such things and subscribe to a thorough understanding of Divine Unity.

A person's conception of himself or herself vis-à-vis God Almighty is an important essential for attaining Divine Unity by attributing everything to the Almighty God. As Bediüzzaman states in the conclusion of "The Twenty-sixth Word," you must say: "O my ostentatious carnal soul! Do not be proud of your services to God's religion. As stated in a Prophetic Tradition,[124] God may strengthen this religion by means of a dissolute person. You are not pure, so regard yourself as that dissolute person."[125] With this example, he reveals how he sees himself as

---

[124] *Sahih al-Bukhari*, Jihad, 182; *Sahih Muslim*, Iman, 178
[125] Nursi, *The Words*, p. 492

nothing and teaches a lesson on how we should view ourselves. Likewise, he addresses his carnal soul in "The Eighteenth Word": "Do not
say: 'I am an object of Divine manifestations. One who receives and
reflects Divine beauty becomes beautiful.' That beauty has not assumed
a perpetual form in you, and so you may reflect it for only a short time."[126]
Given that such a great guide sees himself as nothing, what befalls
upon us is to see ourselves as "nothing in essence."[127]

---

[126] Ibid., p. 242
[127] Ibid., p. 235

The Luminous Spiritual
Bonds between Muslims

Q uestion: *As Bediüzzaman lists the drawbacks against Muslims' progress in his famous Damascus Sermon, he refers to "not knowing the spiritual bonds that attach believers to one another" as an important reason. Could you elucidate "the spiritual bonds between believers"?*

Answer: When Bediüzzaman gave the Damascus sermon, Muslims were going through the most disastrous period in our history. People turned out to be so inefficacious over the long years that they went rusty in the end; they were grimly atrophied in every way and Bediüzzaman sought the ways of revivifying them with all of their spiritual and material, or outward and inward, faculties. Instead of dispiriting people with mournful elegies, he strived to be a source of hope for lifeless willpowers at a time when people could not see any hope for the future and roared with statements such as: "Be hopeful; the highest and strongest voice in the changing world of the future will be the voice of universal truths."[128] I suppose expressing certain facts about hope as a new dawn breaks is not unwise, but it cannot be considered a great merit either. Real merit is being able to utter the words to invigorate people in a period without the slightest sign of dawn.

---

[128] Nursi, *Tarihçe-i Hayat* (İlk Hayatı), p. 126

Bonds of Brotherhood as Many as the Divine Names

Nearly a century ago, Bediüzzaman gave a sermon in the Umayyad Mosque of Damascus. There, he firstly diagnosed the "diseases" that impede progress of Muslims, and then he presented the prescriptions needed for reviving the Islamic world. One of the most important diseases he diagnosed was the ignorance of the luminous spiritual bonds that attach the faithful. Accordingly, the solution he proposed was revivifying the understanding of unity and concord through a spirit of consultation.[129] Actually, he briefly referred to this issue in *The Damascus Sermon* and expounded on it later in some letters[130] and in the treatises he wrote *On Sincerity* and *On Brotherhood*. For example, in the treatise "On Brotherhood," after stating that there are bonds of unity, agreement, and brotherhood between Muslims as many as the number of the Divine Names, he cited some of these shared bonds, such as having faith in God and the Prophet, the *qiblah* (direction of the Prayer), and the lands in which they live. By stating that the number of such bonds can be cited up to ten, a hundred, or a thousand, he drew attention to the significance of the issue.[131]

In one *hadith*, the most noble Messenger of God, peace and blessings be upon him, stated that faith has more than sixty or seventy branches.[132] It is possible to take this number as a round figure indicating a multitude. Every one of those branches is an unbreakable bond that attaches Muslims together. In the same way, each one of the truths stated by the Qur'an is a very powerful bond between Muslims.

On the other hand, when believers are taken as a community, it will be seen that they have so much in common. They are children of the same fate, same lands, same culture, and same moral upbringing. Within these common points, they underwent the same oppression,

[129] Ibid., pp. 86–93
[130] Apart from his book *The Letters*, Bediüzzaman's correspondence with his students was compiled into separate volumes named after the places Kastamonu, Emirdağ, and Barla, where he spent many years in persecution, exile and imprisonment.
[131] Nursi, *The Letters*, p. 283
[132] *Sahih al-Bukhari*, Iman, 3; *Sahih Muslim*, Iman, 57

suffering, and condemnation. Thus, Bediüzzaman underlined how great a wrongdoing it is to present attitude and behaviors to cause disunity, hypocrisy, grudge, and enmity among believers in spite of having so many common points that necessitate unity, concord, love, and brotherhood.[133]

Being Righteous Enough to Give up One's Personal Conception of "Right"

Maintaining these spiritual bonds between believers without any harm depends on every individual's being able to give up their personal conceptions, preferences, and judgments when needed; it depends on living in spite of oneself for the sake of finding common ground. If we put this from the perspective of Bediüzzaman again, if it is possible to agree on "good," there is no point in raising disagreement for the sake of "better."[134] In other words, if seeking the better option will raise disagreement among Muslims, they should stop there and suffice with what is good, without generating any means of contradiction. We know that receiving Divine guidance and assistance depends on having unity and concord. Accordingly, the apparent "good" agreed upon by Muslims is better than the best in actual reality. For this reason, avoiding to make trivial matters into factors of disagreement bear utmost importance in terms of keeping up the spirit of brotherhood. Individuals should be able to give up their own priorities by taking others' feelings into consideration and not let secondary matters result in disagreement.

For example, it is so important to observe the Prayer (salah) in compliance with its truth. As Imam Muhammed Lütfi Efendi of Alvar put it: "The Prayer is the main pillar and luminous light of the religion; the Prayer makes that ship carry on; the Prayer is the master of all the acts of worship..." The truth of Prayer is disregarding one's selfhood and feeling one's standing before the Divine presence, as if expe-

---

[133] Nursi, *The Letters*, p. 281
[134] Nursi, *The Words*, p. 737

riencing a journey of ascent to the Lord (*miraj*). In accordance with the scope of one's horizons of spiritual knowledge (*irfan*), one must clear his or her heart from all considerations other than God while making the intention to pray. They must become oblivious of everything else and then they must establish the Prayer in a state of rapture, as if they were witnessing different manifestations in a different dimension. Most of us are unlettered ones, however. Therefore, the Prayer of such ordinary people is usually formalist and superficial. But it should never be forgotten that if somebody observes the Prayer in compliance with its conditions and requirements, they are considered to have fulfilled their duty with respect to its outward dimension, even if they did in a formalist fashion. At this point, it is decidedly wrong to adopt an accusing language and manner if a certain person does not observe the Prayer with its true meaning and essence. What needs to be done is to accept what happens as it is, even if it is formalist and superficial, and not create disagreement for the sake of targeting the most ideal. Otherwise, one can commit different kinds of ugly acts unintentionally while seeking the better or the best. And this means causing the Divine favor, support, and help to cease.

The same considerations are true for *zakah* (the prescribed alms). For example, for the sake of encouraging people to giving for the sake of God, you may see a *zakah* of one fortieth proportion as "penny-pincher's alms" and tell people to give one twentieth, tenth, or fifth. Although this can be allowed in terms of encouraging more, if this attitude is to give way to disputes, you should suffice with the objective judgments of religion. In fact, when somebody from outside who wished to learn the religion came to the Messenger of God, he told the man to observe the Prayers and fasting, and give the prescribed alms. When the man said he would neither do less nor more, the Messenger of God stated that the man would be saved if he were telling the truth.[135] This case is an example of the point we made. In this respect, if you take subjective standards of seeking the best and see it as the threshold of

---

[135] *Sahih al-Bukhari*, Ilm, 6; *Sunan an-Nasa'i*, Siyam, 1

deliverance for all, you then distance other people with lower standards from you and deprive them certain good acts they possibly would have done. Perhaps, you might evoke a feeling of jealousy and envy towards yourself. You can compare other acts of worship and duties with what has been mentioned.

In conclusion, encouraging people to target high horizons is a different issue; narrowing down the matter only to a certain level is a completely different issue. If you really try to keep up within a certain horizon in terms of your heart and spirituality, then you should try calling others to it. But taking points of agreement as basis and knowing where to stop is more important. In this respect, we should always seek means of unity and agreement, and make every kind of sacrifice to maintain this spirit.

Problems Settled within the Individual and Reforming the Society

Question: *You stated that a person who has not been able to settle the problems within his or her own self is not able to solve the problems related to their environment and the society. Would you explain the relationship between reforming oneself (nafs) and reforming the society.*

Answer: With respect to its dictionary meaning, the word "*nafs*" refers to the essence of something or the thing itself. As a religious term, *nafs*, or the "carnal soul," refers to the essence and center of the potentially harmful feelings like grudge, hatred, lust, wrath, and the like, all of which are placed in human nature for certain wisdom; it is the title for the mechanism that is prone to whisperings and goading of Satan and which functions as a center for him. But it needs to be known that this mechanism has a potential for transformation and progress at the same time; it is the most important means for a person's ascending to spiritual realms. However, its being able to fulfill this desirable mission depends on its being disciplined and purified under the guidance and control of heavenly disciplines, like taming a wild horse before it becomes suitable to ride. Otherwise, if the *nafs*, or carnal soul, is left to its own devices, it will continuously run after its fanciful inclinations and desires, become a slave to animal desires and physical pleasures and go after the evil. In the end, it will cause a person to fall headfirst into eternal ruin.

The Child Who Did Not Give up Sucking Milk

In his famous eulogy, Imam Al-Busiri describes the situation of an undisciplined carnal soul as follows: "The carnal soul resembles a suckling infant. If you do not cease breastfeeding when the time comes, its appetite strengthens and it asks for more. If you can once exert your willpower to cease breastfeeding, then it just stops."[136]

If the carnal soul is made to cease its appetite for breastfeeding by using significant and convincing arguments at the right time, it will then be possible to keep its insatiable appetite under control. But—may God forbid—if the carnal self is left prone to bohemianism and gains strength under the influence of negative thoughts and feelings, it becomes disobedient, spiraling out of control; it begins to continually impose its own desires, fancies, and caprices on the individual, which results in screens between the truth and the individual; a kind of spiritual eclipse occurs. For this reason, a person captivated by the *nafs*, or carnal soul, and burdened heavily with its problems cannot set a good example for others and guide them to goodness. The duty that then befalls the person is to first solve his or her problems within. This can be realized by giving the willpower its due and calling a halt to the endless desires and wishes of the carnal self, making it suffice with the delights within the lawful sphere and not allowing it to step toward transgression. Thus, it will have been saved from the state of "*ammara*"—a soul which continually commands to commit evil, and rise to the level of "*lawwama*"—one that continuously makes self-criticism and questions whether the behaviors are right. Furthermore, it can even ascend to the horizons of "*mutmainna*"—the soul with a clear and satisfied conscience that is content with respect to its relationship with its Creator. In addition, just as people seek refuge in God against so many harmful things and factors, they must, night

136 Altuntaş, 2009, p. 17

and day, seek refuge in Him against their own selfhood and evil-commanding soul, which serve as a center for Satan in human nature. Otherwise, as the carnal soul will not give up generating problems, the individual will not be able to avoid being heavily laden with the many problems of the carnal soul.

The Greatest Striving on the Way of God

While returning from a military campaign, the Messenger of God warned his Companions that they were returning from the lesser jihad, or striving on the way of God, to the greatest one.[137] His use of the term "greatest" is noteworthy, for it indicates the significance of the issue. Furthermore, this intimidating statement was made on the way back from an absolutely critical, great battle for Muslims, and thus it gives us a perspective of comparison between struggling against the carnal soul and engaging in hand-to-hand combat with the enemy. In addition, it is very meaningful that it was uttered at a time when people felt the delight of victory. Sometimes, a very important remark can be made without taking people's mood into consideration (and thus being unable to raise their awareness for that remark). Therefore, it does not have an impact on hearts at the desired level. When seen from this perspective, the timing of this blessed saying is very important in terms of saving Muslims from the dizziness of victory. With this remark, God's Messenger, upon whom be peace and blessings, aimed to keep clear of the possible negative thoughts that may emerge among the victorious military of the Companions while returning back to Medina as the conquering army.

Indeed, we always hold a good opinion of the Companions of the Prophet, in compliance with the meaning of the Qur'anic prayer: *"O Our Lord! Forgive us and our brothers (and sisters) in Religion who have preceded us in faith, and let not our hearts entertain any ill-feeling against any of the believers. O Our Lord! You are All-Forgiving, All-Compassionate (especially towards Your believing servants)"* (al-Hashr 59:10). On

---

[137] Al-*Bayhaqi, Zuhd,* 1/165; Khatib al-Baghdadi, *Tarikh Baghdad,* 13/523

the other hand, as the Pride of Humanity was responsible for their spiritual purification and training, he may have taken their souls into consideration, and he may have intended with his warnings to prevent certain negative feelings from the beginning, even before they emerge. Nevertheless, on the way to Hunayn, it may have occurred to some that their crowded army was an invincible one. Afterwards, they experienced a temporary defeat, but by the extraordinary efforts of the Pride of Humanity, peace and blessings be upon him, the temporary defeat was transformed into a victory again. This example is also closely related to our subject. People may go through much hardship while striving on the way of God, sometimes at the expense of serious losses. And as a consequence, God Almighty might grant them material or spiritual victories. Right at such a moment of victory, it is very important to keep under control certain negative feelings (of arrogance) that may arise in a person. In his treatise on sincerity, Bediüzzaman raises very important arguments against such tendencies of the carnal soul: "O my ostentatious carnal soul! Do not be proud of your services to God's religion. As stated in a Prophetic Tradition, God may strengthen this religion by means of a dissolute person. You are not pure, so regard yourself as that dissolute person."[138] Let alone ordinary people, even saintly figures may not keep up their humbleness in the face of such achievements and triumphs.

Indeed, somebody who does not turn towards his or her own carnal soul for the sake of its taming and gaining of moral virtues loses so much in terms of happiness in both this world and the next. What makes people truly human is not their body but their carnal soul, or their very selves. The noble Prophet once said, "God does not look at your bodies and your physical appearances, but He looks at your hearts and deeds (that stem from the heart)."[139] If one truly possesses a feeling of reverence and respect in his or her heart, this will be reflected in all of that person's attitude and behaviors. Another time,

---

[138] Nursi, *The Words*, p. 492

[139] *Sahih Muslim*, Birr, 34; *Sunan ibn Majah*, Zuhd, 9

the Prophet referred to a certain heedless man and stated that if his heart were in awe of God, so would be his body parts.[140] For this reason, it is very important for a person to turn first toward his or her own human essence, engage in a struggle with the carnal self, and settle the problems within. It is for this significance of the issue that the Messenger of God referred to it as the "greatest struggle."

Blessings That Become a Curse

As the carnal soul can tempt someone into committing sins, sometimes it can cause a person to fall by the way of blessings showering upon that person. As an example, the Qur'an relates the story of Qarun: *"Qarun (Korah) was one of Moses' people, but he betrayed and oppressed them"* (al-Qasas 28:78). He was led astray by the wealth and means God Almighty had granted him, because he had not believed in God in the way that he should have, and failed to settle the problem with his carnal soul. Even though he seemed to have belief, he failed to transform his belief into certainty in faith, never ascending to a horizon of heartfelt acceptance. That is, he did not transform mere information into knowledge of God with practice, nor gain certainty based on or arising from that knowledge, and he had nothing to do with attaining certainty based on being able to see the truth. Therefore, there came a time when he said: *"All this has been given to me only by virtue of a certain knowledge that I have"* (al-Qasas 28:76). Although Korah had spent time with Prophet Moses and lived among his people, he was tempted by worldly means and was among the losers.

Similarly, as-Samiri (the Samaritan), who was from the people of Prophet Moses, was a person who had certain merits of speech and craftsmanship. However, he also abused the gifts God had granted to him by making an image of golden calf to worship, thereby bringing about his own ruin. As stated in the Qur'an, *"(Moses) said: "Be gone, then! (The sentence) upon you is that in this present life, you say 'Touch*

---

[140] Abdurrazzak, *Al-Musannaf*, 2/266; Al-*Hakim at-Tirmidhi, Nawadir al-Usul*, 2/172

me not!' (to warn people against proximity to you)..." (Ta-Ha 20:97). As-Samiri lived in abject misery until the end of his life.

So it seems that when the problem is not settled within the individual, even God's blessings may become curses for people. In other words, things seeming like blessings can transform into retribution unawares: skills, power, opportunity to rule, appreciation of people, and gaining status can all be considered in this respect. When a person gains such means without taming his nafs, he will stray from the path of the Messenger of God to that of the pharaohs without even being aware of it.

I would like to elucidate the issue further with a narration from the time of Prophet Moses, peace be upon him. Actually, certain parables may be questionable whether they really took place or not, but what really matters with parables is the meaning that they convey and the lesson we learn from it. Accordingly, on the way to Mount Sinai Moses sees that somebody has buried himself in sand because he had no clothes to wear. This man asks Moses to pray to God so that he has worldly goods. As Moses petitions God Almighty about it, he learns that the man's present state is better for him. After that, Moses conveys this message to the man, but the man still insists on his wish. Finally, God Almighty commands Moses to help that man. Moses provides him some support and after a while the man has enough money to buy a sheep. In time the man owns flocks of sheep through geometrical increase. One day, when Prophet Moses is traveling to Mount Sinai again, he sees a crowd of people. He decides to get closer to see what is happening. He is told: "There used to be a very poor man. In time, God granted him abundant means. But richness did him no good. He started to drink. One day he got drunk, engaged in a fight, and killed someone. Now the man is going to be executed in retaliation."

In conclusion, as it is seen in history and many examples in our time, a person who does not settle his or her problems within can often make material and spiritual bestowals into means of their own ruin. In fact, if a blessing makes one forget God Almighty and causes that person to become a heedless one, then that seeming blessing is a "curse in disguise." Even if what distances a person from God is a great victory, it should be known that it is a calamity sent by God—it makes one suffer the greatest loss, where it is fairly possible to win (i.e. one could have been among the righteous if he had truly tamed his carnal self). So the way to protect oneself from all of these dangers is never giving up the struggle against the nafs, or the carnal soul, and being constantly alert against its tricks and traps.

Respect for the Sacred

Question: *What is the right stance and attitude that become believers in the face of insults and disrespect against religion and sacred values?*

Answer: When insults and disrespect are directed toward a certain individual, it is a very important virtue in Islam to show patience without reacting, take such "stones" into his or her atmosphere of tolerance and let them disappear, like meteors hurled into the atmosphere of the earth. However, there are such rights as the rights of God, the Prophet, and the Qur'an that, since they are not personal issues to be shown personal tolerance, individual believers are not authorized to forgive insult and disrespect toward these. True believers cannot overlook them, show forbearance, or remain unresponsive. However, as they do in everything else, they must always act in a way that becomes a believer. Their actions should reflect a believer's character; they should show their reaction in a civilized fashion, take their style as their honor, and never consent to lower this down.

Those Who Expect Respect Need to Be Respectful First

Unfortunately, we witness very different forms of extreme behaviors in our time. Every day so many events triggered by grudge, hatred, and animosity are taking place. There are various unbecoming remarks and behaviors coming from different sides. Sometimes, an unfortunate event occurs somewhere; even before the doers are identified, somebody remarks—with a horrible grudge and hatred—that it is necessary to do away with all Muslims. Then another one makes a different insult. At another place you see people trying to provoke others by hanging posters. In all this confusion, one point is being missed: if somebody makes an insult against the Prophets, angels, God Almighty and His Divine Names, he also is insulting all of the people who cherish these values. We can even say that an insult related to certain issues, such as resurrection after death and the otherworldly bliss, disturbs not only Muslims but also followers of other religions as well, because with respect to their essence, such matters of belief are also accepted by people who follow other faiths. For this reason, when you add the followers of other faiths with a belief in the Hereafter to the nearly 1.5 billion Muslims, the total number will amount to 4 or 5 billion people; you can picture the actual scale of the insolence. Therefore, such a person should expect the same scale of a responsive insult toward himself or herself. If someone does not mind stabbing a dagger into the sacred values of 4 or 5 billion people, he or she should not be disturbed by the needle that stings in return. No matter who you are, whenever you insult another person, you trigger a relevant response, whereas showing respect toward that person will elicit respect toward you.

Nevertheless, it is definitely not acceptable for a person to comment on a field in which he or she has no knowledge. For example, if a man who never studied philosophy severely criticizes a certain school of philosophy, he will both expose himself to ridicule and commit disrespect toward those scholarly methods. In the same way, if a man who has nothing to do with music starts making remarks about musical keys like an authority, he becomes an object of ridicule. The same is true for journalism and other fields of expertise. Still, so many people can become experts in such fields after a certain deal of effort and relevant study.

When you view the situation today, however, some people who have no serious knowledge about Islam—a faith that has realized significant transformations and breakthroughs in world history and, at

the same time, conduced to a dizzying renaissance that had continued for about five centuries in a vast territory—are making insulting
remarks about the faith and its followers, and then call it, "freedom
of thought and expression." We are living at a time when there are
fields of expertise. When someone makes offhanded remarks about a
subject without having any expertise whatsoever, it is sheer disrespect toward that field, to oneself, to sound reason, commonsense,
and conscientiousness. If someone who commits such disrespect
receives certain responses from some inflamed people, they should
not complain about it, since they personally presented improper behavior at the beginning. As the scale of the insult covers as many as 4 or
5 billions of people, it is always possible that some people in such a
large population will act upon their emotions.

If Your Home Is Made of Crystal...

The devoted believers, on the other hand, are always supposed to be
very sensitive about their words, attitudes, and behaviors; they need
to consider how the words they utter will be responded to and carefully refrain from sudden outbursts of emotion. It should never be
forgotten that words uttered in an angry mood are always prone to
abuse. And others' feelings need to be taken into consideration before
speaking. If your home is made of crystal, you should not hurl anything harmful toward others people's houses. Otherwise, you indirectly cause damage to your own building. This fact is pointed out in
the Qur'an as follows: *"And do not (O believers) revile the things or
beings that they have, apart from God, deified and invoke, lest (if you
do so) they attempt to revile God out of spite and in ignorance"* (al-
An'am 6:108). If you begin to insult others' deities, they will do the
same for what is sacred to you. Indeed, there is no command or rec-
ommendation in Islamic sources to insult the idols and deities others
worship. Believers always voice the truth and proclaim the Oneness
and Unity of God: this is a different issue. But believers have no responsibility to revile things that bear no value in their sight. In this respect,

I wish we could always speak, write, and act in accordance with the criteria of the Qur'an and Sunnah, because certain attitudes and behaviors that have their root in emotional reactions may cause grave effects with respect to our values. As it will be remembered, the Holy Qur'an was insulted recently. Right after that churches were attacked and buildings were destroyed in another place. Certainly, it is an outrageous behavior to insult the Qur'an. But destroying buildings and places of worship in reaction to such insolence is another type of extremism. Therefore, before resorting to offensive attitudes and behaviors, individuals—whoever they are—need to consider well what the likely results will be, and speak and act accordingly. Those who are subjected to insults should keep their reaction within acceptable limits; they should prefer correcting ugliness through scholarly and legal means, never sacrificing their refined character and adopting mistaken manners. The response toward such an attack should be a civilized one, later regrets will be of no use.

How I wish an international agreement on respecting the sacred could be maintained! I tried to make my voice heard to certain authorities, but I suppose that I failed to express myself properly. Freedom of thought and expression in our time is an issue that has much emphasis placed on it. Unfortunately, as insulting faith, religion, and sacred values are seen as a form of freedom of expression and thought in some circles, similar ugly remarks and comments concerning other fields are not acceptable; on the contrary, they are considered hate crimes. Actually, a real believer, who should be a representative of assurance and trust, must never speak against others for no reason; they should never intend to behave in an offensive and insulting way. However, declaring some acts free in certain fields and forbidding them in some other fields is an obvious double standard; it is a contradiction.

In short, there is serious need for making respect for the sacred a thought owned by the entire humanity and for evoking this feeling in everyone. It is high time international institutions, joined by all nations, settle this issue with clear-cut lines that do not allow further speculation. Certain disciplines to serve as decisive criteria must be decreed. How I wish the whole of humanity could agree on this issue! How I wish everyone knew his or her limits. Because, if the principle of respecting others' sacred values—an important component of peaceful coexistence—is not observed, conflicts arising from such incidents of disrespect will make their presence felt as much more horrible and greater problems in today's globalized and shrunken world.

A Builder of Spirituality: Muhammed Lütfi Efendi, the Imam of Alvar

Question: *Could you share your feelings about the Imam of Alvar (d. 1956), the saintly guide, with respect to his messages for society and his influence on you?*

Answer: Actually, describing that great person properly is beyond the abilities of a humble servant like me. For this reason, I should confess from the very beginning that I do not possess a capacity of discernment to have deep insight into his life, world of thought, or his horizons of heart and spirituality. In addition, when that great personality passed away, I was only 16 years old. Although I spent some time near that pure wellspring, a young man at that age obviously cannot benefit from that great figure with an immense horizon in the real sense of the word. For this reason, it needs to be known that the points I am going to tell will be limited by my narrow comprehension, lack of ability, and childish consideration.

A Lustrous and Fruitful Home

The family of the Imam of Alvar was like a blessed source of spirituality. His father Hüseyin Efendi and brother Vehbi Efendi were very great personalities. I did not see his father Hüseyin Kındığı Efendi, but even one particular event I previously narrated to you will suffice to give an idea about the virtues of that blessed person:

One day, the Imam of Alvar and his father Hüseyin Kındığı Efendi, who are from the lineage of the Prophet, traveled to the city of Bitlis in order to become disciples of Sheikh Kufrawi. As he probably discovered their potential immediately, Sheikh Kufrawi showed special care to them and gave them importance. Without any processes of spiritual journeying or Sufi retreats, the sheikh authorized both of them as spiritual guides, as the true worth of jewels is appreciated by masters of the field. So Sheikh Kufrawi was such a master who recognized the worthy jewels before him, and confirmed that they were eligible to guide people. In the face of this unexpected development, the disciples who had been near to the Sheikh until then expressed their protests at night and began to ask the two newcomers questions to see whether they were really eligible to guide others. In the meantime, the door burst open and the Sheikh came in; he addressed them as follows: "You disciples! Hüseyin and Muhammed Lütfi Efendis did not need me. What brought them here is their very perfection." If a person has nothing to do with spiritual maturity, what difference does it make, even if he owns a treasure equivalent of the Korah (a.k.a. Qarun)!

His brother Vehbi Efendi was also a sea of wisdom. He was predominantly a quiet person, but even his quietness had an influence that would cause different undulations in our souls. Both of my parents had deep respect and loyalty to them. Sometimes those great persons would come and stay in my grandfather's guesthouse. My grandfather had a deep respect for them as well. Vehbi Efendi was older than the Imam of Alvar and passed away when I was about five years old. I think the Imam wrote the lines meaning, "I drifted apart from beautiful ones, now I woe with this longing..." after his brother passed.

The Touching Melodies That Light up Fever in Souls

The Imam of Alvar was a person with a deep inner world, a man of God overflowing with love and enthusiasm. His state at circles of remembrance was a living example of this richness of heart. Both the Naqshbandi and Qadiri orders inspired him, and it was possible to witness both types of remembrance in the Mosque. There used to be a crowded circle in the mosque. In Sufi tradition, the head of the circle goes to the contributors to teach them to say the words of remembrance. Since that blessed person was very old in those days, he would not go through the circle but sit somewhere, like the prime one among prayer beads and behold those in the circle from there. Anyway, a short while later those in the circle would become enraptured and unable to realize their surroundings. There would be some people who choked with tears and some even fainted. Despite his serious health problems, the Imam of Alvar would sit with folded legs (as in the Prayer) on the sheikh's mat for two to three hours. Religious poems, eulogies in praise of the Prophet as well as litanies would be recited from his work, *Khulasatu'l-Haqaiq* (Summary of Truths), with a rhythm of a simple frame drum (*daire*). There was a *hafiz*—memorizer of the Qur'an—with a very beautiful voice in the village. He was the one who beat the frame drum. At that moment, the Imam of Alvar would be oriented to God Almighty with his entire being. Sometimes he would be entranced with the sublime atmosphere generated by the hymns, effect a similar mood in those around him, and would kindle in hearts the fire of love for the Divine. When a few people lost themselves in ecstasy, or someone became enthusiastic with tearful eyes, this would pass to the other participants and form an atmosphere of love and enthusiasm in everyone. Such powerful atmospheres that even though I witnessed these in my childhood, I can say that I am still under their effect.

That blessed man was a devoted lover of the Prophet at the same time. When somebody who returned from Medina remarked near him, "I saw so many creatures with mange," he reacted right away: "Stop that! Do not talk like this even of the dogs of Medina. For the sake of the Prophet, I am ready to be sacrificed for the mange of Medina!" He would say such things from the bottom of his heart, with his entire being, to such a degree that he was virtually melted in the spirituality of the Prophet, and passing into a state of *fana fi'r Rasul* (becoming immersed in the love of the Prophet to the degree of forgetting one-self). This deep love for the Prophet is reflected in his following poem:

> O the Sacred Witness, O the Sun embellishing the universe
> Your clothes are melodious, your eyebrows are lovely
> A strand of your hair is dearer than the entire world
> Your hair disseminates a pure fragrance to both worlds

Such eulogies in praise of the Prophet would often be recited in his presence; he and all the people there would burst into ecstasy. Sometimes he lamented in such a way and his voice rose to such a high pitch while reciting the following stanza that the place where he was would resonate with awe of God and everybody in the circle would shake:

> This heart is so fond of you, O beloved: why?
> Your beauty is shining like the bright day: why?
> Your eyebrow is like the "two bow-length's nearness to God"
> Your face brings to our minds the chapter of Ar-Rahman
> (The All-Merciful): why?

He Appreciated Everybody Virtuous

He was a master of verbal expression. He voiced the inspirations of his soul in different metric styles. However, in addition to being an authority on verbal expression, he would never be disturbed by sayings and poems of other great figures recited in his presence; he would even encourage that. For example, I heard Ketencizade's following poem in praise of his master Sheikh Kufrawi being recited in the presence of the Imam of Alvar:

> My dear master, spiritual guide, shining light,
> My remembrance of God is the illumination in both worlds
> All of my disciples agree with the hopeful prayers
> Help us, O noble Spiritual Pole, the greatest Spiritual Helper,
> the king of all time
> Never neglect these servants, O our dearest Sultan.

Normally, a feeling of envy could easily arise, but the Imam of Alvar trampled such negative feelings under his feet. He would salute any truthful words no matter whom they belonged to. I memorized many poems, including the following ones he would frequently recite:

Does one who seeks the Beloved struggle for his own life?
And can another who seeks his own life be in quest of the Beloved?
We have entered the path of love; we are lovesick,
O my heart, are you ready for this? (By Seyyid Nigari)

I found he had left his home already
The beloved Prophet passed away, leaving his headquarters empty
The bottles of love were broken, and the drinks spilt
The cupbearers left the scene.

* * *

On which mountain can I find that doe?
In what desert should I look for the eyes of that gazelle?
Just like a gazelle that lost her fawn,
wandering indecisively from desert to desert. (By Zihni of Bayburt)

As well as,

Growing tired of my life, doesn't my beloved get tired of the torments?
Heavens burned from my sigh; doesn't the candle of my will burn?
My beloved gives the cure to every patient;
why not me; am I not a patient?
My soul burns at the night of separation; my crying
eyes shed tears of blood
My cries wake people; doesn't my bad fortune wake up, too?
To your rose-like cheek, bloody water falls from my eyes
My beloved, this is the season of roses; do the rivers not blur?
I was keeping my grief secret; they say "Make it known to the beloved"
If I say this, I don't know whether the unfaithful would believe or not
I was not interested in you, you made my mind perish
Wouldn't that careless person reprimanding me be
ashamed when he sees you?
Fuzuli is madly in love, and is always shameful in the eyes of folk
Ask what kind of love this is, isn't he sick of it? (By Fuzuli)

I can even say that he would see these words no different than the fruits of his own mind and appreciate all of them. I think this is an important criterion in terms of giving an idea about his horizons, world of thoughts and feelings, maturity, and greatness.

Salih Özcan, a student of Bediüzzaman, related a memory about the Imam of Alvar, which I find very meaningful in terms of reflecting his maturity and level of thankful contentment. Brother Salih came to Erzurum in early 1950s and visited the Imam of Alvar. He told the Imam about the famous scholar Bediüzzaman and his works on faith. Brother Salih told the imam that they were disciples of Bediüzzaman and were trying to guide youths of the time with the works of their guide. On hearing that the Imam of Alvar responded: "I wish my eyes could see, so that I could join you as well." Real virtue is being able to appreciate others' virtues and being respectful toward them.

The Words Ringing in My Ears

I also would like to relate a few unforgettable memories of my own about that person I deeply feel the honor to have met. Here is one of them:

I was about fourteen or fifteen years old. I had a good friend whom I truly liked. One day he said, "There were such centers of spiritual teaching in Istanbul that they take someone to the top level of spiritual journeying within six months and make them eligible to preach." My friend convinced me with these words. I packed my belongings without asking the teacher who was responsible for me and the great imam, and then left for the train station with that friend of mine. I would learn later that in the meantime another friend of ours, who was the grandson of Vehbi Efendi, warned my relatives about my intention to leave. When I extended my hand to the ticket booth to get my ticket, somebody suddenly caught me by the wrist. It was my father's cousin and he took me back right away. The next day, my teacher told me that the imam wished to see me. I went to his presence shaking with fear. I had never seen him so angry before. He said, "I swear to God, if you had left, you would be perished!" These words he uttered are still ringing in my ears. For years I wondered, "Was my attempt really that bad that I would be perished if I had left?" and could not understand why he had said so. But in time, I started to somewhat understand his reaction. Possibly, he worried that a teenager could easily melt in an immense sea like Istanbul. Besides, leaving his blessed atmosphere without permission could mean losing. In addition, if that guide envisioned a certain duty for you to carry out in the future, you could not be where you should be by leaving for another destination. Therefore, I better understand now the intensity of his reaction and say, "Fortunately he did so and protected me under his spiritual shelter." After making that warning, he made different complimentary remarks considering that I would be brokenhearted. I felt like an excited child whose pockets were filled with candies and decided to stay at that madrasa against all odds. Perfected guides' treatment of others is different. That great figure fathomed the character of people before him well and treated them accordingly.

Here is another memory: We had newly started studying (the reference book known commonly as) *Molla Jami* and I went to him with some of my friends. A group of 5 to 10 rich people of Erzurum was sitting with him. He told them: "Now I am going to ask questions to my student. If he answers correctly, you will give him (this much amount of) money." He asked from the parts I knew best, so I answered everything. Those rich men then gave me the amount that he had told them to give me. I think the total amount was two hundred liras. Considering the currency of those days, it was enough to send a man to pilgrimage to Mecca. He could not see how much I had due to the cataracts in his eyes. He asked how much money there was and I told him. Then he said, "This amount is too much for you. Let me give it to Demirci Osman Efendi so that he spends it for the needs of the students of the madrasa."

While we studied in Erzurum, we were really poor and we sometimes could not find basic foods to eat, like bread and cheese, for a few days. My father gave me modest pocket money from what he earned as an imam, but it was too little to support a student. Most days, we had no money to buy bread. On such a day when we were starving, we went to the Sufi lodge, three or four students together. The Imam's grandson Tayyib Efendi was also with us. There was a shed beside the Sufi lodge used for storing food. Through the spaces of the wooden wall, we saw watermelons inside. The Imam was praying inside. After a while, the door opened and he said, "Come in boys, let me slice a watermelon for you." As we witnessed in very different examples, he was an immense figure of deep spirituality, understanding of others' wishes and what passes through their minds, whose heart could sense beyond the physical reality.

In short, although I failed to fully benefit from him, I am so thankful to my Lord for the blessing of having known him.

I remember the day he passed away. My late father had come to Erzurum and we were resting in the house of my father's aunt. All of a sudden I heard some distant voice saying, "The Imam of Alvar passed away!" I immediately broke into a run toward the madrasa of the Kurşunlu Mosque. When I arrived there, I saw my friends crying. From there, I went to the Imam's house, which was in the neighborhood known as Mumcu. Sadık Efendi, who was the mufti of Erzurum, and the great scholar Sakıp Efendi had also come and personally washed his blessed body, not leaving this honor to anybody else. After the washing in a winter day, the body was taken to the village of Alvar and buried there. All the people attended the burial in spite of the severe winter cold. May God Almighty resurrect that great guide together with His Beloved Prophet and grant him eternal bliss in the highest Paradise of Firdaws, amin!

In Order Not to Feel Remorse
When It Is Too Late

Question: *It is stated in the Qur'an that wrongdoers will feel remorse on the Day of Judgment: "On that Day, the wrongdoer will bite at his hands, saying (with remorse), 'Oh, would that I had taken a way in the company of the Messenger. Oh, woe is me! Would that I had not taken so-and-so for a friend!'" (al-Furqan 25:27–28). What kind of mistakes is this remorse related to? What are the points to be careful about in this world, in order not to feel remorse in the next one?*

Answer: The verse begins by referring to "that day," a dreadful one, and then describes how a wrongdoer will bite at his hands in remorse on such a day of grimace and grief. "Biting at one's fingers" is an idiom in Arabic and it describes a state of remorse in deep feelings of woe, grief, and yearning.

Then the wrongdoer will express his deep regret for not having followed the way of the Prophet: *"Oh, would that I had taken a way in the company of the Messenger."* His regret, however, is not limited with that; he will further express his remorse by saying, *"Oh, woe is me! Would that I had not taken so-and-so for a friend!"* That is, "I wish I had not fallen in with such and such wrongdoers and unbelievers and sided with them. I wish I had not followed in the footsteps of evildoers and transgressors and thus taken the wrong way!" However, saying "I wish" in the next world will not help at all. On the contrary, it will double the remorse. In other words, as it will only mean wasting one's breath, it will only add to the suffering. Just as those words can be uttered in the Hereafter, they might be uttered when the dying person's soul comes up to the throat as he is about to leave this world for the intermediate life of the grave, the first step toward the eternal afterlife. No matter when they are uttered it is definite, however, that these words express deep remorse by somebody who blatantly wasted the great chances that they had.

The Greatest Kind of Regret

Even though there are many sins and wrongs that will burn people within and make them say "How I wish" with a deep sorrow, the foremost of them is unbelief, because the entire universe proclaims God—letter by letter, word by word, phrase by phrase... When somebody leaves aside all biases, gives a fair ear to creation, and tries to read this universe like a book of wisdom, they will discover that everything in the universe points to the Almighty Creator. Owing to this evident truth, the great scholar Imam Maturidi stated that even the peoples who did not have a Messenger from God to guide them are responsible for knowing Him.[141] Nevertheless, even if such people cannot know God Almighty in detail with His Attributes and Names within the framework of a Divine teaching, they can come to the conclusion that this splendid universe has a Creator. Umar ibn al-Khattab's uncle Zayd voiced this thought before the advent of Islam: "I know that there is a Creator, but I do not know what am I supposed to do. If only I knew what He wishes me to do, so that I could exert myself to carry it out."[142] In short, the greatest "I wish..." to make one seized with remorse is to give one's last breath as being devoid of faith.

---

[141] Al-Maturidi, *At-Tawhid*, p. 176
[142] Ibn Hisham, *As-Siratu'n-Nabawiyya*, 2/54; Az-Zahabi, *Tarikhu'l-Islam*, 1/91

Forsaking faith after having found guidance is another grave sin to make one grimly say "I wish..." in the next world. There is a thin veil between belief and unbelief and there is always the risk of finding oneself on the other side with the slightest move. For this reason, we believers ask from God for guidance to the Straight Path[143] forty times in total through the five Prayers we offer every day. And then by stating *"to the Path of those whom You have favored,"*[144] we wish to be on the path of the rightly guided ones. As stated in another verse (an-Nisa 4:69), those whom God has favored are the Prophets, truthful (*siddiq*) ones, martyrs, and righteous (*salih*) ones. This is the wish we repeat forty times a day. Right after that, we seek refuge in His greatness and mercy and ask for being saved from deviating to the path of *"those who have incurred (Your) wrath (punishment and condemnation), nor of those who are astray."*[145] It is nothing but a delusion to be confident for having found right guidance and to see oneself immune to a possible fall or deception by Satan. Nobody has a guarantee to keep on the righteous path until they give their last breath. People who feel confident at this issue put their own faith in danger. A man who does not worry about his end is a man to be worried about his end. For this reason, one must shake with the fear of straying to unbelief after having found guidance and be constantly vigilant about it. A believer should constantly implore God not to leave him or her alone with his or her carnal soul and seek refuge in Him against whisperings and goading of devils. Faith is an invaluable treasure that makes one eligible for Paradise, gains the good pleasure of God, and lets one witness Divine Beauty. There are jinn and human devils lying in wait to steal it. What befalls believers is to treasure their faith, protect it against attacks, and being constantly alert in this respect.

---

[143] Al-Fatiha 1:6
[144] Al-Fatiha 1:7
[145] Ibid.

The Weaknesses That Can Make One Sink into the Ground

Being taken by human and Satanic intrigues (*Hücumat-ı Sitte*, or "The Six Assaults") Bediüzzaman mentions at the end of "The Twenty-ninth Letter" [146] might also make one stray from the Straight Path and say "How I wish..." grimly in the other world. Actually each one of the human weaknesses he explains is powerful enough for a believer's spiritual downfall. Namely, as love of status or fame is such a virus, fear is no less powerful. The same goes for greed, racism, egotism, laziness, and love of comfort. Given that each one has the potential to bring a believer down, having all of these does not make one just fall, but rather makes one sink deep into the ground. Even a person within the circle of faith is under the constant risk of being overtaken by them. For instance, love of fame can easily mar the essence of the good deeds a person does in the name of serving faith. Another person can present distinguished works and secretly wish to become famous, which eventually makes him sink deep into the ground. In addition, giving in to such negative feelings invites other types of negativities as well. For example, if love of fame seizes a person, you cannot know what further sins it will cause that person to commit. All of these are possible dangers within a circle of faith, and they will cause grim remorse in the next world. One who lays personal claim on the success granted by God, as a result of failing to adopt the principles of sincerity[147] as guidelines, will say, "I wish I had not fouled up all of those good deeds for the sake of worldly appreciation and applause; I wish I had not set sail to the void for the sake of nothing! I wish I had not be taken by deadly currents..." They will agonize in useless woes and laments of perpetual remorse. Grimly, their wail will be to no avail; on the contrary, it will only double the suffering of their misfortune.

---

[146] Nursi, *The Letters*, p. 389
[147] Nursi, *The Gleams*, pp. 226–231

Shields to Protect from Feelings of Remorse in Vain

For this reason, believers should act sensibly in this world. On the one hand, they should count being saved from unbelief as the greatest favor of God; on the other hand, they should shun from the alleys that may cost them their faith. As Bediüzzaman stressed, "Each sin has a path that leads to unbelief."[148] The Messenger of God stated that every sin leaves a dark spot on the heart, which can cover the entire heart in time[149] (unless removed through repentance). Every dark spot forming on the heart is an invitation to another one. In the Qur'an, God Almighty refers to the hearts contaminated and darkened with evil: "... *By no means! But what they themselves have earned has rusted upon their hearts (and prevents them from perceiving the truth)*" (al-Mutaffifin 83:14). If people do not remove sins darkening the heart through repentance and asking forgiveness, God Almighty will seal up their hearts: "*God has set a seal upon their hearts...*" (al-Baqarah 2:7) and "*... a seal has been set upon their hearts*" (at-Tawbah 9:87). These hearts become unable to receive anything from the pure message descended from heavens, and they end up continually saying "How I wish..." in the next world. In order not to fall into the grip of useless remorse, what needs to be done here is trying to carry out the responsibilities of servanthood to God without any flaws, in a balance of fear and hope. Realizing this depends on a heart in awe of God. The Messenger of God referred to a certain man and stated that if his heart had been in awe of God, so would have been his body parts.[150] Awe of God in a believer's heart will be reflected in the behaviors of that person; in time, even the body parts of that believer begin to shake with the awe of God—so much so that this shaking can be perceived by some in the iris of their eyes. On the one hand, a believer doubles up on feeling the greatness of God; on the other hand, if he or she trusts the immensity of His mercy and leads a life

---

[148] Nursi, *The Gleams*, 12

[149] *Sunan at-Tirmidhi*, Tafsir as-Surah (83), 1; *Sunan ibn Majah*, Zuhd, 29

[150] Abdurrazzak, *Al-Musannaf*, 2/266; *Al-Hakim at-Tirmidhi, Nawadir al-Usul*, 2/172

of such sensitivity and balance, this will be a means of deliverance from woes and regrets in the next world.

At the same time, people can prevent the negative factors to ruin their afterlife by attending circles of religious talks—or "*sohbet-i Canan*" (talk of the Beloved). As Süleyman Çelebi stated:

"Constantly say God's Name with every breath
It is with God's Name everything becomes complete."

Another Sufi poet (Yahya of Taşlıca) voices the same truth thus:

"I wish my love was shared by all people of the world
If only all of our words could be talk of the Beloved."

If we make mention of Him everywhere we go and make our gatherings blessed with His name, and make our time gain a depth uncontainable by dimensions, then we put a stop to so many negativities that might make us feel regret in the other world.

Saying "I Wish..." in the Sense
of Asking Forgiveness

Question: *Can there be useful examples of "I wish..." as opposed to useless ones? What should be our criteria?*

Answer: As there are useless kinds of "I wish..." to be uttered in the next world, there are positive kinds of "I wish..." that are acceptable, and even laudable, in Islam. Those uttered by our master Abu Bakr are of this type. As it is known, he once said, "I wish I had asked the Messenger of God about the meaning of the verse referring to one who dies leaving behind no lineal heirs, so that I would not leave the issue to the judgment of scholars." He voiced the same regret about the judgment concerning the share of a grandmother's inheritance, as it is not openly stated in the Qur'an. He also expressed similar regrets about some strategic decisions he had to make.[151] In my opinion, such phrases of "I wish..." are uttered as a consequence of deeply felt suffering and a feeling of self-criticism, which stem from comprehending religion correctly and rendering it the spirit of one's life. They took Abu Bakr the Truthful to a great spiritual level beyond our comprehension. Imagine that the Pride of Humanity confirmed Abu Bakr's worth by stating that if Abu Bakr's faith were to be weighed against

---

[151] At-Tabarani, *Al-Mu'jamu'l-Kabir*, 1/62, At-Tabari, *Tarikhu'l-Umam wa'l-Muluk*, 2/354; Az-Zahabi, *Tarikhu'l-Islam*, 3/118

the faith of all people, his faith would weigh heavier.[152] He was the greatest truthful one who realized through God's grace—within two years and ten months (of his caliphate)—what others could not achieve in one and a half centuries. He did not simply overpower different lands as tyrants did, but poured the inspirations of his soul into them. Every place he went or turned his eyes came to life with the teachings of the Prophet. Indeed, he was the one who prepared the ground for the great conquests and breakthroughs realized during the next caliph, Umar ibn al-Khattab. Therefore, his statements of "I wish..." added to the worth of that great figure, whose worth was already greater than the totality of all people.

In the same way, there are positive kinds of "I wish," for every believer to elevate their ranks. For example, "I wish I had made better use of my youthful days in terms of worship! I wish I could spare two hours for a hundred units of Prayer every night! I wish I could save myself from carnal desires! I wish I could thoroughly restrain my hands, feet, sight, and hearing even while carnal desires boiled over at youth. I wish I had not turned my gaze anywhere else and not beheld anything else except for what is oriented toward seeking the good pleasure of God..." Even though one did not fulfill certain things previously, such statements of remorse, which express a resolution to take positive action to make up for what one has missed so far, actually lead to a person's spiritual progress. If left to the other side, it will mean nothing but anguish and misery, whereas those we make here can be considered as *istighfar* (asking forgiveness). We say, "*Astaghfirullah*," at remembering such things; we then feel ashamed of saying it only once and say, "*Alfu-alfi Astaghfirullah*," (I ask forgiveness for a million times) and continuously seek refuge in God with a spirit of heartfelt penitence and remorse (*tawba-inaba-awba*).[153] So when believers knock the door of Divine mercy with all of these "*Astaghfirullahs*", God will hopefully not leave their petitions unanswered and will treat them with His immense mercy and grace.

---

[152] Al-*Bayhaqi*, *Shuab al-Iman*, 1/69; Ibn Asakir, *Tarikh Dimashq*, 30/127

[153] For a detailed explanation of these concepts of *Tawba*, *Inaba*, and *Awba*, see Fethullah Gülen, *The Emerald Hills of the Heart*, Vol. 1.

A Time to Listen to Our Souls:
The Three Months

Question: *What are your suggestions for feeling the elation of the three months, Rajab, Shaban, and Ramadan, within and making the most of their spiritual atmosphere?*

Answer: First, we need to state that the three months are the most important blessed segments of time when believers can attain greatest proximity to God, become eligible for His immense mercy, and journey through the horizons of the heart and spirit by abandoning sins. Every year believers need a process of heavenly rehabilitation to purify the carnal self, discipline the spirit, and purify the heart. These months are a very important means to realize such rehabilitation.

Obviously, a person's being able to rid oneself of carnal burdens, ascend to a certain horizon, and maintain a certain level of spirituality requires a serious process of reflection and contemplative dialogue. However, while doing this, one needs to keep the heart and spirit receptive to religion and spirituality. That is, as people try to grasp matters related to faith and the Qur'an with their mental powers and discussion, they should also try to benefit, sip-by-sip, from the showering of Divine blessings and light.

The One Who Cherishes the Divine Will Be Cherished

So many people have praised those special segments of time and have drawn attention to the various beauties of these blessed months in accordance with their viewpoint and horizons. Analyzing these invaluable works, word-by-word, through reading circles and internalizing their meaning are very important in terms of understanding and sensing the spiritual blessings these months can make one gain. In order to benefit properly from what is written about the three months, it is necessary to leave aside a causal manner of reading and delve into the depths of the issue. Otherwise, if such feeling and way of thinking are not developed, it will not be possible to thoroughly benefit from the sources about the three months.

In addition, for feeling the particular beauties of these three months and their delights that are reflected on human heart, it is necessary first to appreciate them as months of gaining spiritual favors and then seriously try to make the most of their nights and days in devotions, without wasting a second. For example, those who do not determinedly wake up in the night for *tahajjud* prayer and turn to God in devotion, sipping the blessings of the night, cannot profoundly feel the spiritual beauties told about these months, taste them, or feel their delight. If somebody does not seriously maintain a state of metaphysical vigilance and become immersed in devotions with a consciousness of servitude, they cannot sense or feel the meanings these months convey, even if the blessings keep pouring down in abundance. They might even evaluate others' statements about these segments of time according to their limited horizons and see those experiences as mere fantasy.

Benefiting from the abundant blessings of these days depends first on having belief in them and cherishing them. Attentiveness is reciprocal. If you are not attentive to the spirit and meaning found in these months, they will not open their doors to you, and the most enthusiastic statements about these months will remain faint in your sight. Even the touching expressions of Ibn Rajab al-Hanbali or statements of Imam Al-Ghazali that move hearts with enthusiasm do not make sense to you, as the impact of a statement does not only depend on its real worth but also on the listeners' mental and spiritual receptiveness to the issue, together with their viewpoint and intention.

In this respect, one must own the issue to the degree of being permeated by the hue of the sacred months; only then will they be able to hear and feel what those blessed months whisper into the human soul. Indeed, believers cannot rid themselves from superficiality unless they try to gain insight into these months' truths. Those who prefer acting lightheartedly, who do not make an effort for self-renewal at a season of such abundant blessings, and who fail to act seriously can hardly benefit from these months.

Gatherings Becoming for These Heavenly Segments of Time

Another aspect of the issue is related to the societal spirit and general acceptance of the society. Nevertheless, feeling the true depth and immensity of the blessed months is an attainment peculiar to those who have deepened with respect to the horizons of their heart and spirit. It is a reality that Muslims have begun to grow aware of the value of these months, are attending to mosques, and are becoming oriented to God Almighty. Taking this valuable opportunity, it is possible to help people learn certain truths and feel these in their souls by different events and activities. In the same way, it is possible to hold spiritual gatherings to appeal to the believers of this age during the blessed nights of Raghaib, Miraj, Bara'at, and Qadr, with the condition of being true to the spirit of religion. This will mean seizing the opportunity of making people closer to God and feeling the essence of religion within. It is also possible to make different gatherings more meaningful through reading circles or contemplative dialogues. Thus the expectations of believers will have been answered correctly.

I would like to draw attention to one more important thing that I have realized about these programs: all of such activities should be meant for helping people to become one more step closer to God with respect to their world of thoughts and feelings. If such events and activities do not take believers to their own identity and guide them toward finding themselves, then they are nothing but a waste of time. Instead of voicing Divine truths and evoking love for the Prophet, make God bless him and grant him abundant peace, making people enjoy themselves by appealing to their fancies and desires only serves to waste one's time, and even can lead to transgression. Every means that does not take one closer to God Almighty and His Messenger is a delusion. It is not the job of devoted souls to make people have fun.

In addition, it is necessary to be aware that people of our time have a general inclination towards entertainment in terms of their lifestyles. For this reason, their positive response might be deceptive. By looking at their pleased manner, you may think you did a good job. What really matters, however, is whether what you did was right according to the criteria of the Qur'an and Sunnah, rather than catching their interest. In this respect, even if there is no large-scale attendance to a program, one should always seek the right conduct. In other words, what really matters is whether the program stands for anything meaningful in terms of hearts and spiritual life.

At such fruitful periods, when the heavens are filled with blessed light and the earth is adorned with heavenly tables, we should always guide people toward deepening their heart and spiritual life; we should always pursue sublime goals in everything we do. So much so that we should convey a new meaning and spirit into the hearts of people at every time, and let them set sail toward the horizons, always asking for more spiritual journeying.

In order to realize this potential, either traditional hymns, prayers, and poems in praise of the Prophet or new ones can be recited. But no matter what happens, with every gathering and activity, we must always try to evoke a yearning for eternal bliss in people and help them awaken to the spirit of religion.

Asking Forgiveness-1

Question: *In this contemporary age when sins have spread like an epidemic, what does istighfar (asking forgiveness) promise for believers? Would you talk about particular segments of time that may be preferable for seeking God's forgiveness?*

Answer: Every child is born with the pure primordial nature, as stated by the Messenger of God.[154] The essential idea in man's responsibilities in this world is preserving this original nature until the time of death. All of the good acts that can lead one to eternal bliss are apt to protect this original nature, whereas all of the forbidden acts that might lead one to destruction are apt to corrupt it. While believers should build up sound sets and barriers against destructive sins on the one hand, they should constantly seek ways of preserving their original nature in untainted form. Every sin committed is a deformation with respect to human nature. Restoring one's original nature after such deformation is only possible through *istighfar*—asking the forgiveness of God Almighty. Sometimes a heart contaminated by sins may come to the point of inability to fulfill its function.[155] Thus, free-

---

154 *Sahih al-Bukhari*, Janaiz, 80, 93; Tafsir as-Surah (30), 1; Qadar, 3; *Sahih Muslim*, Qadar, 22–25

155 This does not refer to the marvelous blessing of the physical heart in the chest that pumps blood throughout human body, but to its spiritual counterpart.

dom from sins, which take one nearer to unbelief, and clearing up the stains sins leave on the heart are only possible through seeking God's forgiveness and protection from sins.[156]

Preventive Medicine

Indeed, believers must adopt a resolved stance from the very beginning and not step toward even the pettiest kind of sins. They need to strive for an auspicious atmosphere to keep them clean from sins and avoid dangerous grounds, just like one escapes from (the venomous bites of) snakes and scorpions. Such resolution and alertness can be achieved only by those with a believing heart and profound conscience that feel as if he or she is falling into Hell with every sin. If one does not feel disgusted at a sin, then it is possible to judge that that person's heart has already lost its vitality. A heart that does not feel upset and react against one's wrongdoings or a heart that does not cause the person to lose sleep in remorse resembles a dead body. For this reason, a true believer's heart reacts against sin. And the foremost reaction to be shown is *istighfar*—seeking God's forgiveness and protection from wrongdoings.

As a believer says "*Astaghfirullah*" (I seek the forgiveness of God), he or she actually says—with the immense meaning of the Arabic present tense (*mudhari*)—that I seek Your forgiveness all the time as I am now asking and will always ask forgiveness from You. In this way the repentant one renders the wish for forgiveness of a past sin as a petition that includes an entire future. In fact, the All-Forgiving God may accept a single repentance and demand for forgiveness as forgiving of all sins of that person. However, what befalls on us is not sufficing with a single petition but continuing to ask forgiveness for a lifetime and bearing the remorse within. One must think how shameful it is to have committed the sin despite being shown the right guidance, what an insolence it is to dismiss a promise like Paradise and indulge in sin, always feel due shame within, and thus constantly make

---

[156] *Sunan at-Tirmidhi*, Tafsir as-Surah (83), 1; *Sunan ibn Majah*, Zuhd, 29

istighfar, to the degree of asking forgiveness ten thousand times for a single sin. Sometimes one should be unsatisfied even with that much, and say "*alfu-alfi* (a million times) *Astaghfirullah*," trying to feel it within a million times over.

The Elixir That Cuts Out the Root of Inclination toward Evil

As *istighfar* restores the damaged human nature, it cuts out the root of inclination toward evil as well. A person who continuously purifies oneself by *istighfar* eliminates a ground of sins at the same time and no virus to invite others remains in the heart. In addition, God Almighty may curtail the feelings of inclination toward evil in a person who makes *istighfar* continually. In the Qur'an, God Almighty gives the glad tidings about the repentant ones who do good, righteous deeds that He will efface their sins and record righteous deeds in their place (al-Furqan 25:70). As He erases the record of deeds from sins, He can fill those gaps with beautiful things out of His infinite mercy. It is a different manifestation of the fact that His mercy surpasses His wrath.[157] Bediüzzaman interprets this verse with a different approach and states that "our infinite capacity for evil is changed into an infinite ability for good."[158] Accordingly, when a person shows loyalty to God by turning to Him repentantly, He may respond as, "Now that you have turned to Me, I will change your potential for evil into potential for goodness."

Important Time Segments for *Istighfar*

It is a tradition of the Prophet, upon whom be peace and blessings, to ask forgiveness three times right after performing the obligatory (*fard*) Prayers.[159] The following two points can explain the wisdom of asking God's forgiveness right after carrying out this act of worship—which

[157] *Sahih al-Bukhari*, Tawhid, 22; *Sahih Muslim*, Tawbah, 14–16
[158] Nursi, *The Words*, p. 337
[159] *Sahih Muslim*, Masajid, 135; *Sunan at-Tirmidhi*, Salah, 108

is most lovable to God—with the prostrations during which the worshipper is expected to ascend to the nearest proximity to his or her Lord: firstly, people's inability to maintain full concentration at the Prayer, failing to sense standing in the Divine presence but still roaming through their own world and running after their own pursuits. Such attitude constitutes a kind of disrespect toward God, especially during the Prayer, which is, indeed, the believer's ascent to the proximity of God. If one is immersed in personal considerations instead of seeking the meanings the Prophet felt during his Ascension, that person needs to make *istighfar* for such a light hearted attitude.

Secondly, as the Prayer signifies a lofty spiritual state in which requests from God are more likely to be accepted, supplications made right after the Prayers have a different value. Therefore, the Messenger of God recommended using this opportunity and asking forgiveness three times. In this respect, the five prescribed Prayers are important grounds and opportunities for seeking God's forgiveness and protection from sins.

A Qur'anic verse points out an important segment of time for making *istighfar*: "*They used to sleep but little by night (almost never missing the Tahajjud Prayer). And in the hour of early dawn (sahar), they would implore God's forgiveness*" (adh-Dhariyat 51:17–18). This verse expresses appreciation for the believers who get up during the final hours of the night and make *istighfar*, who open up to God imploringly, and who prostrate and nearly forget to rise back up from the prostration position; it announces this appreciation to all dwellers of heavens, spiritual beings, and to all believers. As certain praiseworthy qualities of believers are related by the Qur'an or the Prophet, others who do not yet have those desirable qualities are encouraged to acquire them. Therefore, it is extremely important to rise during the final hours of the night when others are sound asleep and offer servitude to God by two units of *Tahajjud* Prayer, at the least.

Also, there are times when the heart is softened, when one feels the weight of sins on the conscience and overflows with emotion... they must be taken as great opportunities for *istighfar*. We can call them times for breezes of proximity to God. Additionally, turning to God repentantly right after one commits a mistake or sin will mean taking the opportunity of "the first moment of realization that one has stepped into mistake and sin," for such moments are among the time periods when *istighfar* is most acceptable. Sins resemble whirlpools and they pull the individual into them like an addiction. It is difficult to rid oneself of sins after a person is immersed in them. If somebody in such a situation does not give the willpower its due and make resolved efforts to be freed from swamp of evils, that sinner may begin to wish for the non-existence of the Divine commandments that forbid those evils, and this wish might lead to one's ultimate spiritual downfall by losing faith completely. This has been the general pattern for those who fall. This is why it is so important to step back from sin immediately, fearing to come to a point of no return.

Let me conclude with one final point. Even though the times we mentioned above are important opportunities for *istighfar*, it is not necessary to allocate a special time for seeking God's forgiveness and protection from sins; indeed, limiting *istighfar* to those segments of time is wrong. One can and should ask forgiveness from God at any time during night and day, taking every moment of life as an opportunity for it. Whenever possible, one can draw to a corner, sit on bent knees, or prostrate oneself, and turn to God repentantly and ask forgiveness. One can open up to God through *istighfar* while walking somewhere, driving, or waiting for someone; one should make use of every available moment in this respect. Death can come any time, and meeting death with lips mumbling *istighfar* is a very important means in terms of walking to the realms beyond in a purified state.

Asking Forgiveness-2

Question: *What are your recommendations concerning the manners of istighfar, which is a means of purification for believers?*

Answer: While beginning to make *istighfar*, one should first remember the greatness of God Almighty and make due glorification. There are many statements of the noble Prophet, peace and blessings be upon him, related to this issue reported by the Companions. By these reports, we should begin to ask God's forgiveness as follows:

وَحْدَهُ اَللهُ أَكْبَرُ كَبِيرًا وَالْحَمْدُ لِلهِ كَثِيرًا فَسُبْحَانَ اللهِ بُكْرَةً وَأَصِيلًا

لَا إِلَهَ إِلَّا اللهُ وَهَزَمَ الْأَحْزَابَ وَحْدَهُ لَا شَرِيكَ لَهُ عَبْدَهُنَصَرَ

(God is great infinitely, praise be to God abundantly, and glory be to God night and day incessantly. There is no deity but God, He is One. He has supported His servant, and He alone defeated the enemy troops. He has no partners.)

After expressing the greatness of God with these words, invoking blessings on the Beloved Messenger of God is very important in terms of the acceptance of the *istighfar*. *Salawat*, or invoking peace and blessings on the Prophet, is an ever-accepted supplication. Words of *salawat* are a very important means for establishing a connection with the Pride of Humanity. Turning to God by having the Prophet, who ever-turned to his Lord with his prayers, as an intercessor will be a special means for being honored with proximity to God. Also, it is possible to ask forgiveness for all Muslims before beginning *istighfar*, as we do before the Prayer of Need (*Salatu'l-Hajah*). As it is included among the prayers of the saints known as *Abdal*,[160] it is possible to habitually recite the following litany in one's recitations of the dawn and dusk:

$$\text{اَللّٰهُمَّ اغْفِرْ لِأُمَّةِ مُحَمَّدٍ اَللّٰهُمَّ ارْحَمْ أُمَّةَ مُحَمَّدٍ}$$

(My God, forgive the followers of Muhammad! My God, have mercy on the followers of Muhammad!)

Thus you will have made a good wish for all Muslims. In addition, all of these serve as a prelude for making an *istighfar* to be accepted by God. You can even hold the humble consideration of seeing yourself as one the most blameworthy one among all Muslims, adding yourself to the prayer and say: "My God, forgive me and the followers of Muhammad! My God, have mercy on me and the followers of Muhammad!"

Seeking Forgiveness through the Most Beautiful Words

After such an initiation, a believer should turn to God with the petition of forgiveness of his or her sins with the following blessed words of the Qur'an in the form of prayer:

$$\text{لَا إِلٰهَ إِلَّا أَنْتَ سُبْحَانَكَ إِنِّي كُنْتُ مِنَ الظَّالِمِينَ}$$

("*There is no deity but You, All-Glorified are You [in that You are absolutely above having any defect]. Surely I have been one of the wrongdoers [who have wronged themselves].*") (al-Anbiya 21:87)

---

[160] The term *Abdal* (plural for *badal*) is usually translated as "Substitutes." The term is used to describe the "men of the Unseen" who have certain degrees of knowledge of God, who are supported by God, and who, with their refined hearts and purified souls, are open to certain Divine mysteries. These Substitutes are the pure, honest saints who help people with their affairs without being seen and who function as veils in the reflection of Divine Acts. When one of the Substitutes dies, he is replaced by another saintly person.

أَنِّي مَسَّنِيَ الضُّرُّ وَأَنْتَ أَرْحَمُ الرَّاحِمِينَ

("*Truly, affliction has visited me [so that I can no longer worship You as I must]; and You are the Most Merciful of the merciful.*") (al-Anbiya 21:83)

رَبِّ اغْفِرْ وَارْحَمْ وَأَنْتَ خَيْرُ الرَّاحِمِينَ

("*O my Lord, forgive me and have mercy on me [always treat me with Your forgiveness and mercy], for You are the Best of the merciful.*") (al-Mu'minun 23:118)

رَبِّ إِنِّي ظَلَمْتُ نَفْسِي فَاغْفِرْ لِي

("*My Lord! Indeed I have wronged myself, so forgive me.*") (al-Qasas 28:16)

رَبَّنَا اغْفِرْ لِي وَلِوَالِدَيَّ وَلِلْمُؤْمِنِينَ يَوْمَ يَقُومُ الْحِسَابُ

("*O our Lord! Forgive me, and my parents, and all the believers, on the Day on which the Reckoning will be established.*") (Ibrahim 14:41)

رَبَّنَا اغْفِرْ لَنَا ذُنُوبَنَا وَإِسْرَافَنَا فِي أَمْرِنَا وَثَبِّتْ أَقْدَامَنَا وَانْصُرْنَا عَلَى الْقَوْمِ الْكَافِرِينَ

("*Our Lord! Forgive us our sins and any wasteful act we may have done in our duty, and set our feet firm, and help us to victory over the disbelieving people.*") (Al Imran 3:147)

In addition to the prayers mentioned in the Qur'an, there are very beautiful words of prayer that can be recited for making *istighfar*. For example, the great Companion Abu Bakr asked the Messenger of God to teach him a supplication he could recite during the Daily Prayers. The noble Prophet taught him the following one:

اَللّٰهُمَّ إِنِّي ظَلَمْتُ نَفْسِي ظُلْمًا كَثِيرًا وَلَا يَغْفِرُ الذُّنُوبَ إِلَّا أَنْتَ

فَاغْفِرْ لِي مَغْفِرَةً مِنْ عِنْدِكَ وَارْحَمْنِي إِنَّكَ أَنْتَ الْغَفُورُ الرَّحِيمُ

(My God I surely did much wrongdoing to my own soul, and You are the only one to forgive sins. Grant me a special forgiveness from Your side, and have mercy on me. You surely are the Forgiving, the Merciful.)[161]

It is most appropriate to recite this prayer, which can be recited during the Daily Prayers at the prostration position and after the final sitting (*tahiyyat* right before giving the *salam* to both sides), as an important means to seek God's forgiveness.

Another prayer, famously known as *Sayyidu'l Istighfar*, (the master of *istighfar*s) is a very important one in this respect:

اَللّٰهُمَّ أَنْتَ رَبِّي لَا إِلٰهَ إِلَّا أَنْتَ خَلَقْتَنِي وَأَنَا عَبْدُكَ وَأَنَا عَلَى عَهْدِكَ وَوَعْدِكَ مَا

اسْتَطَعْتُ أَعُوذُ بِكَ مِنْ شَرِّ مَا صَنَعْتُ أَبُوءُ لَكَ بِنِعْمَتِكَ عَلَيَّ وَأَبُوءُ لَكَ بِذَنْبِي

فَاغْفِرْ لِي فَإِنَّهُ لَا يَغْفِرُ الذُّنُوبَ إِلَّا أَنْتَ

("O God, You are my Lord, there is no deity but You. You have created me, and I am Your servant. I try my best to keep my covenant with You. I seek refuge in You from the evil of what I have done. I acknowledge Your favors upon me and I acknowledge my sins. So, forgive me, for truly no one forgives sins except You.)"

The Messenger of God, peace and blessings be upon him, stated that whoever recites this prayer at daytime with true belief in its reward and excellence and passes away before the evening, that person will be one of the dwellers of Paradise. And whoever recites this prayer after nightfall with true belief in its reward and excellence and passes away before the morning, that person will also be one of the dwellers of Paradise.[162]

---

[161] *Sahih al-Bukhari*, Adhan,149; Tawhid, 9; Da'awat, 17; *Sahih Muslim*, Dhikr, 47, 48
[162] *Sahih al-Bukhari*, Da'awat, 2; *Sunan at-Tirmidhi*, Da'awat, 15

Keep Imploring until You Really Feel Purified!

It is also possible to prostrate oneself and keep reciting the following prayer until really feeling contentment and being purified:

$$ يَا حَيُّ يَا قَيُّومُ بِرَحْمَتِكَ أَسْتَغِيثُ أَصْلِحْ لِي شَأْنِي كُلَّهُ $$

$$ وَلَا تَكِلْنِي إِلَى نَفْسِي طَرْفَةَ عَيْنٍ $$

(O the Living, O the Self-Subsistent, for the sake of Your mercy I beg for help. Rectify for all my states and leave me not to myself even for the blinking of an eye!)

Some narrators of this prayer made the following addition, "... not even for shorter than that," which means, "Leave me not to myself even for a moment shorter than the blinking of an eye!"

Another prayer of the Prophet that he recited upon waking up can be expressed as the voice of the heart:

$$ سُبْحَانَكَ اللّٰهُمَّ أَسْتَغْفِرُكَ لِذَنْبِي وَأَسْأَلُكَ رَحْمَتَكَ، اللّٰهُمَّ زِدْنِي عِلْمًا وَلَا $$

$$ تُزِغْ قَلْبِي بَعْدَ إِذْ هَدَيْتَنِي وَهَبْ لِي مِنْ لَدُنْكَ رَحْمَةً إِنَّكَ أَنْتَ الْوَهَّابُ $$

(Glorified are You, O God! I seek Your forgiveness for my sins, and I ask You for Your mercy. O God! Increase my knowledge, and let not my heart stray after You have guided me, and grant me Your mercy, for truly You are the One Who bestows.)[163]

Additionally, everybody should take their own mistakes, faults, and sins into consideration and say *astaghfirullah* or *subhan Allah*, thousands of times every day. It is reported that the famous Companion Abu Hurayra said *subhan Allah* 12,000 times a day. When others expressed that it seemed too much, he replied that he was saying it in proportion with his sins.[164] I do not think that blessed Companion

---

[163] *Sunan Abu Dawud*, Adab, 99; An-Nasa'i, *As-Sunanu'l-Kubra*, 6/216; Al-Hakim, *Al-Mustadrak*, 1/724

[164] Ibn Abi Shayba, *Al-Musannaf*, 5/345; Al-Bayhaqi, *As-Sunanu'l-Kubra*, 8/79

had a sin. Abu Hurayra came from Daws[165] and joined the scholarly group of Ashab al-Suffa (People of the Bench), who stayed near the beloved Prophet for a long time. He reported the Prophet's sayings more than any other Companion and was a great source of reference after the Messenger of God himself; I would call him the Lion of Daws. However, with respect to his high level of piety Abu Hurayra saw it as a necessity. When we consider our own life, tainted with sins, even making *istighfar* 30,000 times a day is not too much.

It is also possible to recite the *istighfar*s of great spiritual guides as included in the compilation, *Imploring Hearts* (*Al-Qulub ad-Daria*). For example, Hasan al-Basri was a person of dizzying spiritual depth who severely criticized his soul. If possible, one can read his recitation that he distributed over the days of the week in the same way. After beginning his words by invoking peace and blessings on the Prophet, Hasan al-Basri mentions that he committed so many sins, and then he similarly ends with peace and blessings upon the Prophet.[166] Actually, the prevalent ethos of his time and his personal character would not allow for sins anyway; it was impossible for him to have such sins mentioned in the prayer, one who spent his days and nights worshipping and who was dedicated to striving on the righteous path. Still, it seems that he asked forgiveness even for things that passed his imagination. As we are not better than him in terms of our religious life, we are in no better position in terms of sins. Therefore, it will be too little even if we repeated his nightly recitations twice every night.

When one concludes the words of imploration overflowing from the heart to the tongue, it is better to invoke peace and blessings on the Prophet (*salawat*) again, given that a prayer between two acceptable prayers will be accepted as well;[167] thus, enveloping our petition for forgiveness between *salawat* will make it more likely to be accepted.

---

[165] Daws was one of the tribes of Arabia living in the south of Mecca.

[166] Gülen, *El-Kulûbu'd-Dâria*, pp. 138–156

[167] Al-Qurtubi, *Al-Jami' li Ahkami'l-Qur'an*, 14/235; Aliyyulqari, *Mirqatu'l-Mafatih*, 3/20

Let me mention one final point: every word uttered for the sake of seeking God's forgiveness must be pronounced consciously. As words spoken heedlessly show disrespect to God Almighty, they can also be taken as a lie. For this reason, every word uttered should be coming from the bottom of one's heart, and they should leave a trace when they pass. So much so that when one opens up to God with this consciousness and ask forgiveness, he or she must be uneasy with the shame of their sins, shiver with remorse, and the heart should virtually come to the verge of stopping.

Different Kinds of Tests
the Devoted Souls Go Through

Question: *There are so many different factors that put people to the test. What are the most dangerous of such factors, particularly for the devoted souls of today?*

Answer: Divine Justice puts people to various kinds of tests throughout their lives. As an acid test separates gold from stone and dust, God Almighty, Who already knows our real worth, makes people see it for themselves. By these tests, He makes us see what we can endure until when, what kind of an attitude we adopt before misfortunes, and whether we will be steadfast or complain, which implies covert criticism of Divine Destiny. Worldly tests batter people, apply different filters to them, and put them into melting pots. The saintly dervish Yunus Emre voiced this truth as follows:

> *This road is long,*
> *Many ranges along...*
> *Not even a gate,*
> *Deep waters ahead.*

Difficulty of the Test is Proportional with the Ideals Targeted

God Almighty states that He will test people in different ways and then He gives glad tidings for those who endure:

"We will certainly test you with something of fear and hunger and loss of wealth, and lives, and fruits (earnings); but give glad tidings to the persevering and patient" (al-Baqarah 2:155).

Accordingly, as worship increases a person's spiritual rank, tests and trials of this life—considered as negative form of worship—purify one from sins if patience is not given up; they take the individual to the highest levels. In addition to enduring consecutive tests patiently, what befalls a believer is taking those tests as opportunities to face oneself, ponder upon one's deeds by calling one's self to account, and evaluate one's own performance.

Given that difficulties increase in accordance with the greatness of the consequent reward, then intensity of tests increases proportionally with the value of the ideals sought. For example, becoming a martyr while serving humanity and ascending to a different level of life is an important attainment. However, having this honor depends on serving in the way of God and taking due pains; there must be utter self-sacrifice. It is for this reason that people devoted to a lofty ideal who try to fulfill its requirements must bear any trouble or misfortune that befalls them. They must show due patience and continue their life in spite of themselves.

You can remember the statements of Bediüzzaman concerning the issue: "In my life of more than eighty years, I did not enjoy anything as worldly pleasures; my life always passed in battlegrounds, prison houses, and different places of exile and suffering. There is no torment I haven't been subjected to. I was brought to court-martials and treated like a murderer. I was sent from one exile to another like a vagabond. I was banned from communicating with people for months in the prisons of my country. I was poisoned many times over. I underwent various kinds of insult. There were times when I had gladly preferred death to life. If my religion had not prevented me from suicide, this Said would have become dust long ago."[168] Because the tests he

---

[168] Nursi, *Tarihçe-i Hayat* (Tahlliler), p. 610

went through were so hard, God Almighty took him to the peak of human progress. You never know, maybe due to the troubles he went through enduringly, by the grace of God, he was rendered a guide for those who remain behind.

And There Are People Who Remain Halfway

The life of this world is a chain of tests from beginning to end, but these are not only comprised of troubles and misfortunes. Material and spiritual achievements and bestowals serve as a means of testing as well. People will pass such stages and stations in their lives that some places will make them dizzy; some positions and titles—God forbid—will make them slip, and some germs on the places they pass will infect their spiritual life. In short, individuals will pass through tests sometimes by ease and comfort, and sometimes by glory, fame, status, and applause. Imam Al-Ghazali gives the following example about the tests people face in this world: A man sets off determined to go to a beautiful Garden of Paradise, having heard much about the beauties of his destination. However, he sees an inviting place with babbling rivers, singing birds, and pleasant tree shades, all of which seems so inviting. The man forgets about his destination and decides to settle there. He builds a hut for himself and begins to live there.

Actually, this parable summarizes the life of this world in a striking and pithy fashion. You may picture different versions of the factors that make one forget the true destination. One may be held by many different factors along the way in addition to comfort. However, it is not possible to attain Paradise and good pleasure of God without leaving those places behind.

Greed for Fortune

One of the most important examples of the tests one faces in life is the desire for money and worldly possessions. It can even be said that it is the greatest weakness for most people. The Messenger of God refers to this fact in one of his sayings. Accordingly, if the son of Adam possesses one valley of gold, he would like to have two. And nothing fills his (greedy) mouth but soil. However, God accepts the repentance of the one who repents.[169] Thus, asking for more with an insatiable greed, trying to possess bigger companies and firms, and the desire for taking control of everything are the weaknesses of most. Indeed, such a competition for personal interests and benefits underlies so many fights and clashes in society.

When Muhyiddin ibn Arabi was under pressure in Damascus, he stamped his foot on the ground and said, "The deity you worship is under my feet." Some take these words as a denial of faith. However, he had the opinion that the love of money had seized the hearts of the people he addressed to the degree of worshipping it. As for their deity being under his feet, it turned out centuries later that he had indeed referred to a great treasure of gold buried under the very spot where he stood.

Unfortunately, so many people are virtually dying for it. They begin with, "Let me have a house," and continue with, "Let me have one for my son and one for my daughter" and "There should also be a villa for my grandchild..." You can see so many worldly ones living with these considerations. You may even meet people who set forth to serve humanity for the sake of God but then begin to run after such desires as if they worship money, to the extent that some of those people do not suffice with the payment that they receive, and with the intention of earning more, they abandon services of vital importance for people and faith. Thus, they stray from the path of righteousness to the path of worldliness.

Lusts of the Flesh

Lustful passions constitute one of the most difficult tests in our contemporary age. It has always been a difficult test all throughout history, but it has assumed a much more dangerous form today.

---

[169] *Sahih al-Bukhari*, Riqaq, 10; *Sahih Muslim*, Zakah, 116, 119

Rumi tells a story about weakness of lust in his *Mathnawi*. Satan speaks with God Almighty, or rather he uses an insolent language towards his Lord. The Qur'an and the sayings of God's Messenger relate insolent expressions Satan used demagogically. However, Rumi's parable is different: Satan complains to God that He made him disgraced and suffer deprivation. And then he asks some things he can use for deviating and tempting people. God Almighty grants him factors like wealth, status, and fame. But Satan does not feel happy with any of them. In the end, God gives him the chance to use men and women against one another; Satan feels greatly pleased and begins dancing out of joy.[170]

Even though this parable is not mentioned in essential sources of religion, what really matters here is the truth that it conveys. Particularly for certain character types, lust is the greatest factor of testing in this world. We can take it into consideration together with the following *hadith*: "The Hell is surrounded with lust, and Paradise is surrounded with difficulties and things unpleasant to the carnal soul."[171] There are long roads, many stopovers, forbidding waters, and other obstacles on the path to Paradise, while things pleasing to the carnal soul, such as indulging in food and drinking, lying lazily, and running after carnal desires, are on the way to Hell. A person who gives in to these will keep sinking gradually toward the lowliest levels unawares.

Love of Fame

Running after respect, status, authority, and expecting appreciation are among the tests most people lose. Bediüzzaman refers to "love of fame, post and position"[172] among the six routes of (Satan's) assault in his "Twenty-ninth Letter" and to fame as "poisonous honey"[173] in his *Al-Mathnawi Al-Nuri*. They are among the greatest weaknesses of some,

---

[170] Mevlâna, *Mesnevî*, 5/47

[171] *Sahih al-Bukhari*, Riqaq, 28; *Sahih Muslim*, Jannah, 1

[172] Nursi, *The Letters*, p. 399

[173] Nursi, *Al-Mathnawi al-Nuri*, p. 124

and it should never be forgotten that one who has become a fool for fame will do anything for this sake. May God save us from falling into these deadly pitfalls and make us pass to the next world with a visa of faith and consciousness of ihsan (perfect goodness; living carefully as if one were able to see God, or at least living with a consciousness of being seen by Him).

The Carnal Soul, Satan,
and Those Who Straddle the Fence

Q uestion: *The Qur'an relates the example of an unfor-*
tunate man whom God made well-informed of His signs
and Revelations, but the man cast them aside, and
Satan overtook him. He then became of those who went
astray, following his carnal desires and Satan (al-A'raf
7:175). What are the reasons that cause one to go astray
so gravely while trying to walk on the righteous path?

Answer: The foremost reason for such deviations is forgetting
the fact that this life is a testing ground and everything, at every
moment, is a component of that test. Those who go astray forget this
fact and fall for the deceptions of the carnal soul and Satan. Indeed,
man is always faced with both the internal mechanism of the carnal
soul and Satan who can never be known when, where and how he
will approach and play new tricks on him. These two archenemies
usually approach us with a friendly face and try to misguide us by
making right seem wrong and vice versa. One needs to always be
alert against these tricks. Otherwise, a momentary heedlessness can
take one to deceptions that are difficult or even impossible to overcome. In terms of their appeal to our carnal soul and physicality, you
can see the temptations of this world as tools of illusion used by
Satan, the relentless deceiver. At unexpected moments he makes cer-

tain things seem unpredictably very inviting. However, those things that are seemingly pleasant may have disastrous consequences as pointed out in the verse (which means): *"It may well be that you dislike a thing but it is good for you, and it may well be that you like a thing but it is bad for you. God knows, and you do not know"* (al-Baqarah 2:216). In other words, poisonous honey that you initially enjoy might soon trouble your stomach severely. In the same way, there are certain things people face that they seem bitter and bothersome outwardly, but by putting up with their trouble you can take wing to felicity. For example, Satan wants to make a river in front of your home appear to you as a deep and sinister torrent. However, when you evaluate the issue with sound reason, common sense, and a pure heart and thus gain insight into the issue, this helps to purify you. You see that the river that you feared does not even reach your ankle and furthermore has a purifying quality. As Satan tries to get you into negativities by his illusion, he tries to avert you from doing good by his positive-illusion on the other hand. As the Qur'an states, he is the one that deceives and embellishes;[174] he decks the ugly sins to be appealing.[175]

The Watcher

Satan, the archenemy of humanity, relentlessly watches for our weak moments, figuring out the best time to attack. He takes advantage of weaknesses such as lust, fear, comfort, love for position, or seeking benefit, and topples a person over when he finds the chance.

The Qur'an describes Satan's grudge against humanity: *"Now that You have allowed me to rebel and go astray, I will surely lie in wait for them on Your Straight Path (to lure them from it). Then I will come upon them from before them and from behind them, and from their right and from their left. And You will not find most of them thankful"* (al-A'raf 7:16–17). Other verses also describe this unappeasable enemy (trans-

---

[174] Muhammad 47:25
[175] Al-An'am 6:43; al-Anfal 8:48; an-Nahl 16:63, an-Naml 27:24; al-Ankabut 29:38

lated as): *"Then (I swear) by Your Glory, I will certainly cause them all to rebel and go astray"* (as-Sa'd 38:82). Taking into consideration these and other verses in the Qur'an, we can say that what lies behind all of people's misguidance, transgressions, rebellion against God, and heedless indulgences are the goadings and whisperings of Satan.

Who Suffices with What Is in Hand Is a Deceived One

Undoubtedly, what befalls us in the face of such a relentless enemy is not standing somewhere in the middle but adopting a resolved stance and verifying all the values one believes in with reasoning, judgment, and following the established principles in the Qur'an and Sunnah. That is, one needs to have sound faith and due reliance on God in order to be saved from Satan's evil: *"Surely he has no power over those who believe and put their trust in their Lord"* (an-Nahl 16:99). It is not possible to be saved from Satan and his traps for those who may content themselves only with the acculturation they received from the environment in which they grew up without deepening their faith through reflection and investigation or trying to internalize the values they believe in.

The Situation of a Person Straddling the Fence

As mentioned in the question, the Qur'an gives the example of a person who does not adopt a clear position with respect to faith and following Divine commands: *"Tell them (based on Our Revelation) the story of him whom We made well-informed of Our signs and Revelations, but he cast them off, and Satan overtook him, and he became of those (followers of Satan) who rebel (against God's way) and go astray"* (al-A'raf 7:175).

The Qur'an relates this story to teach us a lesson. That man witnessed manifest signs and had evident works of wonders—to guide him to truth, which would make him see and hear correctly, which would guide his heart to wisdom, but he ignored all this and left everything behind. So it seems this poor man, in spite of being granted certain blessings, failed to define a clear position and take a sound stance; he could not save himself straddling the fence. In other words, although he lived in a suitable environment for practicing faith, he failed to ingrain in himself the truths he had learned from the culture he was raised in. That poor man did not show any personal effort to verify what he inherited, did not ponder it, nor try to rebuild the world of his feelings, thoughts, and beliefs by giving his willpower its due; ultimately, he became a loser. According to the statements of some interpreters of the Qur'an, his knowing the *Ism al-Azam* (greatest Divine Name) and Divine secrets did not do him any good; he did not make them an integral part of his character or nature, and thus they did not belong to him. In this respect, if people do not restore the thoughts they inherit from their ancestry and have an unshakable faith by verifying and internalizing every piece of the information they possess, then Satan can cast doubts and hesitations into them, polluting their hearts and minds.

Talk of the Beloved All the Time

The verse continues by stating, "*If We had willed (to impede the way he chose by his free will), We could indeed have lifted him (towards the heaven of perfections enabled by faith) through those signs and Revelations, but (by his own free choice) he clung to the earth and followed his desires*" (al-A'raf 7:176). That is, he was taken by comfort, physicality, fame, imitation, praises, fancies, and desires, and thus forgot that the bestowals he enjoyed essentially belong to God. When he became oblivious of this fact, God left him to oblivion. The verse then states (translated as): "*So (in his being surrendered to greed), his likeness is that of a dog: if you move to drive it away, it pants with its tongue lolling out (still hoping to be fed more), or if you leave it, it pants with its tongue lolling out*" (al-A'raf 7:176). And a few verses later, the situation of such people is described as: "*They are like cattle (following only their instincts)—rather, even more astray*" (al-A'raf 7:179). Due to their carnal, animalistic desires, they fall down to a status lower than the lowliest creatures.

Humanity is indeed honored with the best pattern of creation, as candidates for exaltedness. Although human essence is potentially even superior to angels, their downfall does not take them to ground zero but to a deep pit much lower than that. That is, a man who has become a slave to his desires and fancies, he cannot even keep the level of an ordinary man but falls to a level below animals. While describing the situation of such a person—owing to the gravity of the matter—the style of the Word of God changes here significantly and the conduct of the person in question is likened to animal behavior. To conclude, if a person is not walking determinedly, not improving his abilities to comply with the needs of walking on this righteous path, and lacking the resolution for constant self-renewal, if he is not upholding the truth of the Prophetic statement, "Renew your faith by *La ilaha illa'llah*,"[176] it is always possible for him to be stopped by one of these obstacles. In order to overcome all of these obstacles and reach their target, individuals must concentrate their powers on retaining their faith; they should build insurmountable walls around it and continuously feed their heart and spirit with good, righteous deeds and attending religious talks.

---

[176] *Al-Hakim at-Tirmidhi, Nawadiru'l-Usul*, 2/204; Ahmad ibn Hanbal, *Al-Musnad*, 2/359; Al-Humaydi, *Al-Musnad*, 1/417

Essentials for Fruitful Criticism

Question: *What do we need to be careful about while making constructive criticism, which is an important means of seeking the better at everything, so that it will be effective and fruitful? What are the essential points to be observed both by those who make and receive criticism?*

Answer: Criticism means criticizing a statement or behavior, revealing its negative and positive sides, and making a comparison between what is and what should be; it is one of the important scholarly essentials that facilitates progress toward the ideal. In this respect, it has been employed since the early generations of Muslims. For example, in the methodology of *Hadith*, a given report would be evaluated with a critical approach in terms of its text and the reliability of its chain of narrators. Indeed, criticism took its place in the methodology of Islamic disciplines from the beginning, in order to unearth the truth at issues such as finding the right meaning to be derived from Divine commandments and interpreting them correctly. This scholarly discipline of criticism served as a sound filter against alien elements incompatible with Islam. As the discipline of *munazara* (comparing and discussing ideas) also developed, the new interpretations that emerged as a consequence of fruitful discussions were also put to criticism, tested with established criteria, and sparkles of truth were attained in the end.

Particularly at questioning the reliability of the chain of narrators in the field of *Hadith*, there was a serious accumulation of literature. Numerous volumes of work sought to help authenticate whether statements reported as *hadith* genuinely belonged to the Prophet, blessings and peace be upon him. But even while making judgment and evaluation at such an important issue, scholars showed the utmost sensitivity at refraining from excessive remarks. For example, Shu'ba ibn Hajjaj, one of the important *Hadith* scholars of the classic period who systemized the subject of criticism (*naqd*) for the first time, once used an interesting term while referring to the critical evaluation of narrators. Addressing a fellow scholar, he said, "Come, let us make some backbiting on the path of God,"[177] drawing attention to both the necessity of doing this vital task and that it must solely be done for the sake of God.

The method of criticism was successfully employed particularly during the first five centuries of the Islamic calendar in the fields of both religious and positive sciences, for the sake of reaching the most appropriate. Therefore, this scholarly method can be employed in our time as well, given that fairness, respect, and mindfulness are maintained. At this point, let's refer to the manners and method of criticism briefly.

Adopting a Fair Attitude and Soft Style

The issue criticized must be presented in a very sound style and utmost care must be shown at using a polite manner of speaking. That is, the criticism is not meant to evoke a negative response, but to be easily welcomed. When you present your alternative thoughts and plausible approaches for solving certain matters, you will be shown respect if you do it in agreeable politeness. For example, suppose that you are stating your opinion on a certain subject and the person you are addressing thinks the opposite. If you say, "This is what I knew about

177 Abu Nuaym, *Hilyatu'l-Awliya*, 7/152; Khatib al-Baghdadi, *Al-Kifaya fi Ilmi'r-Rivaya*, 45; Ibn Battal, *Sharh Sahih al-Bukhari*, 9/247

the matter, but I see that it has a different side as well," that person will likely come to you after a while and confess that your opinion had been more appropriate. And this time, you will respond by thanking that person for being so fair. In this respect, one should know how to—to some degree—dismiss one's ego, experience, and knowledge for the sake of upholding righteousness. In other words, if you expect the reasonable to be met reasonably, you should even evaluate others' not-that-reasonable thoughts within their own reasonability, adopt a welcoming attitude toward them, and form an atmosphere of sincerity where people can be welcoming toward truths.

Making General Statements without Targeting the Person

History has witnessed that, in whatever field, those who do not show respect to others' thoughts and who continuously dismiss others as worthless, ruin so many worthy things without even noticing it. For this reason, whatever is the nature of the element before us, we should adopt the principle of treating them all with a certain degree of respect. This is a very appropriate means of making people before us accept the truths that we present. Otherwise, no matter how great the projects that we offer, statements slammed on others' heads will not be welcomed. When criticism is not expressed politely, it will inevitably be received negatively, even if the matter that we criticize is an obvious mistake of someone that conflicts with the decisive and established teachings of religion. For example, you might witness that your friend has gazed at a forbidden sight. If you jerk into telling his embarrassing mistake to his face in a direct way and reproach him, he may respond by trying to justify some devilish considerations— God forbid! In particular, if the individual in front of you is not ready for a criticism of his attitudes and behaviors, then every criticism of yours will evoke reactionary behavior and disrespect against truths, or even make that person hostile against his own values. Even if such people understand what they hear is true, they will do their best to devise new arguments to get the better of the person before them, owing to the trauma of receiving that criticism like a mighty blow on their head; they will be continuously imagining the best way to answer the criticisms directed toward them, even when they retire to their bed at night.

Thus, matters need to be told indirectly, without taking individual persons as targets. Indeed, when the Messenger of God, peace and blessings be upon him, witnessed a person's wrong, he did not directly criticize that person. Instead, he gathered people together and spoke about that act in general, which allowed the doer to hear the lesson. On one occasion, for example, a man who had been commissioned to collect taxes said, "This amount is the tax I have collected and these were given to me as presents." Upon hearing this, the Prophet addressed his followers from the pulpit and made a general statement about when he commissions a person to carry out a certain commandment of God and that person states that a part of what he collected belongs to the state and the rest is a present to him. To show how mistaken this idea was, the Prophet asked whether those gifts would have been presented had he sat in his parents' home.[178] The issue of who makes the criticism is also very important. If something needs to be told to someone, one should not be too eager to do that personally, but rather leave the issue to another person whom the one to receive criticism loves very much. In such a situation, even criticism from a beloved friend will be taken as a compliment. If it seems likely that a criticism you need to make will receive a reactionary response, you should leave it to someone else because what really matters is not who voices the truth but whether the truth meets with a heartfelt acceptance.

At this point it is useful to relate a relevant parable of the two grandsons of the Prophet, blessings and peace be upon him. Although this parable about Hasan and Husayn does not take place in the reliable sources of Hadith, it conveys important lessons.

---

[178] *Sahih al-Bukhari*, Ayman, 3; *Sahih Muslim*, Imara, 26–29

Accordingly, the two boys came to make ablutions somewhere and they saw a man who splashed water all around but did not wash his limbs properly as required for a valid ablution. These two young talents of keen insight sought a way to show him the way without humiliating him. With this intention, they asked the man to tell them which one of them made ablutions correctly. They made ablutions exactly as they had learned from their blessed father Ali ibn Abi Talib, may God be pleased with him. When they were done, they asked which one of them did it better. With the ease of being free from humiliation, the man calmly replied that they both did it so well and that his own way was wrong.[179] Therefore, it is important to reiterate that the style we use at correcting wrongs bears great importance in terms of acceptance.

Educating Individuals to Accept Criticism

Additionally, making people able to accept criticism and evoking a righteous feeling of respect in them constitute a separate dimension of the issue. The Companions, who had attained an ideal level of righteousness, could comfortably warn one another about any wrong that they had committed without causing any negative reaction at all. For example, during a sermon, Umar ibn al-Khattab, may God be pleased with him, reminded people that it was necessary to keep bridal dues (*mahr*) within affordable limits and told them not to ask for too high amounts. What he suggested was a reasonable solution to prevent possible abuses. Even today, an understanding attitude of this issue will definitely fulfill an important function at solving a social problem. While Umar was drawing attention to this fact, an old woman spoke up and asked the caliph, "O Umar, is there a Qur'anic verse or *hadith* on this issue that you know and we do not? The Qur'an commands, '*But if you still decide to dispense with a wife and marry another, and you have given the former (even so much as amounts to) a treasure, do not take back anything thereof* (an-Nisa 4:20), thus not setting a limit to the amount of bridal dues." In spite of being the caliph governing a

---

[179] Mevlâna, *Fîhi mâ Fîh*, pp. 142–143

great state that challenged the two superpowers of the time, Umar said aloud to himself, "O Umar, you do not know your religion even as much as an old woman."[180] This degree of righteousness caused Umar to be referred as "al-waqqaf inda'l haqq" (one who halts when he meets the truth). That is, when he faces a righteous argument, he stops like a car that suddenly comes to a halt while moving downslope. It is necessary to effect this feeling in people. For this reason, we should make a deal with a certain friend and authorize him or her to comfortably criticize any wrong that arises in our personal attitudes and behaviors.

In conclusion, a person who intends to criticize, or rather to correct certain matters, must first understand the issue well and make a serious effort in terms of making the correct remark. Secondly, the other person's feelings must be taken into consideration and fathom whether that other person is ready to welcome what we are about to say. If a negative reaction seems likely, one should not think, "I definitely want to be the one who expresses this truth," but instead leave the criticism to another person whose remarks will be more influential. Considering the circumstances of our time, when arrogance has become so prevailing and people cannot tolerate even a little criticism, these principles have gained a greater importance. As for those who receive criticism, they should uphold righteousness above everything else and respond to criticisms with gratitude instead of reacting negatively. Bediüzzaman advises us: If someone warns us about a scorpion on our back (in other words, one who warns us about our wrongs), we should only express gratitude, which is an indication of maturity.[181]

---

[180] Al-Bayhaqi, As-Sunanu'l-Kubra, 7/233

[181] Nursi, Mektubat, pp. 66–67

Relation of Living on Pure Sustenance and Doing Good Deeds

Q uestion: *It is stated in a verse (which means): "O you Messengers! Partake of (God's) pure and wholesome bounties, and always act righteously. I have full knowledge of all that you do" (al-Mu'minun 23:51).*

Could you explain the relation between pure sustenance and righteous acts?

Answer: The Qur'an and Sunnah place great emphasis on the issue of forbidden and lawful. Islamic scholars who know this fact well summarize Islam as knowing the lawful and forbidden (as they set the fundamental framework of leading a good, righteous life on both the personal and social levels), and then living accordingly. In a pithier form, we can say, "Religion is in good, righteous acts and dealings." Umar ibn al-Khattab emphasized the importance of this matter as follows: "Do not take a person's prayers and fasting as basis; you should see whether a given person speaks truth, remains faithful about something entrusted to him, and observes what is lawful and forbidden while carrying out worldly affairs."[182] Surely, acts of worship such as the Prayers and fasting are very valuable in the sight of God and extremely meritorious. Nobody can dismiss their worth. However, a person's

182 Al-Bayhaqi, *As-Sunan al-Kubra*, 6/288

being careful about one's food, drink, and clothes, refraining from violating rights of individuals or the public, and leading a righteous
life—that is, showing utmost sensitivity concerning what is lawful
and forbidden—is a must for being truly Muslim, and it can be said
that fulfilling this in practice is more difficult than observing individual acts of worship. Thus, in order to be able to practice Islam thoroughly, one must always stick with the lawful, seek the lawful, stand
firm against the forbidden adamantly, and not let a single morsel of
unlawful food pass down one's throat. If we consider the behaviors and
attitude of great figures it will be seen that they are the spiritual guides
and role models for other believers in this respect as well. They lived
in such a sensitive way and presented such willpower that, God Almighty
protected them from eating something forbidden, even when they
were unaware of it. There are such people that when they extend
their hand not knowing that something is forbidden, they notice that
thing's being forbidden (*haram*) from the shaking of their hand or the
racing of their pulse and are taken aback. In the same way, when some
of them take a forbidden morsel of food to their mouth unknowingly,
they are unable to swallow it. And if they ever learn that such a thing
reached their stomach, they try to regurgitate it right away. The first
two caliphs are examples to this final case. This was what Abu Bakr did
on learning that the food he had eaten had been bought with the money
his servant had earned (in pre-Islamic days) by fortune telling,[183] and
what Umar did on learning that the milk he drank was from the cam-
els donated as *zakah*.[184] They both put their fingers in their mouth and
regurgitated everything, until nothing remained in their stomach. Thus,
such sensitivity against eating anything forbidden and an upright stance
are very important with respect to being truly Muslim.

The Greatest Means of Spiritual Progress

The issue of observing what is lawful or forbidden is also very important in terms of being a manifestation of obeying God's command-

---

[183] *Sahih al-Bukhari*, Manakibu'l-Ansar, 26; Al-Bayhaqi, *As-Sunanu'l-Kubra*, 6/97

[184] Malik ibn Anas, *Al-Muwatta* (Zakah), 31; Al-Bayhaqi, *As-Sunanu'l-Kubra*, 7/14

ments and respecting Him. In addition, every kind of effort one makes for the sake of opting for the lawful and refraining from the forbidden is counted as worship offered by that person. Resisting temptations or suffering misfortunes with patience is counted as a "negative" form of worship (which is not actually performed, but endured and thus leads to sincerity of worship); the same holds true with respect to making efforts in search of the lawful. It is also possible to relate this truth with the verse (which means): *"To Him ascends only the pure word (as the source of might and glory), and the good, righteous action (accompanying it) raises it"* (al-Fatir 35:10). Accordingly, it is revealed that blessed words of praise, glorification, proclamation of God's greatness, and invoking blessings on the Prophet, blessings and peace be upon him, will ascend to God Almighty by means of righteous action only. That is, be it the literal form of worship as prayers, almsgiving, and fasting, or be it "negative" form of worship as taking a stance against forbidden things and making due efforts, both forms of worship are like wings for blessed words to ascend to God. For this reason, the issue should not be seen as something simple, and much sensitivity must be shown with respect to the issue of the lawful and forbidden.

Concerning food, distinguishing pure from impure and not letting the impure pollute the pure, and showing utmost sensitivity in this respect will bring a person otherworldly rewards as if he or she offered worship. If a person reviews the ingredients of a certain medicine or of a product bought from supermarket to determine whether there is anything forbidden by religion, inquires whether the meat he or she buys is in compliance with Islamic rules, and is careful about having completely lawful earnings, these will be a means of spiritual progress for that person. On the other hand, not giving the willpower its due at this issue, and acting in a heedless and lighthearted manner will paralyze the individual's religious life, kill that person's spiritual faculties, and be that person's ruin. Consuming unlawful earnings is referred in the Qur'an while depicting the most corrupt state of a society: *"Listening out for lies and falsehood eagerly, and consuming unlawful earnings greedily"* (al-Maedah 5:42). Nourishment bought by unlawful earnings is mentioned in the verse as "*suht*;" it circulates in one's bloodstream, and it is mentioned in several *hadiths* that even that person's worship and prayers will not be accepted. For example, the Messenger of God pointed this out as follows: "Whoever eats a forbidden morsel, his Prayers will not be accepted for forty nights and his supplications will not be answered for forty mornings. What becomes for every (piece of) flesh developed by the forbidden (food) is Hellfire. And (it should be known that) even a single morsel develops flesh."[185]

The Bitter End of One with Forbidden Food in His Stomach

In another *hadith* recorded in *Sunan at-Tirmidhi*, Abu Hurayra narrated the negative effects of the unlawful as follows: "The Messenger of God described the situation of a prolonged traveler covered in dust and raised his hands to supplicate God, saying 'O Lord, O Lord!' Then the Prophet said, 'What he eats is forbidden; what he drinks is forbidden, and what he wears is forbidden. So how can his supplications be answered?'"[186] In another *hadith*, it is stated that when a pilgrim who came with lawful earning calls out "(*Labbayk*) At Your beck and call O Lord, You have called and we have come," a caller from Heavens will respond as, "Welcome, how glad you are. Your food is lawful; your mount is lawful, and your pilgrimage is accepted; it is not polluted by sin." Whereas, a pilgrim who came with unlawful earnings will be responded by a caller from Heavens as, "No beck and no call, you are not welcome. Your food is forbidden; your earnings are forbidden, and your pilgrimage is not accepted."[187] How can the pilgrimage and supplication of such a person immersed in forbidden things be accepted? How dare can he say, "My Lord! I came here in obedience to You. I am at your beck and call. I am hoping for Your mercy and

---

[185] Ali al-Muttaqi, *Kanz al-Ummal*, 4/8
[186] *Sahih Muslim*, Zakah, 65; *Sunan at-Tirmidhi*, Tafsir as-Surah (2), 37
[187] At-Tabarani, *Al-Mu'jamu'l-Awsat*, 5:251

forgiveness. I expect Your favor and graces!" Even if he does, will not his words be slammed on his face like shabby clothes? For this reason, living within the lawful sphere and eating lawful food are of great importance in terms of letting acts of worship ascend to God. The verse mentioned in the question points to the same fact. That is, a person's consumption of lawful sustenance has a significant effect on the acceptance of his or her worship for God.

There is another thing that needs to be pointed out here. In many verses of the Qur'an, God Almighty commands eating lawful food.[188] This depends on a struggle to seek the lawful from the very beginning. Actually, as every forbidden thing is an invitation to other forbidden things, every lawful thing similarly is an invitation to other lawful things; everything demands things of its own kind, so that they go together well, have the same character, and keep company. As this is true for people as well; our behaviors, works, and actions similarly run after what resembles them. In the same vein, it is pointed out in a verse, "*Corrupt women are for corrupt men, and corrupt men for corrupt women...*" (an-Nur 24:26).

It is also possible to describe this as follows: purity, goodness and wholesome things are invitations to other good things. Likewise dirty, foul, and wicked things always invite dirty things. Therefore, when one pursues the lawful and shows due effort, it will form a "virtuous circle" leading to further good, righteous deeds over time (as opposed to a vicious circle), and that person will live accordingly. For this reason, the distinction of lawful and forbidden must be abundantly clear from the beginning.

Forbidden Things Becoming Common Cannot Be an Excuse

Unfortunately, lawful and forbidden are intermingled in our time, and people have lost sensitivity in this respect. However, it should be

---

[188] Al-Baqarah 2:57, 60, 168, 172; al-An'am 6:118; al-A'raf 7:160; al-Anfal 8:69; an-Nahl 16:114; Ta-Ha 20:181; al-Hajj 22:28, 36; al-Mu'minun 23:51

stressed that a person's neglect of this issue will bring no benefit at all. As Bediüzzaman stated at the end of "The Fourteenth Word," "Do not say 'I am like everyone else.' Everyone befriends you only as far as the grave. The consolation of a common misfortune cannot help you on the other side."[189] Others' eating from the forbidden, looking at the forbidden, engaging in forbidden, and empty talk may look like a consolation while in this world, but they have no use beyond the grave. Having a common misfortune with some others does not alleviate one's misfortune in the next world. What befalls on a believer then is to determine where every morsel he or she eats come from, where it will go, and what troubles it might cause that person to face. It should not be forgotten that being heedless on this issue and leading a carefree life will cause serious troubles in the next world. On the Day of Judgment, people will be called to account even for (something as little as) one seventh of a grain of barley. Although we aphoristically say "one seventh of a grain of barley," the Qur'an refers to the same truth with a *dharrah* (smallest piece of matter): *"...whoever does an atom's weight of good will see it; and whoever does an atom's weight of evil will see it"* (az-Zilzal 99:7–8). Accordingly, as one who does an act of goodness as little as an atom's weight will see what it corresponds to, and one who commits this amount of evil will also see for sure what corresponds to it. Individuals will be called to account for everything: the words that came out of one's mouth, the food and drink that went into the stomach, words a person listened to, sights he or she looked at... If a person does not watch one's step carefully in this world, the reckoning in the Hereafter will be painstaking and—may God protect us—a grim one. Thus, those who have lost their sensitivity in this respect must reconsider what they eat, drink, earn, and spend, and face themselves anew.

Let me make a final point: there is no reason to become pessimistic by looking solely at certain people's lighthearted attitude. If particularly, those who seem on the fore show scrupulous attention to leading a vigilant life, their state will pervade their surroundings, and

---

[189] Nursi, *The Words*, p. 185

this consciousness and sensitivity will be embraced by the society in time, given that we as believers can rid ourselves from superficial practice of Islam and become intent upon distinguishing the lawful and forbidden, or the beautiful and ugly in everything, by considering seriously and pondering deeply.

Considerations of *Eid*

Question: *What are your recommendations to thoroughly feel the blessings of Eid, the holy days of rejoice, and benefit from them in compliance with religious commandments?*

Answer: In Islam, every form of worship or issue bears a special meaning of its own. Feeling this meaning profoundly depends first on a person's faith and subsequently on his efforts of renewal by making efficient use of willpower against the human tendency to take blessings for granted. Those who can constantly renew themselves with respect to their belief and thoughts can feel everything afresh. In other words, feeling something anew depends of keeping pure. As in the Divine command, *"If He so wills (for the fulfillment of His purpose in creation), He can put you away and bring another generation"* (Ibrahim 14:19), God Almighty puts emphasis on people who do not lose color, become weary, take blessings for granted as a result of familiarity, and who can always feel faith with all its depth freshly in their souls. It is for this reason that other issues, such as appreciating the value of Ramadan or *Eid* and trying to benefit from them efficiently, first of all depends on a sound faith and constantly renewing one's faith. It is very difficult for those who reduce Islam to a culture of repeating certain practices they learned from their ancestors to experience *Eid* in heartfelt purity.

Relation between Ramadan and *Eid*

Although it can be questionable according to the criteria of authentication, the Messenger of God is thought to have said, "Renew your faith by *'La ilaha illa'llah.'*"[190] This conveys that you must frequently revise your relationship with the Divine Essence together with your perspective of both the creative commands and the commandments of religion, and try to continue your life with pure faith by constantly coming to grips with yourself and making a new start in the Name of God. This is similar to the meaning of the *hadith*, "One whose two days are equal is in loss."[191] Accordingly, it is a very significant matter for a person to make progress in terms of his spiritual state every passing day and feeling beauties of faith better; those who pursue this goal are the ones to feel the essence of Ramadan and *Eid* in its true sense.

On the other hand, as *Eid al-Fitr* contains the essence of an entire month of Ramadan, feeling *Eid* in all its beauty depends on one's resonance with Ramadan; only those people can become truly resonant with *Eid*. The hearts that become tuned to Ramadan spend the month in devotion solely for their faith in God, fulfilling the acts of worship—the fast, *Tarawih* Prayers and others—with a consciousness of responsibility and obedience to Divine commandments. Still, they humbly say, "O God, we tried to worship in the month of Ramadan, but we are afraid of having wasted it. We wonder whether we have been able to observe fasting, which the beloved Prophet described as a shield[192] against hellfire, properly and spent the month behind that shield." On the one hand, they feel sad with the possibility of not having given the due of Ramadan; on the other hand, they see *Eid* as a chance of being forgiven by God, and being filled with feelings of hopeful expectation.

---

[190] Al-Hakim at-Tirmidhi, *Nawadiru'l-Usul*, 2/204. *La ilaha illa'llah*: There is no deity but God.

[191] Ad-Daylami, *Al-Musnad*, 3/611; As-Sahawi, *Al-Maqasidu'l-Hasana*, 631

[192] *Sunan an-Nasa'i*, Siyam, 43; Abdurrazzak, *Al-Musannaf*, 4/307

Eid: A Ground for Remembrance and Thankfulness

The days of *Eid* are a magical segment of time when heavenly blessings and bestowals come showering down on the servants of God. What needs to be done in the face of these Divine graces is to overflow with feelings of praise, gratitude, and zeal. Otherwise, it is not correct to take the days of *Eid* only as a time for being merry; each of them is a chance of forgiveness granted as a Divine favor. Then, the wise thing to do is to spend these blessed days in vigilance of the heart and feelings, with their otherworldly depth and metaphysical immensity. Bediüzzaman also underlines this point in "The Twenty-eighth Gleam": "... For this reason, the noble Prophet strongly encouraged giving thanks to God and remembering Him on religious festive days so that heedlessness should not prevail or lead to acts forbidden in religion.[193] It is hoped that through thanksgiving and God's remembrance, the bounty of joy and happiness on these days may be transformed into thankfulness, which in turn may cause that bounty to continue and increase. Giving thanks increases bounty, but heedlessness dispels it."[194]

Traditions of *Eid* within the Lawful Sphere

As a matter of fact, neither at the time of the noble Prophet nor in the following periods there were no activities—as it happens today— transgressing the lawful frame drawn by religious sources about *Eid*. That is, in the earlier period of Islam there were no traditions of trips, festivals, fireworks, and visiting all relatives and children expecting pocket money from elders. However, as Turks accepted Islam, they tested their own traditions according to the established criteria of religion, and they continued certain traditions that did not contradict those criteria. Therefore, certain traditions like kissing the hands of elders (as a sign of respect), visiting relatives, and welcoming people

---

[193] *Sahih Muslim*, Dhikr, 2–4; *Sunan at-Tirmidhi*, Zuhd, 63; *Sunan Abu Dawud*, Jihad, 14;
 Sahih Muslim, Munafiqin, 79–81; *Sunan Abu Dawud*, Adab, 110
[194] Nursi, *The Gleams*, p. 399

with a smile have continued up to our time since they did not go against the essential teachings of religion.

A Warm Atmosphere of Tolerance That Embraces Everyone

As the days of *Eid* are a blessed and bountiful segment of time where deeds are rewarded so generously, every moment of theirs needs to be efficiently spent in friendly love, brotherhood, sisterhood, and acts of goodness. For example, the welcoming atmosphere of *Eid* which embraces everyone can be taken as a chance for eliminating bitter feelings, organizing activities to bring people closer, visiting the elderly and win their hearts, making children happy with good words and gifts, and also for building bridges of dialogue with non-Muslims in a peaceful atmosphere and break the ice. Undoubtedly, respect toward faith, religion, and the truth the Messenger of God stands for has a separate place and significance. On the other hand, honored with the best pattern of creation, being human has dignity in its essence and deserves to be respected. Particularly, at such a time when brutality is rising tremendously, bombs are being used against humanity, and when man-made viruses are unleashed as biological weapons, the world is in desperate need of a general peace based on this understanding. In order to save humanity from being destroyed between collisions of lethal waves, certain breakwaters need to be built to stop them.

Such activities did not take place in the time of the beloved Prophet or thereafter, and them not being included in the religious sources of reference is not an obstacle to our taking these blessed days as important chances for organizing certain goodwill activities. Apart from the sacred quality of the blessed nights, there were no special activities or particular acts of worship for these nights. Together with that, it is commendable to spend them in devotion by praying, reading the Qur'an, touching beads, and supplicating to God. As those precious days resemble envelopes, they greatly add to the value of the deeds offered in them. The same goes for the location. You can pray to God anywhere; however, praying in Arafat purifies a person in such a way that he virtually becomes sinless as in the day he was born. If there are any stains that still remain, Muzdalifa takes them away. Similarly, circumambulating the Ka'ba is a means of a separate purification. As it is seen, this is realized by the envelope of "location" adding a transcendent value to deeds. In this respect, it is of great importance to turn to God Almighty in certain blessed locations or blessed segments of time in the Islamic calendar, and also to strive for friendly love, brotherhood, and humanity in order to attain God's good pleasure.

References

Abdurrazzaq, Abu Bakr Abdurrazzaq ibn Hammam (d. 211 AH), *Al-Musan-naf*, I-XI, [Ed. Habiburrahman al-A'dhami], Al-Maktabu'l-Islami, Beirut, 1983.

Abu Dawud, Suleyman ibn Ash'as as-Sijistani (b. 202–d. 275 AH), *As-Sunan*, I-V, Çağrı Yayınları, 2nd ed., İstanbul, 1992.

Abu Nuaym, Ahmad ibn Abdillah al-Isbahani (d. 430 AH), *Hilyatu'l-Awliya wa Tabaqatu'l-Asfiya*, I-X, Daru'l-Kitabi'l-Arabi, Beirut, 1985.

Ad-Daylami, Abu Shuja' Shirawayh ibn Shahradar (b. 445–d. 509 AH), *Al-Musnadu'l-Firdaws bi Ma'suri'l-Khitab*, I-V, [Ed. Muhammad as-Said Basyuni az-Zaghlul], Daru'l-Kutubi'l-Ilmiyya, Beirut, 1986.

Adh-Dhahabi, Shamsuddin Muhammad Ahmad (d. 748 AH), *Mizanu'l-I'tidal fi Nakdi'r-Rijal*, I-VIII, [Ed. Ali Muhammad Muawwaz, Adil Ahmad Abdul-mawjud.] Daru'l-Kutubi'l-Ilmiyya, Beirut, 1995.

_____, *Tarikhu'l-Islam*, [Ed. Umar Abdussalam], Daru'l-Kitabi'l-Arabi, Beirut, 1987.

Ahmad ibn Hanbal, Abu Abdillah Ahmad ibn Muhammad ash-Shaybani (b. 164–d. 241 AH), *Al-Musnad*, I-VI, Muassasatu Cordoba, Egypt, nd.

Al-Ajluni, Ismail ibn Muhammad (b. 1087– d. 1162 AH), *Kashfu'l-Khafa wa Muzilu'lilbas*, I-II, Muassasatu'r-Risala, Beirut, 1985.

Al-Baghawi, Abu Muhammad Muhyissunna Husayn ibn Mas'ud, (d. 516 AH/1122 CE), *Ma'alimu't-Tanzil*, I-IIX, Daru'l-Ma'rifa, Beirut,1987.

Al-Bayhaqi, Abu Bakr Ahmad ibnu'l-Husayn (b. 384–d. 458 AH), *As-Sunanu'l-Kubra*, I-X, [Ed. Muhammad Abdulqadir Ata], Maktabatu Dari'l-Baz, Mecca, 1994.

_____, *Shuabu'l-Iman*, I-IX, [Ed. Muhammad as-Said Basyuni az-Zaghlul], Daru'l-Kutubi'l-Ilmiyya, Beirut, 1990.

_____, *Az-Zuhdu'l-Kabir*, [Ed. Amir Ahmad Khaydar], Muassasatu'l-Kutubi's-Saqafiyya, Beirut, 1996.

Al-Bazzar, Abu Bakr Ahmad ibn Amr ibn Abdilkhaliq (b. 215–d. 292 AH), *Al-Musnad*, I-IX, [Ed. Mahfuzurrahman Zaynullah], Muassasatu Ulumi'l-Qur'an/Muassasatu'l-Ulumi wa'l-Hikam, Beirut-Medina, 1989.

Al-Buhari, Abu Abdillah, Muhammad ibn İsmail (d. 256 AH), *Sahih al-Bukhari*, I-VIII, Al-Maktabatu'l-Islamiyya, İstanbul, 1979.

Al-Ghazali, Abu Hamid Muhammad ibn Muhammad (b. 450–d. 505 AH), *Ihya Ulumi'd-Din*, I-IV, Daru'l-Ma'rifa, Beirut, nd.

Al-Hakim, Abu Abdillah Muhammad ibn Abdillah an-Naysaburi (d. 405 AH), *Al-Mustadrak ala's-Sahihayn*, I-IV, [Ed. Mustafa Abdulqadir Ata], Daru'l-Kutubi'l-Ilmiyya, Beirut, 1990.

Al-Hakim at-Tirmidhi, Abu Abdillah Muhammad ibn Ali ibn Hasan (d. 360 AH), *Nawadiru'l-Usul fi Ahadisi'r-Rasul*, I-IV, Daru'l-Jil, 1st ed., [Ed. D. Abdurrahman Umayra], Beirut, 1992.

Al-Haythami, Nuraddin Ali ibn Abi Bakr (d. 807 AH), *Majmau'z-Zawaid wa Manbau'l-Fawaid*, I-X, Daru'r-Rayyan li't-Turas, Cairo, 1987.

Al-Humaydi, Muhammad al-Azdi (d. 249 AH), *Al-Musnad*, [Ed. Subhi al-Badri as-Samarrai, Mahmud Muhammad Halil as-Saidi], Maktabatu's-Sunnah, Cairo, 1988.

Al-Husayn, Abdulqadir Muhammad, *Imam Ahli'l-Haq Abu'l-Hasan al-Ash'ari*, Al-Mashriqu li'l-Kitab, Damascus, 2001.

Al-Jurjani, Ali ibn Muhammad as-Sayyid ash-Sharif (d. 816 AH), *At-Ta'rifat*, [Ed. İbrahim al-Abyari], Daru'l-Kitabi'l-Arabi, Beirut, 1985.

Al-Kurtubi, Muhammad ibn Ahmad ibn Abi Bakr ibn Farah (d. 670 AH), *Al-Jami' li Ahkami'l-Qur'an*, I-XX, Daru'sh-Sha'b, Cairo, 1372 AH.

Al-Kushayri, Abu'l-Qasim Zaynulislam Abdulkarim ibn Hawazin (d. 465 AH/1072 CE), *Ar-Risalatu'l-Kushayriyya fi Ilmi't-Tasawwuf*, [Ed. Mustafa Zurayk], Al-Maktabatu'l-Asriyya, Beirut, 2001.

Al-Maqdisi, Muhammad ibn Ahmad ibn Abdil Hadi ibn Qudama (d. 744 AH), *Al-Uqudu'd-Durriyya*, Daru'l-Kitabi'l-Arabi, Beirut, nd.

Al-Maturidi, Abu Mansur Muhammad ibn Muhammad (d. 333 AH/944 CE); *Kitabu't-Tawhid*, Daru'l-Jamiati'l-Misriyya, Alexandria, nd.

Al-Munawi, Zaynuddin Muhammad Abdurrauf ibn Taj'il-Arifin ibn Ali (d. 1031 AH/1622 CE), *Fayzu'l-Qadir Sharh Jamii's-Saghir*, I-VI, Al-Maktabatu't-Tijariyyatu'l-Kubra, Egypt, 1356 AH.

Ali al-Muttaqi, Alauddin Ali ibn Abdulmalik ibn Qadi Han al-Hindi (d. 975 AH/1567 CE), *Kanzu'l-Ummal fi Sunani'l-Aqwal wa'l-Af'al*, I-XVI, [Ed. Mahmud Umar ad-Dimyati], Daru'l-Kutubi'l-Ilmiyya, Beirut, 1998.

Aliyyulqari, Abu'l-Hasan Nuraddin Ali ibn Sultan Muhammad (d. 1014 AH/1606 CE), *Al-Asraru'l-Marfua fi'l-Akhbari'l-Mawdua*, [Ed. Muhammad ibn Lutfi Sabbagh], Al-Maktabu'l-Islami, Beirut, 1986.

_____, *Mirqatu'l-Mafatih Sharh Mishkati'l-Masabih*, I-XI, Daru'l-Kutubi'l-Ilmiyya, Beirut, 2001.

Altuntaş, İhramcızâde Hacı İsmail Hakkı, *Niyâzî-i Mısrî, Kaside-i Bürde Tesbîi*, n.p., 2009.

An-Nasa'i, Abu Abdirrahman Ahmad ibn Shuayb (b. 215–d. 303 AH), *As-Sunan*, I-VIII, Çağrı Yayınları, 2nd ed., İstanbul, 1992.

_____, *As-Sunanu'l-Kubra*, I-VI, [Ed. Abdulghaffar Sulayman al-Bundari], Daru'l-Kutubi'l-Ilmiyya, Beirut, 1991.

An-Nawawi, Abu Zakariyya Yahya ibn Sharaf (b. 631–d. 676 AH); *Sharh Sahih Muslim (Sharhu'n-Nawawi ala Sahih Muslim)*, I-XVIII, Dar'ul-Ihya Turasi'l-Arabi, Beirut, 1392 AH.

As-Sahawi, Abu'l-Khayr Shamsaddin Muhammad ibn Abdurrahman (d. 902 AH/1497 CE), *Al-Maqasidu'l-Hasana*, [Ed. Muhammad Uthman] Daru'l-Kitabi'l-Arabi, Beirut, 1985.

As-Sarakhsi, Abu Bakr Muhammad ibn Sahl (d. 483 AH/1090 CE), *Al-Mabsut*, I-XXX, Daru'l-Ma'rifa, Beirut, 1986.

At-Tabarani, Abu'l-Qasim Sulayman ibn Ahmad (b. 260–d. 360 AH), *Al-Mu'jamu'l-Awsat*, I-IX, [Ed. Tariq ibn Iwazillah ibn Muhammad, Abdulmuhsin ibn Ibrahim al-Husayni], Daru'l-Haramayn, Cairo, 1994.

_____, *Al-Mu'jamu'l-Kabir*, I-XXV, [Ed. Hamdi ibn Abdulmajid as-Salafi], Maktabatu'z-Zahra, Musul, 1983.

At-Tabari, Abu Jafar Muhammad ibn Jarir (d. 310 AH), *Jamiu'l-Bayan fi Tafsiri'l-Qur'an*, I-XXX, Daru'l-Fikr, Beirut, 1985.

_____, *Tarikhu'l-Umam wa'l-Muluk (Tarikhu't-Tabari)*, I-V, Daru'l-Kutubi'l-Ilmiyya, Beirut, 1987.

At-Tirmidhi, Abu Isa Muhammad ibn Isa ibn Sawra (b. 209–d. 279 AH), *Al-Jamiu's-Sahih*, I-V, Çağrı Yayınları, 2nd ed., İstanbul, 1992.

Gülen, M. Fethullah, *Çekirdekten Çınara*, Nil Yayınları, İstanbul, 2013.

_____, *El-Kulûbu'd-Dâria*, Nil Yayınları, İstanbul, 2011.

_____, *Ümit Burcu*, Nil Yayınları, İstanbul, 2013.

Ibn Abdi Rabbih, Ahmad ibn Muhammad (d. 328 AH), *Al-Iqdu'l-Farid*, I-VII, Dar'ul-Ihya Turasi'l-Arabi, Beirut, 1999.

Ibn Abdilbarr, Abu Umar Yusuf ibn Abdillah an-Namiri (d. 463 AH), *At-Tamhid*, I-XXIV, Wizaratu'l-Awqaf wa'sh-Shu'uni'l-Islamiyya, Maghrib, 1387 AH.

Ibn Abi Shayba, Abu Bakr Abdullah ibn Muhammad (d. 235 AH), *Al-Musannaf fi'l-Ahadis wa'l-Athar*, I-VII, [Ed. Kamal Yusuf al-Hut], Maktabatu'r-Rushd, Riyad, 1989.

Ibn Asakir, Abu'l-Qasim Sikatuddin Ali ibn Hasan ibn Hibatillah (d. 571 AH/1176 CE); *Tarikh Dimashq*, I-LXX, Daru'l-Fikr, Beirut, 1996.

Ibn Battal, Abu'l-Hasan Ali ibn Halaf ibn Abdi'l-Malik (d. 449 AH), *Sharh Sahih al-Bukhari*, I-X, Maktabatu'r-Rushd, Riyad, 2003.

Ibn Hibban, Abu Hatim Muhammad ibn Hibban ibn Ahmad at-Tamimi al-Busti (d. 354 AH), *Sahih Ibn Hibban*, I-XVI, [Ed. Shuayb al-Arnawut], Muassasatu'r-Risala, Beirut, 1993.

Ibn Hisham, Abdulmalik ibn Hisham ibn Ayyub al-Himyari (d. 213 AH/828 CE), *As-Siratu'n-Nabawiyya*, I-VI, [Ed. Taha Abdurrauf Sa'd], Daru'l-Jil, Beirut, 1991.

Ibn Kathir, Abu'l-Fida Ismail ibn Umar ibn Kathir ad-Dimashqi (d. 774 AH), *Tafsiru'l-Qur'ani'l-Adhim*, I-IV, Daru'l-Fikr, Beirut, 1981.

Ibn Maja, Muhammad ibn Yazid al-Kazwini (b. 207–d. 275 AH); *As-Sunan*, I-II, Çağrı Yayınları, 2nd ed., İstanbul, 1992.

Ibnu'l-Mubarak, Abdullah ibnu'l-Mubarak al-Marwazi (b. 118–d. 181 AH), *Az-Zuhd li'bni'l-Mubarak*, (Ed. Habiburrahman al-A'zami), Daru'l-Kutubi'l-Ilmiyya, Beirut, nd.

Khatib al-Baghdadi, Ahmad ibn Ali Abu Bakr (b. 393–d. 463 AH), *Al-Kifaya fi Ilmi'r-Riwaya*, Al-Maktabatu'l-Ilmiyya, Medina, nd.

_____, *Tarikh Baghdad*, I-XIV, Daru'l-Kutubi'l-Ilmiyya, Beirut, nd.

Malik ibn Anas, Abu Abdillah al-Asbahi (b. 93–d. 179 AH), *Al-Muwatta*, I-II, Daru'l-Hadith, Cairo, 1993.

Mevlâna, Celaleddin-i Rumi (Mawlana Jalaluddin Rumi) (d. 672 AH/1273 CE); *Mesnevî: konularına göre açıklamalı*, I-VI, [Tr. Şefik Can], Ötüken Neşriyat, İstanbul, 2001.

_____, *Fîhi mâ Fîh*, [Tr. Ahmed Avni Konuk], İz Yayıncılık, İstanbul, 2009.

Muhammad Abduh, *Al-A'malu'l-Kamila*, I-V, [Ed. Muhammad Imara], Daru'sh-Shuruq, Beirut-Cairo, 1993.

Muslim, Abu'l-Husayn al-Hajjaa an-Naysaburi (b. 206–d. 261 AH), *Sahih Muslim*, I-V, [Ed. Muhammad Fuad Abdulbaqi], Dar'ul-Ihya Turasi'l-Arabi, Beirut, nd.

Nursi, Bediüzzaman Said (b. 1877–d. 1960 CE), *Emirdağ Lâhikası*, Şahdamar, İstanbul, 2010.

_____, *İşârâtü'l-İ'câz*, Şahdamar, İstanbul, 2010.

_____, *Mektubat*, Şahdamar, İstanbul, 2010.

_____, *Münazarât*, [Ed. Abdullah Aymaz], Şahdamar, İstanbul, 2006.

_____, *Tarihçe-i Hayat*, Şahdamar Yay., İstanbul, 2010.

_____, *The Gleams*, Tughra Books, New Jersey, 2008.

_____, *The Letters*, The Light, New Jersey, 2007.

_____, *Al-Mathnawi al-Nuri*, Tughra Books, New Jersey, 2007.

_____, *The Rays*, Tughra Books, New Jersey, 2010.

_____, *The Words*, The Light, New Jersey, 2010.

Index